The Canons

THE CANONS

Cathedral Close Encounters

Trevor Beeson

scm press

British Library Cataloguing in Publication data

A catalogue record for this book is available
from the British Library

0 334 04041 8/978 0 334 04041 5

First published in 2006 by SCM Press
9–17 St Alban's Place,
London N1 0NX

www.scm-canterburypress.co.uk

SCM Press is a division of
SCM-Canterbury Press Ltd

Typeset by Regent Typesetting, London
Printed and bound in Great Britain by
William Clowes Ltd, Beccles, Suffolk

Contents

Preface

Since my brief lives of *The Bishops* and *The Deans* were said to be entertaining as well as, in some instances, edifying, it would have been churlish of me to neglect the canons – not least because among these cathedral dignitaries are to be found, during the years 1830–2000, some of the most remarkable priests the Church of England has ever produced.

An author seeking to chronicle the lives and careers of these men has a wide choice. They outnumber the bishops and the deans of their times by about four to one, but it would be misleading to suggest that they were all outstanding or even interesting. Emphatically, they were not, and those selected by me are simply examples of special treasures who adorned the Church in a more leisurely cathedral age.

I have deliberately omitted those, a no less interesting band, who became bishops or deans, and any canons who are, happily, still alive, but I have ventured to suggest some ways in which the gifted cathedral canon may continue to flourish in changing times for the Church as well as for the nation.

I am grateful to the Very Reverend David L. Edwards, the Very Reverend Alexander Wedderspoon, the Very Reverend Ingram Cleasby and Canon Howard Root, who afforded me assistance with particular chapters, and to the Reverend Robert L. Glover for sight of his Glasgow University dissertation on the life and writings of W. H. Vanstone. Kathleen James has used her computer to work wonders on my untidy manuscript and, once again, Fiona Mather has miraculously tracked down long-hidden research material. Timothy Bartel, an erudite and fastidious editor, has been of the greatest assistance. I wish to thank them, too.

TB

I

Introduction

Canons in the Church of England are of four kinds. Canons residentiary are clergy, usually three or four in number, who, under the leadership of a dean, are responsible for the administration and day-to-day life of a cathedral. Honorary canons, of whom there may be 20–30 in a diocese, are parish clergy, and sometimes diocesan officers, who have a loose association with their cathedral but no responsibility for its running. In some cathedrals they are known as prebendaries. Minor canons, of whom relatively few now remain, are clergy who exercise a special ministry in cathedrals, usually as musicians, but have no over-all responsibility for its life. They do not have the title of canon. Lay canons, usually three or four, and a new breed dating only from 2000, are laypeople with particular skills or experience who join the dean and the canons residentiary in the administration of the cathedral. Because of their other responsibilities they are not normally involved in its day-to-day business, unless they are members of the cathedral's salaried staff, and they retain their lay titles. This book is concerned solely with canons of the residentiary sort.

In Saxon England the missionary bishop initially moved from place to place, driven either by external hostility or strategic need. He sur-rounded himself with a small community of priests who constituted his *familia*. These worshipped with him, served as his counsellors and shared in his mission. Sometimes the communities consisted of monks bound together by the requirements of the religious life, but often they were ordinary priests committed to the observance of a disciplined rule drawn up by the bishop. These were known as canons (derived from the Greek word meaning 'rule'), but the distinction between the two groups of clergy was not as great then as it became later.

From the seventh century onwards the bishops began to base their work on permanent buildings, some of them eventually quite sizeable, which became known as cathedrals since they housed their *cathedra* (chair) – the symbol of their teaching authority. During the eleventh and twelfth centuries these were replaced by massive Norman structures, but though the bishops became less involved in their daily life, being busy about many other things, including administrative functions at the court, cathedrals continued to be the chief centres of worship, mission and, increasingly, education in the bishop's territory, or diocese, and to be served by communities of clergy who related to him. These were housed in buildings adjoining the cathedral, and were financed by the income from landholdings, gifts, and, where there was the shrine of a saint, the offerings of pilgrims.

By the thirteenth century the English cathedrals were organized on two distinct lines – Canterbury, Carlisle, Durham, Ely, Norwich, Rochester, Winchester and Worcester were monastic and, apart from Carlisle, which was Augustinian, governed by the Benedictine rule. Their monks were known as canons regular and lived in obedience to an abbot. The other cathedrals – Chichester, Exeter, Hereford, Lichfield, Lincoln, London, Salisbury, Wells and York – were administered by colleges of secular canons, under a dean. Most of these adopted the rule of St Augustine and were identified with the other communities of Augustinian canons which sprang up throughout western Europe during the Middle Ages.

In England it became impossible as the Middle Ages advanced to maintain the ideal of a common life in the collegiate cathedrals. The canons began to live in separate houses in the precincts and the cathedral estates were divided into separate manors, each providing an income for a member of the college. These portions of land were known as prebends (from the Latin word for 'a grant'), and their holders began to be known as prebendaries, rather than as canons. There were often a large number of them: Lincoln had 58, Salisbury 52, and even Lichfield, one of the poorer dioceses, had 32. Not all of these resided and worshipped in the cathedral permanently, so the major responsibility for its day-to-day life lay with the dean, who had considerable authority and often great wealth; the precentor, who was responsible for the worship, the music and the song school; the chancellor, responsible for scholarship and education; and the treasurer, responsible not, as might be expected, for the finances, but the treasures – relics, silver, vestments – and also for the provision of candles, incense and bread and wine for the altars.

Several other prebendaries were usually on hand to assist them, or deputize for them when away, and in some cathedrals where the dean was frequently away, the sub-dean acquired considerable power. The rest of the prebendaries came and went as it suited them, and often spent most of their time on their estates, where they were required to provide, in person or through a deputy, a ministry to the local parishioners. In due course it was decided that, besides the dean and the chief officers, a certain number of prebendaries should be required to reside in the precincts and carry out cathedral duties for certain portions of the year – hence the designation prebendary (later canon) residentiary.

The organization of the monastic cathedrals was different inasmuch as it was determined by the Benedictine rule, and there was no possibility of the monks living outside the cloister and being sustained by personal manors. Although the bishop was still officially the abbot, because of his growing responsibilities elsewhere he had delegated the rule of the monastery, and therefore of his cathedral, to the prior, who usually had a separate substantial lodging and lived in considerable style. From this time onwards the authority of the bishop in his cathedral, whether monastic or secular, declined sharply and has never been recovered. The number of monks varied from place to place and at different periods of history. Seventy was usually regarded as ideal, though this was exceeded in some major monasteries and often declined during periods of plague. As many as 25 monks, known as obedientiaries, had specific responsibilities within the community's life, which included the managing of a farm and associated rural activity. Much of the manual work was carried out by lay servants and this, together with the presence of schools and hospitals and their welfare work, made the monasteries akin to villages. At the heart of them the round of daily worship was maintained by the choir monks, and the scholars pursued their studies in what were often substantial libraries.

The dissolution of the monasteries at the Reformation in the sixteenth century brought this way of cathedral life to an end – but not the cathedrals themselves. King Henry VIII recognized their value and, although the shrines of saints were dismantled and much else confiscated, they were substantially endowed for future ministry. The monastic cathedrals were required to embrace constitutions similar to those of their collegiate counterparts and all with substantially reduced numbers of clergy. Royal charters granted in 1541 provided for the appointment of a dean and twelve prebendaries, most of whom came from compliant former monks who were academically qualified to undertake educational work. Provision was also made for six minor canons, twelve lay clerks and ten choristers to lead the worship. New cathedrals were created at Bristol, Chester, Gloucester, Oxford, Peterborough and Westminster. These, together with the former monastic establishments, became known as cathedrals of the new foundation, and those of the former collegiate organizations as cathedrals of the old foundation – designations that are still used.

Overall, it was a constructive transformation, and in spite of various ups and downs during the reign of Queen Mary Tudor and the Protectorate of Oliver Cromwell, the arrangements initiated by Henry VIII survived virtually unaltered for the next three centuries. During this time the English cathedrals became important centres of learning and among their deans and prebendaries were some of the country's leading scholars. But as they prospered materially, so corruption eroded the integrity of their life and witness. The modest demands of residence – perhaps only two months of every year and even this possible of delegation – enabled the prebendaries to accumulate other well-endowed posts and become rich men. This made their stalls coveted appointments, thus encouraging their patrons – the Crown and the bishops – to favour their relatives and friends, who might or might not (mostly not) take their cathedral duties seriously. Edward Pyle, who was a prebendary of Winchester from 1756 to 1776, wrote, 'The life of a prebendary is a pretty easy way of dawdling away one's time: praying, walking, writing and as little study as your heart would wish.' At the Winchester funeral of Bishop Brownlow North in 1820 it was noted that, of the twelve prebendaries who acted as pallbearers, eight were related to him.

By this time it could hardly be disputed that the cathedrals were, if not actually corrupt, at least a very long way from fulfilling the purposes for which they were brought into being. They were in fact kept locked except at the time of divine service, and after attending Winchester Cathedral on Sunday, 30 October 1825 William Cobbett wrote: 'The "service" was now begun. There is a dean and God knows how many prebendaries belonging to this immensely rich bishopric and chapter and there were at this "service" two or three men and five or six boys in white surplices, with a congregation of fifteen women and four men.' This pattern was replicated in cathedrals in every part of the country, but its days were numbered. The remarkable burst of reforming zeal which led to the Great Reform Bill of 1832 soon spread to the Church of England, where there was concern, not only about the state of the cathedrals, but also about the almost total spiritual neglect of the huge and growing populations of the towns and cities. The repair of this neglect required large amounts of money and the affluent bishoprics and cathedrals were the obvious places in which to seek it.

A commission of enquiry appointed by the prime minister, Sir Robert Peel, in 1834 became a permanent Ecclesiastical Commission two years later and was given responsibility, with increasing power, for the administration of the Church of England's financial assets. An Act of Parliament in 1840 required the deans and chapters of cathedrals to turn over to the commission the greater part of their estates, and to reduce substantially the number of clergy on their books. Besides the dean there were to be no more than four prebendaries (six at Canterbury, Durham and Ely, five at Exeter and Winchester) – all to be renamed canons residentiary – and no more than six minor canons. The stipend of the deans was fixed at £1,000 and that of the canons at £500 and the reduction in the size of establishments was to be effected gradually through death or retirement. In the end 382 cathedral offices were abolished. The displaced prebendaries were succeeded by 20 or so honorary canons (in the old foundation cathedrals the title of prebendary was sometimes retained) and these offices, carrying little responsibility, even if no pay, became much coveted by the parish clergy.

It was not to be expected that administrative and financial reforms of this kind would hasten the renewal of the spiritual life of the cathedral. The immediate effects were demoralization and the beginning of protracted litigation in the unsuccessful defence of historic endowments. It was not until the latter decades of the century, when the renewing influence of the Evangelical and Tractarian movements began to be felt throughout the Church of England, that some of the cathedrals showed signs of new life. A number of new cathedrals were created from large parish churches to serve new dioceses in industrial areas. And as the nineteenth century advanced there were to be found among the canons residentiary a number of outstanding churchmen who used the freedom still afforded by their offices to deploy their gifts for the benefit of a much wider constituency than their still somnolent cathedrals. Scholarship became once more an important, though never an essential, qualification for appointment to a stall.

During the twentieth century the renewal of cathedral life was accelerated by the ministries of Dean Frank Bennett at Chester in the 1920s and 30s and Provost Bill Williams at Coventry in the 1960s and 70s. So great was their influence that by the 1980s the vibrant life of the cathedrals was one of the Church of England's few 'success stories', and the scale of their activities was bringing their administrative resources and methods under increasing and sometimes unmanageable strain. This led to the setting up at the request of the cathedrals of an Archbishop's Commission which published in 1994 a 262-page report, *Heritage and Renewal,* containing 104 recommendations. The chief of these became law in 2000 and now require deans and chapters to incorporate into their membership not less than two and no more than seven other people, of whom two-thirds must be laity. A professional administrator with financial expertise is required and may, or may not, having voting rights.

The choice of canons residentiary is still made by the bishop (in some instances by the Crown) but only after consultation with the chapter and with the duties of each canon clearly defined. They may hold office for a term of years or be given a freehold until the age of 70 – the decision in each case to be made locally. The dean and chapter is accountable to a cathedral council consisting of a lay chairman, the dean and 11 to 19 other members drawn from the chapter, the honorary canons, the cathedral congregation and the wider church and community. The bishop may attend and speak, but not vote, and the council, which has limited powers, must meet at least twice a year to receive (not approve) reports and accounts, and, if it so chooses, to make proposals. The chapter is required, after consultation with the bishop, to formulate proposals for the general direction and mission of the cathedral and to submit these to the council for advice.

Thus the English cathedrals entered a new millennium with new constitutions designed to enable them to meet new opportunities and new challenges more effectively. As always, however, the effectiveness of their response will depend on the faith and skill of the men and women called to serve them.

Westminster Abbey and St George's Chapel, Windsor are royal peculiars, not cathedrals, but their capitular organization is much the same and they have had a number of outstanding canons whose omission from the pages that follow would have been a serious loss. Hence their inclusion.

2

The Whig
Sydney Smith, Bristol and St Paul's

I must believe in the Apostolic Succession, there being no other way of accounting for the descent of the Bishop of Exeter from Judas Iscariot.

The observances of the church concerning feasts and fasts are tolerably well kept upon the whole, since the rich keep the feasts and the poor the fasts.

How can a bishop marry? How can he flirt? The most he can say is 'I'll see you in the vestry after the service'.

What is real piety? What is the attachment to the church? How are fine feelings evinced? The answer is plain: by sending strawberries to a clergyman.

There have been many extraordinary canons of St Paul's but never another like Sydney Smith, who was there from 1831 until his death in 1845. Born during the reign of King George III, he lived long enough to preach a sermon on what he believed to be the duties of the recently crowned Queen Victoria and to witness the first stirrings of a more serious age. He belonged to what Leslie Mitchell has helpfully described as the 'Whig World' – in reality an exclusive coterie which extended somewhat wider than the relatively small number of active Whig politicians. This embraced many of the oldest and wealthiest aristocratic families who owned what are still some of the most fashionable parts of London's West End, as the names clearly testify – Cavendish Square, Holland Park, Russell Square, Grosvenor Square, Bedford Square and several others.

Whigs had a metropolitan outlook. They resorted to their great country houses for a spell in the summer, but were happiest when in London. Smith was of the opinion, characteristically exaggerated, that:

the parallelogram between Oxford Street, Piccadilly, Regent Street and Hyde Park, encloses more intelligence and human ability, to say nothing of wealth and beauty, than the world has ever collected in such a space before.

Freedom, especially to enjoy the good things of life, was instinctively valued and relentlessly pursued by Whigs. They were at heart reformers and supported both Roman Catholic emancipation and the 1832 Reform Bill, but were in no sense democrats who envisaged universal suffrage. A sound education and ownership of property were for them the only conceivable qualifications for exercising the vote. Their approach to decision-making was controlled by a mixture of the rational and common sense, with little room for religion, least of all when it had a markedly emotional content.

Smith was co-opted into this Whig world. Neither by birth nor wealth did he qualify for automatic citizenship, but there was often room for bright young lawyers and writers, and in his case even for a clergyman of unrivalled wit. The composition of lively dinner parties was a vital element in Whig lives, but although Smith's outlook and Latitudinarian beliefs made him quite at home at Whig tables, he was not averse to consorting with Tories when, as during his years in Yorkshire, he could do no better:

> Tory and Whig in turns
>   shall be my host;
> I taste no politics
>   in boil'd and roast.

He made no bones about enjoying the best of food and the finest of wines, as his huge belly eventually testified, and his wit was liberally shared. At home his wife and children were often in stitches of laughter as he told a story, recounted an experience or simply exuded merriment. Like most entertainers, however, he endured times of acute melancholy and his 20-item prescription for handling depression, offered to Lady Georgiana Morpeth in 1828, drew on his own experience:

Nobody has suffered more from low spirits than I have done, so I feel for you. 1. Live as well and drink as much wine as you dare. 2. Go into the shower-bath with a small quantity of water at a temperature low enough to give you a slight sensation of cold – 75 or

80 degrees. 3. Amusing books. 4. Short runs of life not farther than dinner or tea. 5. Be as busy as you can. 6. See as much as you can of those friends who respect and like you; 7. and of those acquaintances who amuse you. 8. Make no secret of low spirits to your friends but talk of them fully; they are always the worse for dignified concealment. 9. Attend to the effects tea and coffee produce upon you. 10. Compare your lot with that of other people. 11. Don't expect too much of human life, a sorry business at the best. 12. Avoid poetry, dramatic representations (except Comedy), music, serious novels, melancholy sentimental people, and everything likely to excite feeling or emotion not ending in active benevolence. 13. Do good and endeavour to please everybody of degree. 14. Be as much as you can in the open air without fatigue. 15. Make the room where you commonly sit gay and pleasant. 16. Struggle by little and little against idleness. 17. Don't be too severe upon yourself, or underrate yourself, but do yourself justice. 18. Keep good blazing fires. 19. Be firm and constant in the exercise of rational religion. 20. Believe me, dear Lady Georgiana, very truly yours, Sydney Smith.

'Rational religion' – that is what he believed in. It belonged more to the eighteenth than to the nineteenth century, had no concern for dogma, church order or liturgy, and emphasized the importance of being good and doing good. This, combined with a fair dose of common sense, provided the content of Smith's preaching and writing on religious subjects. Yet he was not without spiritual insight:

There are many occasions in life where it is possible to effect by forgiveness every object which you propose to effect by resentment.

Life is to be fortified by many friendships. To love, and to be loved, is the greatest happiness of existence.

Tolerance was one of his cardinal beliefs but it did not extend to Methodists because of what he perceived to be among them 'the growing evil of fanaticism'. Even worse, they were against fun. The rise of Tractarianism also greatly alarmed him, again because of its apparent irrationality – 'inflexion and genuflection, posture and imposture, bowing to the east and curtseying to the west'. Roman Catholics could be treated differently, since their number in England was small, and those in Ireland would cease to be a threat to the stability of English society provided they were emancipated from their unjust disabilities.

As a wit, Smith has been compared to Swift, Carlyle and Wilde, but he had his own distinctive style and doubtless was even better heard than read. His gift was that of making picturesque analogies, using unexpected associations between contrasting ideas to demonstrate the absurdity of particular ideas or persons. He was also a master of irony and had an extraordinary ability to stand an argument on its head, with hilarious effect. He specialized in the ludicrous and, although his barbs sometimes angered their victims, he was a kind, amiable man whom it was difficult not to like. At dinner parties – his main theatre – he was unusual among his sort in that he did not treat the rest of the company as an audience. He was happy to listen carefully to the conversations of others until the chance came to seize on a remark, then add comments and anecdotes of his own. These would invariably reduce all present to uncontrollable mirth, some even rolling helplessly on the floor.

As a writer he had an unusual command of the English language, expressing it always in the elegant style of the eighteenth century. Some of his phrases, such as 'a square peg in a round hole', have passed into common usage, and his many correspondents made a point of retaining his letters. Thus the wit and wisdom of the Smith of Smiths – a title bestowed on him by his friend Thomas Babington Macaulay – remains available without much loss of meaning or mirth to a world far removed from his own. But not all the recipients of his letters found them amusing. When in 1844 a question arose regarding the allocation of tickets to livery companies for seats outside St Paul's at the time of a visit to the cathedral by Queen Victoria, one of the company clerks suggested:

Perhaps, Mr. Smith, all these details had better be left to us. We will form a little committee of our own and spare you all further trouble in the arrangements. Too many cooks, you know, spoil the broth.

Mention of cooks and broth was dangerous territory on which to engage an epicure canon and his response was swift:

Very true, Sir, but let me set you right in one particular: here there is but one cook, myself; you are only a scullion and will be good enough to take your directions from me.

Appointment to a canonry of St Paul's came late in life – he had kept the wrong political company – but it was just right and gave him the 15 happiest years of his life. He chose not to occupy the official residence but settled instead in Green Street, off Grosvenor Square and within the magic parallelogram. He was now in his element and glad to be rid of his Bristol canonry, though he did not relinquish the parish of Combe Florey in Somerset, where he continued to spend a substantial part of the year.

Smith did not, however, treat his St Paul's office as a sinecure. The age of cathedral reform had not yet dawned, though questions were being raised about their finances, and St Paul's was still enjoying its long siesta. Yet the new canon, with the ready consent of his colleagues, with whom he always had the most cordial relations, took the administration in hand and laid foundations for the development of the cathedral's life later in the century. H. H. Milman, who went to the deanery four years after Smith's death, wrote:

I find traces of him in every particular of Chapter affairs; and on every occasion when his hand appears I find stronger reasons for respecting his sound judgement, knowledge of business, and activity of mind; above all the perfect fidelity of his stewardship . . . His management of the affairs of St Paul's (for at one time he seems to have been *the* manager) only commenced too late and terminated too soon.

He installed fire-fighting equipment and caused St Paul's to be the first cathedral in the country to be insured. A close eye was kept on all funds and he maintained close contact with the Surveyor of the Fabric, with whom he had some disagreements over restoration costs, and with the Chapter Clerk, who described him 'one of the most strictly honest men I have ever met in business'. A request from the organist to increase the number of boys in the choir was rejected – 'It is a matter of perfect indifference to me whether Westminster bawls louder than St Paul's. We are there to pray, and the singing is a very subordinate consideration.'

The Whig radical who had been so active in the causes of Roman Catholic emancipation and the 1832 Reform Bill proved to be much less open to change when it threatened the privileges and especially the income of St Paul's. In 1837 the Home Secretary, Lord John Russell, asked that the twopence admission charge to the cathedral outside service times should be dropped since the building was a national treasure. But Smith, who wanted the money to help pay the vergers, would have none of this and sent a stinging response to the Home

Office, arguing that an admission charge was necessary for keeping out the disorderly and thus preventing the church from becoming 'a Royal Exchange for wickedness as the other Royal Exchange is for commerce'. Almost one hundred years would pass before admission charges were abolished, only to be reimposed towards the end of the twentieth century.

Much less successful was his attempt to resist the proposal of the Church Commission, established in 1836, that a substantial portion of the large income of St Paul's should be diverted to help finance new parishes in the East End of London and to improve clergy stipends generally. The driving force in the Commission was the Bishop of London, Charles James Blomfield, whom Smith described as 'a man of very great ability, humane, placable, generous, munificent, very agreeable, but he has an ungovernable passion for business and a constitutional impetuosity'. He launched his attack in three published 'Letters to Archdeacon Singleton', which are pure Sydney Smith in their use of irony and humour to make serious points about principles and policies.

He voiced two main objections to proposals that would, among other things, halve the stipends of the dean and canons (though not in the lifetimes of their existing office-holders). The first was that, although the bishops had agreed to some reduction in their own emoluments, this was not sufficient to preclude them from continuing to live in high style and scandalize true reformers. His second point was that if the Church of England's entire income were to be equally divided between all its clergy, it 'would not give to each clergyman an income equal to that which is enjoyed by the upper domestic of a great nobleman'. This was no way to attract the brightest and best into the Church's ministry – 'The offices of the church would then fall down to men little less coarse and ignorant than agricultural labourers – the clergyman of the parish would soon be seen in the squire's kitchen; and all this would take place in a century where poverty is infamous.' Such an argument hardly reflects a high view of priestly vocation, but more recent experience of the equalization of clergy stipends indicates some truth in Smith's case.

His father retired early from business in order to travel the world, mainly in America, and had shortly before this displayed his waywardness by marrying the daughter of a French Huguenot refugee, then abandoning her at the church door to go off to America. On his return, when he had made some more money, he found his wife patiently waiting and began a delayed family life of somewhat itinerant character. Over a period of years he bought, and it was said spoiled, 19 houses and reared four sons and a daughter.

When young Sydney was born in 1771 the family chanced to be living in Woodford, Essex, but they soon moved to Southampton and after attending a local school Sydney went to Winchester as a scholar. The college was at the time at a low ebb and was described by him as full of abuse, neglect and vice. He was bullied and hated the place, but nonetheless won most of the prizes and ended up as prefect in Hall, that is, head of the school. Later he attacked the inadequacy of the public school system, as well as that of Oxford and Cambridge.

Moving as a scholar to William of Wykeham's other foundation, New College, Oxford, he was able at the end of his second year, under the curious system then prevailing, to exchange his scholarship for a fellowship worth £100 a year. This enabled him to support himself without help from his father. Since New College was exempt from university examinations, it is impossible to tell how seriously he took academic life, though it is known that he spent some time in Normandy, becoming fluent in French, and that he attended some lectures on anatomy and medicine, which he turned to good use when dealing with the maladies of his future parishioners. He wished, in fact, to go to the Bar but his father was unwilling to finance this and said that he must become either a tutor or a parson.

In 1794 therefore he became curate of Nether Avon on a remote part of Salisbury Plain, where, the rector being an absentee, he was effectively in charge of the parish. After twelve months he recorded, 'Nothing can equal the profound, the unmeasureable, the awful dullness of this place in which I lie dead and buried, in hopes of a joyful resurrection in the year 1796.' But the squire, Michael Hicks Beach, valued him and provided money for work among the victims of the deep poverty of the parish. He established a Sunday school – at that time a new idea for providing general, rather than specifically religious, education – and also a school for poor girls, teaching them how to knit and sew. Smith's own financial position was also precarious so, having retained his New College fellowship, he returned to Oxford for a time to earn money from tutoring.

Relief came in 1797 when the squire made him travelling tutor to one of his sons, who was just leaving Eton. It was originally intended that they should go to Germany and experience something of the literary life of Weimar, but continental war made this impossible and they went instead to Edinburgh. This determined the course of the rest of Smith's life. He immediately fell in love with the city. The Georgian new town was under construction and, besides the university, there were excellent libraries and several dining clubs attended by academics and young lawyers. He was quickly accepted into their company, sharing the prevailing Whig, reformist outlook, and when not supervising his pupil, took the opportunity to attend medical lectures and the local hospital, where, as he put it, 'I learned the elements of a puke and the rudiments of purging.'

Before long he was proposing to a small group of literary people and academics that they should publish their wide-ranging interests and reformist concerns in an independent quarterly magazine. The first issue of the *Edinburgh Review* appeared under his editorship in October 1802 and, although he was obliged to vacate the chair when he moved to London in the following year, he continued to contribute to its pages for the next 25 years. By this time he concluded, somewhat oddly, that its political slant was too dangerous for a clergyman to be associated with. He may have had possible preferment in mind.

The *Review* contained essays and reviews of a very high literary quality, while at the same time campaigning vigorously for political and social reform. Sir Walter Scott was among the early contributors and became a friend. A scathing review of an archdeacon's published sermon, penned by Smith for the first issue, offers an enticing example of a style that was to stimulate, entertain and sometimes infuriate his readers for years to come:

A clergyman cannot be always considered as reprehensible for preaching an indifferent sermon; because, to the active piety and correct life, which the profession requires, many a man may not unite the talents for that species of composition: but every man who prints imagines that he gives to the world something which they had not before, either in matter or style; that he has brought forth new truths, or adorned old ones; and when, in lieu of novelty and ornament, we can discover nothing but trite imbecility, the law must take its course, and the delinquent suffer that mortification from which vanity can rarely be expected to escape, when it chooses dullness for the minister of its gratification. . . . He may be a very hospitable archdeacon, but nothing short of *a positive miracle* can make him an acute reasoner.

It was perhaps hardly surprising that the publication soon attracted a wide readership and before long it became the chief organ of the Whig party. It also set a pattern for other nineteenth-century reviews and until it ceased publication in 1929 attracted contributions from most of the leading writers and critics of the nineteenth and early twentieth centuries.

Two years before the launching of the *Review* Sydney had married Catherine Pybus, a friend of his sister, whom he described as having:

> a good figure, and to me an interesting countenance, extremely good sense, very fond of music and of me – a wise amiable woman such as without imposing, specious qualities will quietly for years and years make the happiness of her husband's life.

Time proved it to have been a good choice and during the early years there was the bonus of a marriage settlement of £8,000, the income from which, together with his tutor's fees, enabled them to get by in Edinburgh. His own contribution to their joint assets was six small silver teaspoons. They had five children, one of whom died in infancy, and another when about to embark on a legal career.

In 1803 Catherine persuaded him that his proper place was in London so, aided by the sale for £500 of the jewels given to her by her mother, they moved to a small house in Doughty Street, just off Gray's Inn Road. Preacherships were obtained at the nearby Foundling Hospital and also at the Fitzroy and Berkeley proprietary chapels, where his controversial sermons attracted large congregations. On the strength of this he was invited to give three courses on Moral Philosophy at the Royal Institution and although he was no philosopher his lectures attracted audiences of 600 to 800 people. He mixed commonsense morality with anecdotes and amusing stories and, although the numbers fell during the later courses, the lectures established his London reputation. He was candid enough to describe them as 'without exception the most perfect example of impudence in history'.

The generous fees offered by the Royal Institution enabled him to move to a larger house in Orchard Street, off Oxford Street, where he began to hold weekly supper parties along the lines he had so much enjoyed in Edinburgh. He was now sufficiently well known to be able to invite leading people from London's literary circle, young lawyers and politicians, provided they were Whigs. And he found himself drawn into a wide social circle that included, most significantly, Holland House, the social centre of the Whigs during the early nineteenth century. He was often there several times a week and became an intimate friend of the imperious Lady Holland as well as an adviser and envier of her husband, a nephew of Charles James Fox – 'Think of his possessing Holland House and that he reposes every evening on that beautiful structure of flesh and blood, Lady H.' Among his other friendships that with Lord John Russell, the Whig statesman, who played a leading part in the passing of the 1832 Reform Bill and was twice Prime Minister, was of special importance, though they had sharp disagreements over church reform.

This exciting social life was all very well, but he lacked an adequate income to sustain it indefinitely and, because of his political views, had no hope of substantial preferment in the Church. In the end the Lord Chancellor, and at the request of Lady Holland, appointed him in 1806 to the rectory of the small parish of Foston, about eight miles from York. He had not the slightest desire to move from London to a rural area of Yorkshire, but initially he was not required to reside in the parish so he took the £500 per annum stipend and paid a little of it to the curate of a neighbouring parish who agreed to take the services at Foston. Sydney paid occasional visits but entertained the hope that he might be able to exchange the parish for one nearer London. This he was unable to achieve before a new and more diligent Archbishop of York decided to enforce the 1803 Clergy Residence Act and require Smith to move into Foston, which had not had a resident priest for over 150 years.

There was however the problem that the parish lacked a rectory, having only what Smith described as a 'hovel'. So he was obliged for a time to live in nearby, but still inconvenient, Heslington. Further attempts to exchange the living for one in the South having proved unsuccessful, he set about the task of building a new parsonage. A typical Sydney Smith saga followed. A York architect designed an attractive house but the estimated cost, £3,000, was too high for the rector to meet, even with the aid of a loan from Queen Anne's Bounty – 'You build for glory, Sir; I for use,' he told the architect when returning the plans. But he kept close to these plans after he engaged a builder and a carpenter to erect the house under his own supervision and with his own considerable contribution:

I then took to horse to provide bricks and timber; was advised to make my own bricks of my own clay; when the kiln was opened, all bad; mounted my horse again, and in twenty-four hours had bought thousands of bricks and tons of timber. Was advised by neighbouring gentleman to employ oxen; bought four – Tug and Lug, Haul and Crawl; but Tug and Lug took to fainting, and required buckets of sal-volatile, and Haul and Crawl to lie down in the mud. So I did as I ought to have done at first, took the advice of the farmer instead of the gentleman; sold my oxen, bought a team of horses, and at last, in spite of a frost which delayed me six weeks, in spite of walls running down with wet, in spite of the remonstrances of friends who predicted our death, in spite of an infant of six months old, who had never been out of the house, I landed my family in my new house, nine months after laying the first stone, on 20th of March 1814 . . . a feat, taking ignorance, inexperience into consideration, requiring, I assure you, no small degree of energy.

This 'small parsonage', as Smith called it, housed a succession of rectors until it was gutted by fire in 1962 and it was then sympathetically restored in accordance with its original design.

Smith occupied the house for some 14 years and, having acknowledged that further preferment was improbable, even if always hoped for, settled down to the life of a conscientious, albeit highly unusual, country parson. The church building was small and undistinguished but the congregation – usually about 50 strong – were led in well-ordered worship and treated to vigorously delivered sermons. He recounted later:

When I began to thump the cushion of my pulpit on first coming to Foston, as is my wont when I preach, the accumulated dust of 150 years made such a cloud that for some minutes I lost sight of my congregation.

In his parish work he regarded himself as much a doctor as a pastor, drawing on his attendance at medical lectures in Edinburgh, and had a remedy for most maladies, sending to London for the latest medicines. He also recognized the importance of diet and once expressed the hope that he would become 'the master cook, as well as the master pastor of the parish'. He divided several acres of his glebe into sixteenths and let these at very cheap rents to enable parishioners to grow their own vegetables or even keep a cow. Most of the rest of the glebe – almost 300 acres – he farmed himself with tolerable success, using a large speaking trumpet to instruct his labourers in the field, and a telescope to observe their activities.

All of which still left him with time to serve as a magistrate, being nothing if not unconventional in his dealing with crime, and on two occasions chaplain to the High Sheriff of Yorkshire. The local clergy did not make much of him, nor he of them, but he enjoyed a warm

friendship with Archdeacon Francis Wrangham, a scholar, bibliomaniac and, like Smith, a supporter of Roman Catholic emancipation,
who had a parish nearby. The Earl of Carlisle welcomed him regularly
to Castle Howard and he made an annual pilgrimage to Lord Grey at
Howick. His sparkling wit took him to the tables of many other north
country houses, to which he travelled in an ancient, rickety carriage,
and the Duke of Devonshire improved his income by presenting him to
the parish of Londesborough, about 25 miles distant. This was offered
on the understanding that he would relinquish it as soon as the Duke's
nephew was old enough to be ordained and appointed. Meanwhile,
Smith was allowed to employ a curate to look after the parish.

There remained, however, his need for the kind of lively social life to
be found only in Whig circles in London. He went there whenever he
could afford to, and his visits became more frequent after an aunt left
him £400 a year. But for a priest of metropolitan outlook, who shared
the Whig disdain for rural life, Smith's 24-year tenure of Foston had
some of the marks of the heroic. He made the best of his circumstances
and his gifts.

Relief came in 1828 when the Lord Chancellor – a Tory but a personal friend – made him a canon of Bristol Cathedral. Curiously as
it seems today, news of the offer was conveyed to him by the Lord
Chancellor's wife. No more than three months of residence at Bristol
was required every year, together with attendance at relatively infrequent chapter meetings, but a parish in distant Yorkshire was a wholly
impracticable place from which to commute and he was fortunate to
be able to exchange Foston, which now had an above-average income,
for Combe Florey in Somerset.

Smith was delighted by the arrangements at Bristol, not least the
accommodation, which he described to Lady Holland as 'An extremely comfortable prebendal house, seven-stall stable, room for four car-
riages, so that I can hold all your cortège when you come.' He quickly
established good relations with his colleagues on the chapter, noting
that one of them was 'deaf, tottering, worldly-minded, vain as a lawyer, noisy and perfectly good-natured and obliging'. He lost no time in
disturbing their peace. His first period of residence chanced to include
Bristol's annual civic service, at which he was required to preach. The
issue of Roman Catholic emancipation was still being hotly disputed
and strongly opposed by the Protestant mayor and corporation, who
were treated to a hugely controversial sermon on the subject of toleration – 'such a dose of toleration as will last them for many a year'. The
civic dignitaries were outraged and a Bristol friend who was present

at the service and in touch with him during his future residences later told his daughter,

> At Clifton [where he lived] and Bristol you may readily perceive that he was much more wondered at than liked. All their prejudices were against him; and they were totally incapable of appreciating his talents, or of comprehending his character.

Combe Florey, where apart from his spells at St Paul's he was to remain for the rest of his life, was, he thought, 'a better sort of Foston' but he never really took to it. He appreciated the beauty of the Somersetshire countryside but found the village and most of the local gentry dull. The chief virtue of the place was its proximity to Bristol and relative ease of access to London – something that was to become increasingly important to him. During his early years there he did, however, play a significant part in the political life of the county, speaking at meetings in favour of the 1832 Reform Bill. In October of the previous year, shortly after the House of Lords had rejected the Bill, he made a notable and telling short speech at a meeting in Taunton:

> As for the possibility of the House of Lords preventing ere long a reform of Parliament, I hold it to be the most absurd notion that ever entered into human imagination. I do not mean to be disrespectful, but the attempt of the Lords to stop the progress of reform reminds me very forcibly of the great storm of Sidmouth, and of the conduct of the excellent Mrs. Partington on that occasion. In the winter of 1824 there set in a great flood upon that town – the tide rose to an incredible height – the waves rushed in upon the houses and everything was threatened with destruction. In the midst of this sublime and terrible storm, Dame Partington, who lived upon the beach, was seen at the door of her house with mop and pattens, trundling her mop, squeezing out the sea-water, and vigorously pushing away the Atlantic Ocean. The Atlantic was roused. Mrs. Partington's spirit was up; but I need not tell you that the contest was unequal. The Atlantic Ocean beat Mrs. Partington. She was excellent with a slop or a puddle, but she should not have meddled with a tempest. Gentlemen, be at your ease – be quiet and steady. You will beat Mrs. Partington.

The audience did not need to be told that the good Dame Partington represented the Duke of Wellington, the prime minister and chief opponent of the Reform Bill. Neither did the *Taunton Courier* reporter who, after his paper had printed an account of the meeting, passed the story to *The Times*, in which it was reprinted. Cartoonists and print-sellers ensured that it would continue to entertain the nation for several weeks. But the passage of the Bill in 1832 marked the end of Smith's political activity and there would be no more fun of that sort.

That was not, however, the end of his ecclesiastical career. His attitude to preferment was always ambivalent. The recognition by so many influential people of his undoubted gifts as a writer and speaker naturally led him to believe sometimes that he was destined for a moderately high position in the Church. If many of those same people had doubts as to whether his style, outlook and wit would be acceptable in a bishop or a dean, this would not have surprised him. He was hardly 'a safe pair of hands'. Again, there was a political factor inasmuch as the Tories were in office during long periods of his ministry and he knew perfectly well that there was no chance of a Whig such as himself, especially one who had used his wit to excoriate them mercilessly, receiving high office at their hands. Often he seemed indifferent to these matters, but he spoke and wrote about them frequently enough to indicate that he was not unambitious, and he sometimes went as far as asking his friends to promote his cause. He would probably have liked the offer of a bishopric in order to have the pleasure of turning it down. In 1830, before the Dame Partington incident, he felt drawn to write to the Duke of Wellington asking for consideration and basing his claim on his long campaigning for Catholic emancipation:

> In the fluctuations of life, every man must be content to be sometimes up and sometimes down, but it is a sad life to be always down. I have for twenty years been the uncompromising advocate of that question which you have so lately and so honourably settled. I have published a good deal upon the subject, and in all meetings of the clergy and on every public occasion which fairly presented itself, have been its strenuous, and often its solitary defender.
>
> The misrepresentations, abuse and obloquy to which I have in consequence subjected myself, I need not state to your Grace. If the splendour of your life could not guard you, you may easily conceive to what a country clergyman must have been exposed.
>
> It is not, I think, presumptuous to say I might have advanced my fortunes if I had defended error with half as much earnestness as I have contended for truth and justice. May I now ask you for some preferment in the church?

No reply to this appears to have been forthcoming but the Whig Lord Grey, who succeeded the Duke of Wellington in 1830, was quick to act and appointed him to a residentiary canonry of St Paul's, which he described in his offer as 'A snug thing, let me tell you, being with full £2,000 per annum.'

News of the appointment did not please everyone and the Bishop of Gloucester ventured to suggest that he had not been appointed for his piety and learning, but because he was 'a scoffer and a jester'. Smith responded by expressing surprise at the bishop's strong comments, which he considered 'as rather too close an imitation of that language which is used in the apostolic occupation of trafficking in fish'. His chief *bête noire* however, at least for a time, was Bishop Blomfield – the church reformer.

In a long 'Open Letter to the Bishop', published in *The Times* on 5 September 1840, Smith referred to a Blomfield speech in the House of Lords in which he had recounted his distress whenever passing by St Paul's on the way to the East End:

> I see there a dean and three residentiaries, with incomes amounting in the aggregate to between £10,000 and £12,000 a year. I see, too, connected with the cathedral 29 clergymen, whose offices are all but sinecures, with an annual income of about £12,000 at the moment and likely to be much larger after the lapse of a few years. I proceed a mile or two to the east and north East, and find myself in the midst of an immense population in the most wretched state of destitution and neglect, artisans, merchants, labourers, beggars, thieves, to the number of at least 300,000.

Smith suggested that if, instead of going east and north-east the bishop had crossed London Bridge and proceeded in a south-westerly direction, he would have found in Lambeth:

> a vast palace, containing, not a dean, three residentiaries and 29 clergymen, but one attenuated prelate with an income enjoyed by himself alone, amounting to £30,000 per annum, twice as great as all of those confiscated clergymen put together; not a penny of it given up by Act of Parliament during his life to that spiritual destitution which he so deeply deplores.

And just in case Blomfield missed the point, he went on to suggest that when Blomfield had refreshed himself with 'the beautiful and consistent' scene at Lambeth, and recovered a little from 'those pictures of spiritual destitution which have been obtruded upon you by the sight of St Paul's', he might then continue his promenade, resting for a while at his own palace in St James's Square, 'no scene of carnal and secular destitution', before reaching his second palace at Fulham, 'where I think your animal spirits will be restored and the painful theme of spiritual destitution for the moment be put to sleep. £20,000 per annum to the present possessor increasing in value every hour, not a shilling legally given up during life to "the masses who are living without God".' So he went on – a prod here, a dig there – but it was to no avail. The necessary legislation went through Parliament and cathedral revenues were substantially reduced.

By the time he reached his seventieth year, in 1840, Smith was beginning to feel his age and reported from London to one of his friends, a Yorkshire squire:

I dine out eight or nine times every week. If people will talk across the table it is agreeable but I hate whispering to the lady next to me – when I have asked her whether she has been lately to the opera, I am knocked up entirely and don't know what else to say – and I know she hates me for being a large fat parson and for not being slim and elegant. One of the greatest evils of old age is the advance of the stomach over the rest of the body. It looks like the accumulation of thousands of dinners and luncheons. It looks like a pregnant woman in a cloth waistcoat and as if I were near my time and might reasonably look for twins.

His health gradually deteriorated and he was put on 'that most detestable of a human diet – light and innocent puddings'. His ordained nephew looked after Combe Florey parish, leaving him free to concentrate on the chapter affairs at St Paul's, but he went downhill quickly in the early weeks of 1845 and died in his Green Street home on 22 February.

During the previous summer he had described himself to a Frenchman:

I am seventy-four years of age; and being Canon of St Paul's in London, and a rector of a parish in the country, my time is divided equally between town and country. I am living amongst the best society in the metropolis, and at ease in my circumstances; in tolerable health, a mild Whig, a tolerating Churchman, and much given to talking, laughing and noise. I dine with the rich in London, and physic the poor in the country, passing from the sauces of Dives to the sores of Lazarus. I am, upon the whole, a happy man, have found the world an entertaining world, and am thankful to Providence for the part allotted to me in it.

3

The Bibliomaniac
Francis Wrangham, York and Chester

Francis Wrangham, who was a canon of both York and Chester in the early part of the nineteenth century, exemplifies a pattern of Christian ministry which, as the century progressed, came to be seen as unacceptable, if not actually scandalous. He was a pluralist. Besides his cathedral stalls, he was the incumbent of two parishes, one in Yorkshire, the other in Cheshire, and from 1820 onwards was also Archdeacon of Cleveland, then of the East Riding. His ministry in all these spheres was exemplary, and he had time enough to spare to become a reputable poet, an epigrammatist, a translator from Greek, Latin, French and Italian, and an editor of classical texts, as well as a prolific writer of pamphlets on church and social matters. To which must be added his activities as a remarkable bibliomaniac who accumulated upwards of 15,000 books, a large proportion of which were rare, curious and usually a combination of both.

He was born at Raysthorpe, near Malton in Yorkshire, in 1769. He was the only son of a farmer who was not particularly rich but could afford to pay for him to be educated by three scholarly local clergymen. When he was 17 he went to Magdalene College, Cambridge and during his third term won a Gold Medal for Greek and Latin epigrams, but he then moved to Trinity Hall as a minor scholar and in 1790 graduated as Third Wrangler, second to Smith's Mathematical Prizeman, and winner of the Chancellor's Classical Medal – a combination of honours believed at the time to be unprecedented in the history of the university.

He remained in Cambridge for a time, took pupils, spent about 18 months as private tutor to one of the Duke of Manchester's sons, and returned to Cambridge in 1793 to take his MA and to secure the testimonial required for his ordination by the Archbishop of York. This accomplished, he applied for a fellowship in Divinity at Trinity Hall, which had just fallen vacant and for which he appeared to be eminently well qualified. A teacher of Divinity was not then required to be a highly skilled theologian, and Wrangham, being a former minor scholar of the college, was, according to its founder's intention, entitled to preference.

Yet the fellowship went to the Reverend John Vickers, who was not even a member of Trinity Hall and was said to be 'far from prepossessing in appearance, awkward and uncertain in manner and with classical attainments of an inferior order'. Moreover he was disqualified from election as he held an office of profit in the Church – something he put right by resigning from it when the obstacle was discovered. Wrangham appealed to the Lord Chancellor, who wondered at first if he had any jurisdiction over the matter, but in the end assumed the office of College Visitor in order to deal with it.

After much legal argument and appeal to classical authorities he judged, no doubt correctly, that the fellows were entitled to choose whomsoever they wished to join their company. They for their part had simply explained that they considered Vickers to be a fit and proper person to become a fellow of the college, whereas Wrangham was not. In support of this they spread a rumour, which reached the Lord Chancellor's ears, that Wrangham was in sympathy with the French Revolution and that his loyalty could not be taken for granted. This was quite untrue – he was in fact a moderate Whig – but the rumour hardly served his interests.

The incident became for a time a cause célèbre in Cambridge and far beyond, and various theories were advanced to explain Wrangham's rejection. There was the suggestion that snobbery was involved since Vickers came from a social background judged to be superior to that of a Yorkshire farmer's son. Others believed the villain of the piece to be the President of Queens' College, Dr Isaac Milner, who was the leader of the Tory and Evangelical parties in Cambridge and had considerable influence in Trinity Hall. It seemed hardly accidental that Vickers was a Queens' man. Then there was the undisputed fact that Wrangham was known to have written, under a pseudonym, a small book, *Reform: a farce, Modernised from Aristophanes* (1790), which was critical of contemporary politicians, charging them with over-fondness for money and place-hunting. Since several of the non-resident fellows of Trinity Hall were Members of Parliament, this essay could not have pleased them and the offence was compounded by what could be interpreted as Wrangham's approval of the views of Tom Paine – the hated radical who had attacked Christianity from a Deist standpoint. There was also the small matter of an epigram that had poked fun at the Senior Tutor's eccentric efforts to improve the layout of the college garden.

Whatever the explanation, Wrangham was deeply wounded by the rejection, which turned him away from the possibility of an academic career and towards the life of a country parson, with sufficient leisure for the pursuit of scholarship and none of the distractions and back-biting of common rooms. He abandoned Trinity Hall and became a member of Trinity College, Cambridge. Urgently needing an income, he took a curacy at Cobham, in Surrey, where he also had three pupils – all of them sons of West Indian parents wealthy enough to pay him the not inconsiderable sum of £200 per annum for their tuition. After only three months of this, however – early in 1796 – he was appointed by a friend of his father to the vicarage of Hunmanby with Folkton, not far from Filey on the North Yorkshire coast. This had an income of £600 per annum and, although he was only 27, it was there that he stayed for the rest of his life, leaving only temporarily to carry out his Chester duties from 1828 onwards.

A tall man, albeit slightly built and gentle in manner, he had an attractive personality that combined dignity, humour and courtesy with a strong determination to get things done. For most of his life he was endowed with youthful good looks. Three years after his institution to Hunmanby he married Agnes Creyke, daughter of the squire of Marton, not far away, but within a year of their marriage she died in childbirth, aged 21, leaving the surviving baby daughter. In the following year Wrangham remarried – this time to an heiress, Dorothy Cayley, who was a direct descendant of King Edward I and Eleanor of Castile and brought with her an income of £700 per annum, giving them a joint annual income of £1,300 – riches in those days. She also gave him entry into aristocratic society, which he much enjoyed, and bore him five more children, ensuring many grandchildren and a family life which he found immensely satisfying.

In the parish Wrangham saw himself as being responsible for the material as well as the spiritual needs of the people and he had a special concern for those who were sick or poor. He started a free dispensary for the poor and a savings bank to encourage thrift. A small parish library was founded in the church vestry and for half an hour before the beginning of the Sunday morning service the schoolmaster was on hand to manage the exchange of 15 to 20 volumes – a number that gradually increased. A village Cow Club was inaugurated to enable poor cottagers to accept the offer of a piece of ground on which to graze a cow. This was in effect an insurance scheme, providing, in return for a monthly subscription of half a penny per pound of the cow's value, a guaranteed five-sixths of its value in the event of its untimely death. These social welfare projects were innovative at the time, but soon spread to other parishes in many different parts of the country, assisted by Wrangham's readiness to preach and address meetings about them. He used his own money to pay for the restoration of the church building.

Preaching was always something Wrangham took very seriously, devoting as much time and care to his village sermons as he did to university sermons and the Assize Sermons he was called upon to preach during three separate years when he was chaplain to the High Sheriff of Yorkshire. His sermons expressed a liberal and tolerant understanding of the Christian faith which was uncommon in his time, and he could be courageous, as when he encouraged the editors of *The Examiner*, the brothers John and Leigh Hunt, and promoted subscriptions to their lively weekly literary magazine. This had a radical political section, strongly supporting social and political reform and frequently ridiculing the Prince of Wales and future Prince Regent. All of which often got the editors into trouble with the law and both were fined £500 and sent to prison for two years following a libel action initiated by the Prince. There were few country clergymen, apart from Wrangham, among their backers. Yet his liberal views did not extend to approval of the relationship between Nelson and his mistress, Lady Hamilton, and in a memoir of the great hero he faced this candidly and deemed it improper. Neither was he tolerant of the Deists, who believed that God, having created the universe, then allowed it to continue, as it were, under its own steam without further divine intervention.

He was fortunate enough to have among otherwise dull clerical neighbours none other than Sydney Smith, already noted as a wit and now exiled from London to a small country living. The two men had a lot in common, including Whig sympathies as well as their liberal beliefs, and they became firm friends. Both also belonged to the country gentry and although Wrangham was in no sense ambitious – he didn't need to be – Smith recorded that he had an encyclopaedic knowledge of the Church of England's benefices and their incomes, and was always aware of plum livings that were about to become vacant. None of which, unfortunately, facilitated Smith's longed-for return to the South.

In 1814 Archbishop Vernon Harcourt of York made Wrangham one of his examining chaplains – responsible for testing the academic credentials of ordination candidates – and six years later appointed him Archdeacon of Cleveland. The stipend of this senior post averaged no more than £18 per annum, so the archbishop gave him the living of Thorpe Bassett, near Malton, in place of Folkton, which had been linked with Hunmanby. The archdeaconry embraced the northern part of Yorkshire and extended westwards across the Pennines as far as the Deanery of Rydal in the Lake District. Unlike the twenty-first century archdeacon, Wrangham was not expected to travel the length and breadth of his territory to hold the hands of dispirited parish clergy, but was required by law to hold periodic visitations to ensure that they were carrying out their duties efficiently. A feature of his visitations was an extensive questionnaire which the clergy and churchwardens were required to complete and submit to him before their encounter. These displayed his high expectations of their care of the buildings and also of what took place within them. Is there any Parish Library? Are the Seats, Reading Desk etc. in good order? Has the pulpit also a decent Cushion? What is the Average Number of Communicants? Is the Sacrament Money duly distributed? Are there any Daily, Sunday or Infant Schools? Are there any Dissenters, how many, and of what description? What are the regular Services? Do the Churchwardens keep good order on the Lord's Day? – and many more, all indicating that the standard of church life in the late eighteenth and early nineteenth century was not everywhere as deplorable as it was once alleged to have been.

From time to time the clergy and churchwardens of a number of rural deaneries were summoned to convenient centres to hear an Archdeacon's Charge, which drew largely on the facts revealed by answers to the questionnaires, but also in Wrangham's case included expressions of his liberal approach to wider issues in Church and state – the importance of education, the need to remove the political and social disabilities suffered by Roman Catholics, the need for simplicity of thought and language in sermons – all very uncommon views at the time.

Archbishop Harcourt greatly valued Wrangham's work and, after telling Sydney Smith that the archdeacon was 'an ornament to the diocese', he became known for a time as 'Ornament Wrangham'. More significantly, he was appointed by Harcourt in 1823 to a canonry of York Minster, which increased his income without adding to his responsibilities. He went to York for his periods of residence, which were relatively infrequent since the Minster had many canons – almost all of them non-resident and occupying one or more parishes. The quarterly chapter meetings were largely concerned with the sharing among the canons of the Minster's surplus revenue, though in 1828 Wrangham was in a minority of one in his opposition to a petition rejecting Catholic emancipation.

In 1825 the archbishop displayed his generosity towards his archdeacon by appointing him to a canonry of Chester Cathedral which had chanced to fall vacant and was at his disposal. This also enabled its occupant to become, at his own convenience, rector of nearby Dodleston, which he elected to do in 1827, having resigned from Thorpe Bassett in favour of his eldest son, who was also ordained. A house in Chester was bought to enable him to carry out his minimal duties at the cathedral while also giving some attention to Dodleston parish.

Any fear that he might be overtaxed by his fivefold responsibilities in Chester and Yorkshire must have been quickly dispelled when in 1828 the archbishop got him to leave the Archdeaconry of Cleveland and to take over the much larger Archdeaconry of the East Riding – a post he held for the next 12 years. There was still time for him to play a prominent part in the public life of the county, particularly in the promotion of education and in health and hygiene issues. He virtually founded the North Sea Bathing Infirmary at Scarborough and contributed to a multitude of guidebooks and local histories.

Wrangham was also well known in literary circles and a close friend of William Wordsworth, whom he once admonished for the illegibility of his handwriting – 'Why is it those who can write well in one sense, write generally so ill in another?' His own handwriting was small and neat, and easily legible, but then, his work as a poet and writer was in a league different from that of Wordsworth. He was prolific and highly competent, especially in the handling of the classics and in translation, but, in spite of a distinctive style expressing strong convictions, he cannot be said to have been an inspired writer. Over 100 books, pamphlets, monographs, visitation charges and sermons, and contributions to guide books and historical studies appeared under his name, assisted sometimes by the fact that he could afford to have work privately printed. None of these could be described as substantial, and their subjects were often, to modern eyes at least, esoteric. But he was a good editor and abridger and his handling of a six-volume British edition of *Plutarch's Lives* won widespread praise. His contribution to *Blackwood's Magazine* on classic subjects had an appreciative following, while his membership of the Roxburghe and Bannatyne Clubs took him into the company of the literary elite. In 1804, and for reasons not now clear, he became a Fellow of the Royal Society.

As a collector of books Wrangham was without peer and his passion for books justifies the description 'bibliomaniac', though his knowledge and handling of books was both scholarly and astute. The walls of every room in the vicarage ('from cellar to garret', it was said) were lined with shelves and at the time of his death these were occupied by 15,000 volumes. Shortly before his death he handed over to Trinity College, Cambridge 10,000 pamphlets bound in 996 volumes.

Wrangham delighted in all books, even though the contents of most of his collection were of no interest to him, but he had a special passion for volumes which had been privately printed and for those produced on coloured paper. When his own books were being printed he usually asked for a few to be done on coloured paper and this, recalled a contemporary, 'made of his personal bibliography a phenomenon of rainbow complexity'. Poets and dramatists of the sixteenth and seventeenth centuries took up a great deal of shelf space and much of his pleasure was derived from the tracking down of rare and highly unusual books. He knew what he was looking for and had money enough to purchase most of what he was after. Curiously, he had little interest in typography and his own books, produced by non-specialist printers, were often poorly designed and printed. Reflecting on the contents of his library, which included some very valuable items, such as a first edition of the King Edward VI Prayer Book and the works of Sir Thomas More, he once remarked that he measured its worth 'not by the total of its value, but by the number of ingenious discoveries and lucky caprices'.

When, following his death, the library was despatched to London for auction, the sale, arranged in 5,758 lots, occupied 20 days. The catalogue remains an important record of books that existed in pre-Victorian England. His own final book, written in January 1842 – the year of his death – was entitled *A Few Epigrams attempted in Latin Translations by an old pen nearly worn to the stump.*

4

The Tractarian
Edward Bouverie Pusey, Oxford

Edward Bouverie Pusey was a canon of Christ Church, Oxford from 1828 until his death in 1882, and during this time also held the Regius Chair of Hebrew annexed to his canonry. But it is not as a Hebraist or as a cathedral dignitary that he is now remembered. He was a holy priest who, more than anyone else, symbolized and led the revival in the Church of England of that Catholic element in Anglicanism which had been strongly emphasized by Archbishop Laud and his followers in the seventeenth century but largely lost during the Hanoverian era. So successful was the Oxford Movement, as it came to be called because of the location of its origin, or the Tractarian Movement, because of its propagation by a series of tracts, that it changed the beliefs and practices of a significant part of the Church of England during the latter part of the nineteenth century. Its emphasis on the Incarnation, the Church and the Eucharist later came to be accepted in most parts of the entire Anglican Communion.

Yet Pusey was not a charismatic leader who stumped the country, preaching his beliefs and winning supporters for his cause. On the contrary, he rarely left Oxford and for long periods hardly set foot outside his home in Tom Quad at Christ Church. His teaching was far from immediately attractive, since he had a grim view of human nature which strongly emphasized its depravity and utter dependence on the gracious love of God for its redemption. His spirituality was austere in the extreme, leaving little space for that abundance of life which Christ offered his followers, and his self-hatred was so intense that its causes have to be sought in psychological, as well as theological, categories. These are not difficult to locate.

That said, there can be no doubting that Pusey lived close to God, and that this is the explanation of his immense influence, exercised through his preaching and writing, and the counsel he gave to the multitudes who went to him for confession and spiritual advice. He now has a place in the Church of England's calendar of saints and, like many others on that roll of honour, his personality was lopsided – hence its power. Moreover, his apparent preoccupation with the dark side of human nature had many precedents, not least in the writings of St Paul. In many ways his outlook was deeply conservative, and he strongly resisted cathedral reform, yet he longed for the renewal of the Church's worship and witness. His suggestion that colleges for the training of the clergy should be established in association with cathedrals was eventually adopted and most of these survived until the latter part of the twentieth century.

Pusey was born in 1800 into an aristocratic family. Both his grandfathers were peers and his father, the Honourable Philip Bouverie, took the name Pusey when he inherited the family estate of that name in Wiltshire. Young Edward, who was a cousin of the future Lord Shaftesbury, grew up in the world of hunting, shooting and fishing and throughout his life had a great deal of money at his disposal. But his father was a benevolent despot who ruled over his family with such severity that Edward grew up seriously repressed and with a guilt-ridden personality that controlled the remainder of his life. From his mother, however, he learned of God's immanence and of the real presence of Christ in the Eucharist. And when his father died he was so devastated that he felt unable to attend the funeral.

After attending a private school in Mitcham in Surrey, he went to Eton, where he was said to be the last boy to be taught dancing. His father was evidently dissatisfied with the academic education his son had received in the still unreformed college, so he sent him for 15 months of intense study under Dr Edward Maltby, who later became Bishop of Durham. This worked, for although his pupil spent too much of his first two years at Christ Church, Oxford, hunting, he nonetheless took a First in Classics in 1822 and was elected to a coveted fellowship at Oriel College. During his time at Eton he had felt challenged by a friend who questioned the truth of the Christian faith and eventually became an atheist. This led Pusey to go to Germany in order to study the philosophical and literary systems on which the current opposition to Christianity was largely based. While at Göttingen and Berlin, however, he also encountered a new breed of Christian scholars who were applying the 'higher criticism' to the Bible and using a deeper knowledge of Semitic languages to understand and interpret the Old Testament. Their theological outlook was, in consequence, strongly liberal. On his return to England he went into residence at Oriel, where he undertook an intensive study of Semitic languages, which he completed in Germany, and by 1828 he was one of the very few scholars in England who were competent in this field, and also one of the few English theologians to be fluent in German.

This turned out to be an exciting year. It saw the publication of his first book, his ordination as deacon, then priest, his appointment as Regius Professor of Hebrew at Oxford, to which was annexed a residentiary canonry of Christ Church – and his marriage. Soon after leaving Eton and going up to Oxford he met and fell deeply in love with Maria Barker, of Fairford Park in Gloucestershire. She was said to have been tall and beautiful, with a strong personality and decided views freely expressed. Some thought she was a trifle odd; everyone agreed that she could hardly have been more different from her beloved. It was, however, one of those unions of contrast that can work, though nine years were to pass from their first meeting to the day when Pusey's father was prepared to give his 27-year-old son permission to become engaged. During the intervening years they corresponded but did not meet, and anxiety about the outcome of his eventual proposal led to a complete breakdown of his health, requiring four months' recuperation in Brighton after she had accepted him. They were married in the following year and four years of idyllically happy marriage followed, with four children to prove it. She undoubtedly dominated him, but this is what he needed, or at least liked, and although her outbursts of temper caused him pain, their love for each other ran deep enough to make them bearable.

For one reason or another – ignorance or deliberate suppression – this important period of Pusey's life found no place in H. P. Liddon's monumental biography or in lesser portraits of him and emerged only in 1983 in a volume of essays titled *Pusey Rediscovered*. David W. F. Forrester, a Roman Catholic scholar, had become suspicious of Liddon's handling of the marriage and decided to undertake further research, which led to the discovery in the library of Pusey House, Oxford, of 113 letters from Pusey to Maria and 81 letters from Maria to Pusey. These are discussed by Father Forrester in his essay and indicate that during the early years of his marriage Pusey experienced the bliss of knowing something he had hitherto believed to be impossible: that he could be loved – unconditionally loved – for his own sake. Shortly before their marriage and after a brief meeting in London Pusey wrote to Maria expressing his conviction that:

whatever defects one so softly, beautifully, gently kind may discover in me, she will still look as favourably upon them, and that we shall go hand in hand, alternately perhaps assisting, reminding, comforting each other until the time come when both shall be translated to the presence of a pure and holy God. Everything shews me more and more how great a treasure God has given me in you.

This is not the Pusey bequeathed to us by earlier church historians and is scarcely credible, but the letters indicate clearly that the spell cast over him by his father was broken. But not for long. In 1832 his ten-month-old daughter, Katherine, died and he became convinced that this was a punishment for his sins, he being utterly depraved. By then his father in God and spiritual guide, Bishop Charles Lloyd of Oxford, had also died, causing him unusual distress. His first book had been heavily criticized because it seemed to indicate much sympathy with German liberal theology. The consequence of all this was that Pusey reverted to the outlook and style of his father, imposing a harsh regime on the life of his family, inflicting Maria with his own deformed religious scruples and making his children thoroughly unhappy. His explanation was that 'Our system, if it is worth anything, must be contrary to the world's system.' Maria escaped by dying in 1839 – a devastating blow from which he never really recovered. He told John Keble in 1842,

My dear wife's illness brought to me, what has since been deepened by the review of my past life, how, amid special mercies and guardianship of God, I am scarred all over and seared with sin, so that I am a monster to myself; I loathe myself, I can feel of myself only like one covered with leprosy from head to foot; guarded as I have been there is no one with whom I do not compare myself, and find myself worse than they.

He refused to accept that Maria's early death was anything other than further punishment for his own sins, a belief reinforced by the death of another daughter. He would not enter the drawing room of his Christ Church home where they had all spent so many happy times. The hour of Maria's death was observed daily, and as time passed the intensity of his morbid remorse increased, rather than decreased. He came to believe it wrong to smile or to delight in nature. He wore haircloth next to his skin, beat his shoulders with a five-cord whip and, whenever possible, ate the most horrible food. He drank only cold water to remind him that he was 'only fit to be where there is not a drop to cool the flame' and made it a rule 'always to lie down in

The Canons

bed, confessing that I am unworthy to lie down except in Hell but so praying to lie down in the Everlasting Arms'. It was his deep faith in these final words that enabled him to survive and there was something essentially Pauline in the violent intensity of his contrasting experiences of despair and hope. In one of his published *Parochial Sermons* on Christ and justification he said of the Holy Spirit:

> How could any Comforter be better for us than he? . . . we rest in him; himself our hope, himself whom we hope for; himself the fountain of eternal light, whereby we see his light; himself the earnest of our everlasting inheritance; himself our portion, and possession, and inheritance of which he is the earnest.

Pusey's spirituality, rooted in the Bible, the early Fathers and the Christian tradition, owed a good deal also to the French Counter-Reformation spirituality he encountered and translated into English. He was largely responsible for the revival of the sacrament of confession in the Church of England, though his own use of this sacrament was delayed for some years because he believed, characteristically, that his sins were so vile that any confessor would be bound to be deeply shocked. His remarkable published sermons were sometimes thought to be overlong even in his own day but are replete with deep insights into the mysteries of the Incarnation and the crucifixion. There was a problem, however, inasmuch as his own spirituality and devotional practices owed so much to continental Roman Catholicism. This proved to be a hindrance to their usefulness within the Anglican tradition and, although he played a major part in the re-establishing of women's religious orders in England – the first was started in Regent's Park village in 1845 – the guidance he provided for the sisters often inhibited true growth in the life of the Spirit. It was also unfortunate that the church in Leeds he had financed in memory of his wife and daughter, and designed to represent the Anglo-Catholic tradition in that city, was so extreme in its witness that its first priests had no difficulty in converting to Roman Catholicism, taking many of their parishioners with them.

Pusey was only 28 when he became Oxford's Regius Professor of Hebrew. There was no requirement to give lectures, though soon after his appointment he gave two courses at Oriel College – one for beginners, the other for those with some knowledge of the language. This he continued to do for many years and was always ready to encourage undergraduates to take up Hebrew, financing from his own pocket a number of scholarships to facilitate this. But eventually he reached the conclusion that, while a modest competence would always be helpful in the devotional use of the Old Testament, the Authorized Version translation would serve for most students. The scholarly examination of the text required a great deal of time-consuming study and should, he said, be confined to specialists.

He himself devoted a lot of time to the correction of the AV translation during his early years in the chair, and hoped to produce a new version which was never, in fact, completed. His later commentaries on the Minor Prophets and Daniel were said to be learned but ultra-conservative. His chief contributions to the field were indirect, but led to the revival of Hebrew scholarship in Oxford. The first was a result of a visit to Germany when he was shown a Hebrew lexicon and grammar — the work of a scholar named Gesenius – which was far in advance of anything available in Britain. Pusey introduced this to Oxford, via America, and it became, after some editing, the standard reference work for the next hundred years. The other contribution came later when he was one of the curators of the Bodleian Library and organized the purchase from Germany of major collections of Semitic literature. He catalogued the library's Arabic manuscripts.

It was understood in Oxford that the Regius Professor of Hebrew would have a concern for the wide realm of theology, and this came to occupy most of Pusey's thinking and writing. In 1838 he edited a new translation of St Augustine's *Confessions*, this being the first volume in what became the monumental *Library of the Fathers*. Forty-two years later he published *What is of Faith as to Everlasting Punishment* (1880) – a rejoinder to F. W. Farrar's more liberal contribution to the subject. Most influential, however, were his relatively brief, but always meticulously learned, contributions to *Tracts for the Times*.

Pusey was not involved in the early stages of the Oxford Movement, and there is some dispute as to what factors took him in its direction and away from his earlier attachment to certain aspects of theological liberalism. Some believe that during a period of emotional turmoil in the 1830s he was attracted by the security apparently provided by traditional orthodoxy. Others believe that he was influenced by his work on the early Fathers of the Church, or by his encounter with John Henry Newman. Yet more are of the opinion that he came to regard orthodoxy as the only secure bastion against the eroding effects of liberalism.

When during a casual conversation Pusey told Newman that he was being too hard on the Evangelicals, the response was that he, Pusey, should write something about this in a tract, several of which had already been published. The resulting *Thoughts on the Benefits of the System of Fasting Enjoined by Our Church*, published as Tract 18, was not quite what Newman had expected, but Pusey thought it might appeal to Evangelicals with its emphasis on the crucial importance of the personal relationship of the soul to God. Towards the end of his life he confessed, 'I loved the Evangelicals because they loved our Lord. I loved them for their zeal for souls.' There is no evidence as to their response to the tract, but the immediate effect of its publication was to give a great boost to the Movement, since it was the work of a prominent member of the university, a deeply spiritual priest and, moreover, one with good family connections. Three more tracts, all on *Scriptural Views of Holy Baptism*, followed in 1836 and the saintly Dean Church, in his *History of the Oxford Movement*, described their appearance as 'like the advance of a battery of heavy artillery on a field where the battle has hitherto been carried on by skirmishing and mus-ketry'. They were in fact much more than tracts, having the character of learned treatises.

The wide circulation achieved by Pusey's tracts and the debate they produced had the effect, outside Oxford anyway, of making him appear to be the leader of the movement, and its adherents became known as Puseyites – a title that was to stick. There was however never a leader in the sense of someone at the head of a highly organ-ized campaign, but when Newman left the Church of England in 1841 Pusey became the revered figure to whom most looked for guidance, and whose opinions were treated by some as almost infallible. What Dr Pusey thought became synonymous with truth.

No more tracts came from his pen but in 1865, after the Privy Council had judged in favour of the authors of the controversial *Essays and Reviews* (1860), he wrote a letter to his close friend, John Keble, which was published as *The Church of England a Portion of Christ's One Holy Catholic Church, and a Means of Restoring Visible Unity: An Eirenicon*. This was answered immediately and negatively by Newman, and led four years later to a second *Eirenicon*, which was mainly on the Immaculate Conception and written as a riposte to Newman. A third, *Is Healthful Reunion Impossible?*, appeared in 1870 and dealt mainly with the doctrine of purgatory, but included also material on the deutero-canonical books in the Bible and on the Roman supremacy. For many years Pusey believed that if the true catholic character of Anglicanism could be recovered, some sort of union with the Roman Catholic Church might be achieved without forfeiture of Anglican authority, and this led him to send copies of his third *Eirenicon* to many of the bishops then attending the First Vatican Council. His hopes were however rudely dashed by the Council's definition of Papal infallibility.

Further disappointment came to him in 1870 when a Royal Commission set up to deal with the vexed question of permissible ritual in the Church of England suggested, among other things, that the Athanasian Creed should no longer be used in public worship. This led Pusey to threaten resignation from all his offices in the Church and the university, but after much agitation the Convocation of Canterbury agreed in 1873 that this so-called creed should be kept in use. His university sermons also tended to cause a stir and *The Holy Eucharist, a Comfort to the Penitent* (1834), which dealt with the issue of the real presence and in its published form attracted considerable publicity, was condemned by the Vice-Chancellor and six Doctors of Divinity and led to a two-year suspension from the university pulpit. When he returned to it in 1846 with *The Entire Absolution of the Penitent* he spoke of the importance of sacramental confession, and later in *Will Ye Also Go Away?* (1867) he returned to the subject of the real presence and went on to consider the place of ritual in worship.

The matter of university reform came to a head in 1852 with the publication of a Royal Commission report on the subject. No one doubted the need for reform, since Oxford, in common with many other historic institutions, was essentially corrupt and a very long way from fulfilling the intentions of its founders and benefactors. But the Commission's proposals were controversial inasmuch as they favoured radical, rather than moderate reform. They involved a shift of emphasis in teaching from the college to the professors and a general raising of academic standards through common examinations. Such changes would affect the teaching of every subject, but most especially theology, which was not taught as a separate subject. Every undergraduate was required to have some knowledge of theology, but not very much, with the consequence that it was not dealt with in any depth and even those going forward to ordination were left with little more than a rudimentary grasp of its essentials. The Commission proposed that theology should henceforth have its own faculty and that its professors, of whom more would be required, should actually give lectures on their own fields of study. This was not in itself controversial but the consequences were, inasmuch as teaching would no longer be confined to the college fellows and tutors. What is more, these might be laymen or even Dissenters. All of which was strongly opposed by Pusey and the heads of houses – the latter because it would involve loss of power

and the former because it would inevitably dilute the clericalized religious context in which education was provided.

Pusey was quite frank – 'The Church of England will lose Oxford' –
but in spite of lengthy correspondence with the prime minister, W. E.
Gladstone, and many other representatives on the issue, which raised
some fundamental questions about the nature of university education,
the reformers won the support of Parliament. Yet, in the event, the
changes were effected only very slowly and for a long time were barely
perceptible, apart from the appointment of a few more professors; and
the balance of power has remained largely unaltered to this day, since
professors never aspire to heavy teaching commitments. Pusey, having
recognized that the battle had been lost publicly, got himself elected
on to the Hebdomadal Council in order to continue the fight against
liberalism in the university. The liberals thought his election scandalous, since his status as a professor counted for little in the running of
the university, but he remained a very active member of the Council,
serving on its committees until the end of his life and succeeding in
thwarting some reforms.

In 1832 Lord Henley, a prominent Evangelical and brother-in-law
of Sir Robert Peel, the prime minister, published a *Plan of Church
Reform*. In this he attacked the cathedrals, with their great wealth
and indolent clergy, and proposed the redistribution of this wealth
to finance the building of new churches and the creation of new parishes in the largely neglected industrial towns. Noting that the cathedral clergy absorbed more than one-sixth of the total amount paid
to the parish clergy, Lord Henley recommended that cathedral services should be maintained only by the dean, assisted if necessary by
chaplains, and that neighbouring city parishes in the gift of the dean
and chapter should be annexed to active prebends, while the remainder of the stalls, occupied by sinecurists, should be abolished. Pusey
responded in the following year with *Remarks on the Prospective and
Past Benefits of Cathedral Institutions*. He recognized the need for
reform but strongly objected to the destructive character of Henley's
proposals, arguing that the right approach was not to destroy the life
of the cathedrals but, rather, to consider what constructive changes
were needed to enable them to complement the ministries of bishops
and the parish clergy.

Pusey had no doubt that what he called 'the healthful condition of
the church' required a better-trained priesthood. Oxford and Cambridge could not provide this, yet in Germany he had found no fewer
than 23 theological seminaries which provided as complete an aca-

demic and practical training for pastors as anyone might wish. The Church of England must, therefore, require 12 conveniently located cathedrals with sufficient facilities to establish seminaries that would each provide a two-year postgraduate course for 70 to 80 ordinands. Five of the cathedral clergy, themselves learned scholars, would be professors of the main theological subjects, while able, experienced priests from the city would teach pastoralia. Pusey was, however, concerned with more than clergy training and believed that the cathedrals should once again become important centres of sacred learning where scholars could pursue their studies in ways that were impossible in busy parishes. Something less ambitious than any of this gradually came into being in a number of cathedral closes, usually with about 30 students and a staff of three or four teachers. They were largely independent of deans and chapters and served the Church of England well for over a century.

Lord Henley's proposals also raised for Pusey the question of trust. Any reforms must first involve the ascertaining of the original wishes of the cathedrals' founders and later benefactors and be designed to ensure that these wishes were better carried out. The diversion of property and endowments from the offering of edifying worship, the cultivation of learning, and the life of a Christian community to other purposes – no matter how worthy – was, he believed, nothing short of robbery. Moreover, if this was to be carried out by Act of Parliament it could only represent a wholly improper interference by the state in the affairs of the Church – an issue which would soon ignite the Oxford Movement over the proposed suppression by the government of ten Irish bishoprics.

When Pusey was 70 he still celebrated Holy Communion in his study daily at 4 a.m. and this continued on Sundays and saints' days until virtually the end of his life. First appointments – mainly for penitents and others seeking spiritual counsel – began at 7 a.m.; the last ended at about midnight. During the winter of 1872/3, however, his health declined seriously and he became subject to attacks of bronchitis. From then onwards he rarely ventured from his house in Tom Quad, which he had occupied for 54 years, though he went sometimes to a house in Ascot, close to a convent with which he was associated. Eventually he became almost stone deaf and penitents had to catalogue their sins on paper. He died in the convent on 16 September 1882, and Dean Church said, of him:

No man was more variously judged, more sternly condemned, more tenderly loved.

5

The Novelist
Charles Kingsley,
Chester and Westminster

Of the many extraordinary personalities who invigorated the public life of Victorian England, none was more variously gifted than Charles Kingsley. His occupancy of the canonries of Chester (1869–73) and Westminster (1873–75) were but brief postscripts to a relatively short life, based on a small North Hampshire parish, in which he ministered for 34 years. There he expressed, in a unique combination, the gifts of a priest, pastor, preacher, lecturer, novelist, poet, polemical journalist, social reformer, geologist and naturalist – a clerical polymath, if ever there was one.

These gifts were infused with a deep religious faith, a burning passion and a dramatic power that brought him national fame, wide influence and considerable achievement. There was a compulsive element in his make-up and A. C. Benson, who knew him well, described him as:

> a strong, spare, active figure, with very marked features, a big nose, a great mobile, compressed mouth, eyes deeply set, but with a flash-ing light in them that told you he was no ordinary man. His face was worn and deeply marked, showing that he had not found life an easy business.

He once said that laughter and humour belonged to the nature of God himself, and he was often elated and full of fun, but there were also periods of acute melancholy and in the end he died burnt out and exhausted. It was marvellous while it lasted and, besides a bust in Westminster Abbey, two of his novels, *The Water Babies* and *Westward Ho!*, remain in print as a living literary memorial.

A quarter of a century after Kingsley's death, Cosmo Gordon Lang, then Bishop of Stepney and destined to become Archbishop of Canterbury, reflected on the course of his own life and wrote about his call to ordination:

The mention of Kingsley is the mention of the only personality which had so far got a hold of such religious life as I had. I remember reading his life in my dingy little lodgings . . . Well, that book spoke to me as no living voice had, and I remember distinctly closing it with the feeling that had I been good enough I should have liked to take Orders and witness to the Kingsley ideal of Christianity.

It is not altogether clear, however, whether the unmarried Lang, whose views on marriage and divorce were to bring him unwelcome notoriety at the time of King Edward VIII's abdication, was aware of the degree to which Kingsley's religious passion was inseparable from his sexuality. The two-volume biography of Kingsley written by his devoted widow Fanny naturally did not venture onto this territory, but it was tackled head-on by Susan Chitty in *The Beast and the Monk* (1975). She unearthed some of his startling unpublished erotic drawings of himself and Fanny and learned from an assistant at the British Museum that they possessed a number of his drawings that constituted 'the most disgusting exhibition in the whole collection'.

Towards the end of his time as an undergraduate at Cambridge, when he had fallen deeply in love with Fanny, he felt driven to confess to his previous lapses from celibacy:

You, my unspotted, bring a virgin baby to my arms. I, alas, do not to yours. Before our lips met I had sinned and fallen. Oh, how low! If it is your wish, you shall be a wife only in name. No communion but that of mind shall pass between us.

But that was a very long way from her wish, since her own sexual needs were no less urgent than his. They had a blissfully happy marriage in which the physical expression of their love for each other always had a central place. Some of his writings and poems, and the drawings that accompanied them, were also nothing if not erotic and his public quarrels with the Tractarians and Roman Catholics were to a considerable degree focused on their claim, which was utterly anathema to him, that celibacy was a purer form of Christian discipleship than matrimony.

Charles Kingsley was born in 1819 in Devonshire, where his father, who had once been a wealthy but unwise landowner, was now an impoverished curate, though he eventually became rector of the rich living of St Luke's, Chelsea. Young Charles, who had a sickly child-hood and from an early age experienced the dreams and nightmares that were to be a permanent feature of his life, was initially educated at home by his father. When 12, however, he and his younger brother Herbert were sent to a preparatory school in Bristol, and while there he witnessed the 1831 riots which followed the rejection by the House of Lords of the first Reform Bill. He was horrified by the degree of violence displayed by the rioters and his first reaction was to side with the Tories and aristocrats, but later he became much more sympathetic to the claims of the poor.

He completed his schooling at Helston Grammar School, where he had the devastating experience of losing his beloved brother to rheumatic fever. He then went to the junior department of King's College, London to prepare for entry to Magdalene College, Cambridge. His Cambridge years, however, were more notable for their social and sporting activities than for industrious study – he once confessed to being 'very idle and very wicked'. Riding, rowing, long walks and fishing claimed much of his time, and often he would climb out of the college for a dawn spell on the banks of the river. A prizefighter taught him how to box. Study tended to depress him and he was at one point tempted to leave 'to become a wild prairie hunter'. His broad plan was to enjoy himself during the term, then try to catch up with his studies during vacations.

But even these demanded their breaks and it was while riding in the Oxfordshire countryside that he met the beautiful Fanny Grenfell. It was love at first sight for both of them, but it would be some years before her wealthy father would consent to their marriage. She had, in fact, been seriously considering the possibility of entering a religious order recently founded by Dr Pusey in London's Regent's Park, and although she now gave this up she remained a devout young woman and had a sobering effect on her student lover. She urged him to work hard for their future together and, besides writing letters of advice to him on his religious development, sent him books by Thomas Carlyle and Samuel Taylor Coleridge. A copy of F. D. Maurice's controversial *The Kingdom of Christ* had a profound effect upon him, and Fanny's influence led to his decision to seek holy orders. This also had the useful effect of assuring her father of his sobriety and social standing, and after a final six months of intense cramming he managed to scrape a First in Classics and a good Second in Mathematics.

In 1842 Bishop Sumner of Winchester ordained him to a curacy at Eversley – the North Hampshire parish he was to serve for the remainder of his days. It was not the most exciting assignment in the Church of England, the parish consisting of three small villages on heathland bordering the Windsor Forest. The small, very impoverished popula- tion included deerstalkers and gypsies. But Kingsley loved the place and, shortly after leaving the parish to marry Fanny, he was delighted to be invited back as rector. The incumbent he had served was obliged to flee the country to avoid prosecution for his too close involvement with some of his women parishioners. The parish had become very run down. Few people went to church, most could neither read nor write, and Nonconformity had taken over. The rectory was dark and damp, the ground floor being often flooded in the winter.

Kingsley tackled all this in the spirit of George Herbert, though the personalities of the two priests could hardly have been more different. His style was that of a country gentleman in holy orders. He dressed in rough grey cloth, wore knickerbockers and a black tie, and visited the homes of the parish assiduously – sometimes three or four times a day when there was sickness, or if death was lurking. He talked with the men working in the fields, advised their wives on domestic prob- lems and entertained their children with his stories. When diphtheria appeared for the first time in England, this created a minor panic in Eversley, but Kingsley went in and out of the cottages armed with large bottles of gargle and taught the inhabitants how to gargle their throats as a precaution against infection. If anyone was seriously ill he would cancel his outside engagements in order to minister to them. Being himself an inveterate smoker of long clay pipes, he bought these in large quantities and secreted a supply of them at various key points in the parish so that if on his rounds he became desperate for a smoke there was always one ready to hand. He insisted that smoking and fishing were essential tranquillizers, and rode to hounds on a horse 'picked up cheap for a parson's work'.

From his earliest years Kingsley was affected with a stammer. He overcame this partly by means of controlled breathing exercises which he often recommended to other sufferers, but also by tone of speech, which gave his voice a distinctive timbre. None of this restricted his power as a preacher and teacher. He spoke passionately of the things close to his heart – of the love of God, of the beauty and holiness of nature, of the compassion of Christ for the poor, the sick and the oppressed. The effect on congregations was electrifying and both preacher and people were often in tears, though the 'manliness' of his Christian calling was a constant theme and a course of Evensong ser- mons opposing Bishop John William Colenso's controversial views on the authorship of the Pentateuch must have lowered the temperature somewhat. From far and wide people began to travel to Eversley to see and hear the rector in action on Sunday morning. Edward White Benson, Master of the newly founded Wellington College, lived near enough to walk over with his family. From somewhat further afield came Queen Emma of the Sandwich Islands, who stayed for a weekend and gave the villagers their first sight of a black face. Officers and cadets walked from Sandhurst and Aldershot to hear rousing sermons on patriotism and the vocation of the Christian soldier. He was fascinated by military matters and never failed to be moved by the clank of swords and spurs in the aisles. On one occasion when A. C. Benson, the son of Edward White Benson, was in the congregation, news was brought of a serious fire at the nearby great house at Bramshill. Kingsley ordered the women to stay and the curate to finish the service, while he, still in surplice and hood, ran across the churchyard, seized a small axe and led the men to the scene of the conflagration, which they managed to put out.

Yet life was not always so exciting. When the curate took the service Kingsley sat in the rector's pew unrobed and simply stood at the end to give the blessing. Or if Mattins was to be followed by Holy Communion he would leave the first service to the curate and sit behind the heavy Jacobean screen unseen and unheard until the sound of his voice reciting the Lord's Prayer indicated that the Eucharist had started. But the crowds took their toll – 'I cannot bear having my place turned into a fair on Sundays, and all this talking after church,' he wrote to F. D. Maurice, who had become a friend. In the end, to avoid meeting people he had a small back gate made into his garden, so that immediately after the service he could escape through the vestry door and go straight back to the rectory. The continuation of excitement and emotional exhaustion evidently required a time of quiet for recovery. He was a restless man who composed most of his sermons and writings while walking about the parish or with long strides around the rectory lawn. He never seemed able to settle and during meals would often rise to wander about the house, or even the garden.

A lending library was started and reading classes were held in the rectory. A savings scheme encouraged thrift among those who had anything to spare for saving, and in all the pastoral and social work his wife was also deeply involved. Besides this she had four children and suffered a number of miscarriages. He was himself often away for quite long periods, preaching, lecturing and attending meetings, and was for a time Professor of English Literature at Queen's College, Harley Street in London – an educational establishment for governesses of which F. D. Maurice was the president. This involved weekly lectures but ill-health made him give up after 12 months. A sermon in a London church on 'The Message of the Church to the Labouring Man' drew an immediate protest from the vicar, who objected to its socialist tendency, and the Bishop of London, learning from the press of the ensuing controversy, forbade him to preach in the diocese, though he retracted after reading the published text.

Kingsley was closely associated with J. M. F. Ludlow, F. D. Maurice, Tom Hughes and the other founders of the Christian Socialism Movement and was sometimes accused of being a Chartist. He contributed a regular column under the pseudonym Parson Lot to a newspaper called *Politics for the People*, which was launched in 1848 and published 17 issues before it ran out of money. He used the same pseudonym for a pamphlet, *Cheap Clothes and Nasty* (1850), which exposed the iniquities of the rag trade, and also wrote for the *Christian Socialist* during its brief life. His novels protested loudly against social injustice. Yet he was, like F. D. Maurice, a social reformer, rather than someone who sought radical change in the political and economic order. Indeed, his ideal was a feudal society in which the different social classes recognized responsibility for those beneath them, leaving no one uncared for and everyone with sufficient for their needs – limited though these might be deemed to be.

Kingsley recognized that there could be no return to such a society but, unlike some of his associates, he strongly defended the traditional role of the House of Lords and there were those who accused him of deserting the socialist cause. His views on race were also somewhat suspect. He once declared that England was for Englishmen, not for Jews, and there was a considerable furore in 1865 when he spoke at a dinner in Southampton in honour of Edward Eyre, a returned Governor of Jamaica who had dealt with a black uprising on one of the plantations with the utmost severity. This led to a breach of friendship with Ludlow and Hughes.

As he got older Kingsley's denunciation of social evil became less shrill and his associations with the upper classes more frequent, but some of the problems about which he had once felt strongly were now on the way to solution and his concern to improve the lot of the poor never wavered. Chief among his campaigns was a plea for better sanitation. He had an obsession with water and washing, which may perhaps have found expression in *The Water Babies*, but he was a long way ahead of his time in recognizing the connection between sanitation and health. He lost no opportunity of raising the subject in sermons, addresses and articles and at the first meeting of the Ladies' Sanitary Association in 1859 he described the enterprise as 'one of the noblest, most right-minded and practical conceptions that I have come across for some years'.

Kingsley was a compulsive writer and at the end of his life his collected works filled 47 volumes. He often wrote very late into the night and this, on top of a full day in the parish and involvement in other enterprises, frequently caused exhaustion. But he always explained that he was driven by the need for money and certainly the income at Eversley was insufficient for the public school education of three children. Yet his vision of how life ought to be lived needed a larger audience than anything that might be achieved by sermons and lectures and his creative urges demanded an outlet.

He was a prolific novelist, though not a great one, even if *The Water Babies* and *Westward Ho!* became classics and remain in print a century and a half after their first publication. The problem, from the literary point of view, is that Kingsley was essentially a propagandist and everything he wrote was an extension of his sermons. Thus his first book, which he started soon after taking his degree, was a life, in poetic drama form, of St Elizabeth of Hungary (1848), but it also expressed his views on contemporary religious and social issues.

While his life of St Elizabeth was going through the press he started a novel, *Yeast*, which first appeared also in 1848 in instalments in *Frasier's Magazine*. This expressed his sympathy with the rural poor, and drew heavily on his own experience at Eversley, but it was not what the well-off readers of the magazine wanted and the editor found himself engulfed in a storm of protest. Kingsley was therefore driven to change publishers for his next novel, *Alton Locke* (1850), which was concerned with the plight of the urban poor, particularly those employed in tailors' sweatshops. Carlyle described it as 'a fervid creation still left half chaotic'. Again it was published anonymously, though by this time few of its many readers were unaware of the author's identity. *Westward Ho!* (1855) was an expression of patriotism with plenty of unsavoury sea dogs, stimulated by the Crimean War and fed by violent anti-Catholicism. George Eliot in her review complained that 'Kingsley sees, feels and paints vividly, but he theorises illogically and moralises absurdly'. Nonetheless, it was widely read and, besides putting the newly founded Macmillan publishing house on its feet, made its author both famous and respectable.

The Water Babies (1863) was written for his youngest son Granville and, after first being serialized in *Macmillan's Magazine*, became a runaway publishing success. Queen Victoria greatly admired it and often read it to her own children. Many generations of children learned to love the story of Tom, an unfortunate chimney climbing boy, who escaped from his dire plight and was transformed into a 'water baby' who lived for some time with the creatures of a river, before emerging to become a happily married engineer. Kingsley was, of course, making a point about a great social evil and, perhaps coincidentally, the employment of climbing boys was made illegal in the year following the book's publication.

In addition to other novels, Kingsley wrote a large number of poems, songs and ballads, which for the most part had less social content but became immensely popular. 'The Sands of Dee', 'For men must work and women must weep' and 'Be good sweet maid, and let who will be clever' were among those recited or sung until well into the next century. Again, the literary quality was not of the highest, but Kingsley's gift as a communicator enabled him to touch people of every social class throughout the English-speaking world. Curiously as it must seem later in a financially driven world, his remarkable success never made him rich.

He was often asked to review books and, although he was somewhat reluctant to tackle volumes 7 and 8 of Anthony Froude's *History of England* for the January 1864 issue of *Macmillan's Magazine*, he eventually dashed off a piece that was to cause him a great deal of trouble, with unforeseen consequences. It included two sentences that were deemed even by his friends to be unwise, if not reckless:

Truth, for its own sake, has never been a virtue of the Roman clergy. Father Newman informs us that it need not, and on the whole ought not to be: that cunning is the weapon which heaven has given to the saints wherewith to withstand the brute male force of the wicked world which marries and is given in marriage.

Newman complained to the publishers and a bitter public controversy ensued, during the course of which Kingsley's family and friends thought it best to get him out of the country. He was very happy to accompany Froude on a visit to France, but not before attempting to defend himself by pointing out that Newman, before his conversion, had himself said something similar about the Roman clergy. In the end, however, Kingsley was widely thought to have misjudged the subtlety of Newman's views and to have come off the worst in the dispute. But this was not quite the end: Newman, challenged by Kingsley to state what he really believed, wrote *Apologia pro vita sua* – often said to be the greatest autobiography in the English language. Kingsley said that he had read *The Dream of Gerontius* 'with awe and admiration'.

In 1860 the prime minister, Lord Palmerston, ill-advisedly offered Kingsley the chair of Modern History at Cambridge, and after some hesitation Kingsley no less rashly accepted it. He had made no academic study of history and was simply not up to the post's demands. Yet for nine years he tried hard and spent a tremendous amount of time over the preparation of his courses of lectures. These were always crowded – mainly by undergraduates who fell under the spell of his eloquence and novel ideas – but the senior members of the History Faculty were less impressed. E. A. Freeman, a distinguished historian who was disappointed not to have been given the chair, complained that 'Pages on pages of these lectures are simply rant and nonsense – history, in short, brought down to the lowest level of the sensational novelist.' A century later, Owen Chadwick's negative verdict, in *The Secularization of the European Mind in the Nineteenth Century* (1975), was more gently stated, but hardly less destructive.

In spite of the heavy work involved, Kingsley always enjoyed his visits to Cambridge, where he was given attractive rooms in Trinity College and was generous in giving time to undergraduates who needed his help. Among these was the Prince of Wales, the future King Edward VII, who, it was said, learned more from his tutor than anything otherwise imparted to him during his year spent at Cambridge. But after nine years Kingsley resigned, declaring that he would have done so much earlier had he not needed the money.

The Prince of Wales showed his gratitude by making him one of his chaplains, which led to an invitation to attend the future king's marriage to Princess Alexandra of Denmark at Windsor in 1863. Not long after the wedding the happy couple went to Oxford to receive the formal congratulations of the university and the Prince to exercise his privilege of nominating a number of worthy people to receive honorary degrees. Among these, it became known, was Charles Kingsley, nominated for a DCL. The Tractarians, who had been gravely offended by his intemperate denunciation of their views, indicated to the university authorities that their leader, Dr Pusey – the Regius Professor of Hebrew – would openly object to the Prince's nomination. His grounds for doing this would be the immoral character of Kingsley's latest novel, *Hypatia*.

Set in fifth-century Alexandria, shortly after the fall of the

Roman Empire, Kingsley's novel – as always – included a discussion of nineteenth-century problems in England. His intention was to demonstrate, albeit in a very roundabout way, that Christianity is the religion of the poor and underprivileged, but it ends with a violent scene in which Hypatia, a woman pagan philosopher, is torn in pieces by a fanatical Christian mob. At one point the unfortunate woman

> shook herself free from her tormentors and springing back, rose for one moment to her full height, naked, snow-white against the dusky mass around – shame and indignation in those wide, clear eyes, but not a stain of fear.

It was this image of a naked woman that cost Kingsley his honorary doctorate for, on hearing of Pusey's opposition, he declined the offer to avoid royal embarrassment. He took his deep disappointment well, but never again did he set foot in Oxford, declining all invitations to preach or to lecture. He also resolved to refuse any public office that might involve him in controversy, and to concentrate on what he regarded as the vital tasks of popularizing science and opening the eyes of the world to the need for adequate sanitation.

Kingsley's appointment to a canonry of Chester, made by Gladstone in 1869, came shortly after his resignation from Cambridge and provided him with the four happiest years of his life. Since there were three other canons and a single house for occupancy in turn by the one in residence, it was not necessary for Kingsley to resign from Eversley, which he left to the care of a curate when he was absent. The dean, J. S. Howson, was one of the nineteenth century's early cathedral reformers and more energetic than most, but he was apprehensive when advised of the identity of his new colleague. He had been shocked by Kingsley's first three novels and the report that he had once declared himself to be a Chartist. The two men had got on well during a brief encounter in Cambridge, but the radical image remained and Howson feared that an agitator would shortly disturb the tranquillity of the close.

He need not have worried. Kingsley proved to be a most congenial collaborator, and quickly became a very popular figure in the close and the city. His appointment to Chester was timely inasmuch as the professional class had acquired the Victorian appetite for intellectual stimulation and new knowledge, especially of the sciences. On his arrival he was invited to give a course of lectures on a scientific subject and, having chosen botany and decreed that they were open only to men, gave twelve weekly lectures which attracted such large audiences that the original venue had to be changed. The lectures in fact alternated between the hall and visits to fields, where the content gradually extended to geology, natural history, evolution – and, of course, morality. The fee for the course was three shillings and Mrs Kingsley paid for any who could not afford this.

Such was the success of the venture that in the following year Kingsley convened a meeting of city intellectuals which led to the founding of the Chester Society of Natural Science. He got his famous friends and contacts in the scientific world to join as honorary members and declared the project to be 'the dream of the year'. A *conversazione* in the Town Hall attracted over 300 enthusiasts, who were shown a variety of natural history specimens and other exhibits. This led to the planning of a city museum.

Within the cathedral itself, Kingsley met the other canons only at changeover of residence or when a chapter meeting was convened. He and the dean became friends, and long queues formed outside the cathedral whenever he was preaching. For more than a year the nave was closed but with Kingsley in the pulpit the remaining part of the building was always full to capacity. His sermons were invariably reported in the local press and, being a national literary celebrity, he was lionized wherever he went. He, for his part, always looked forward to his periods of residence and, although these totalled no more than twelve months in four years, he grew to love the people of Chester and they certainly loved him.

When in 1873 Gladstone offered Kingsley a canonry of Westminster he told him he was aware that this would, as he put it, 'injure the people of Chester' but he felt the time had come for his voice to be heard in the Abbey. The prime minister had not, in fact, intended to make the offer to Kingsley, but the dean, A. P. Stanley, was very keen to have him on the chapter and the Dean of Windsor applied the necessary pressure on the prime minister, explaining it to be the Queen's wish that he should go to Westminster. Kingsley, for his part, was reluctant to give up Chester and told a friend that he had accepted the Westminster stall because it would double his capitular income and he felt that he had a financial responsibility to his children. But he was also conscious of the honour and considered the canonry to be more desirable than either a deanery or a bishopric. The increased income would, he hoped, free him from the need to write so much.

In the event, he occupied the stall for only two years, until death intervened, and since there were six canons, he was required to be in residence for no more than two months of each of these years. Yet, once more, he made a remarkable impact. Although his months of residence – September and November – were unfashionable in London's social calendar, the Abbey was always packed whenever he was preaching, and there were those who wondered how the crowds would have been handled had he been allocated more popular months. Kingsley told Dean Stanley that moving to the Abbey was 'like coming suddenly into a large inheritance of unknown treasures', and, since he was allocated his own house in the Little Cloister, he was able to be involved in the life of the Abbey even when not officially in residence. A curate took care of Eversley whenever he was in Westminster, and his contribution to the life of the Abbey was eloquently expressed by Stanley at the time of his death:

> When Charles Kingsley was first appointed to the stall in Westminster there was a great sense of triumph that a famous name was enrolled in the number of our body. When he came to live among us, this feeling was deepened into a no less unusual sentiment of grateful attachment. Everyone felt that in him they had gained a friend. Everyone was delighted with him, because he was delighted with everything . . . I was myself absent during the largest part of his Residence – but I could judge of its effects from the glow on the hills after the sun has just set.

When Kingsley first moved into the Little Cloister his wife was too ill to join him, and for most of the next two years he was himself dogged by ill-health. He was still only in his early fifties, yet evidently burned out, but in the hope of recovering his strength he embarked on an extensive tour of America, accompanied by his daughter, Rose. In order to meet the cost of this he was obliged to undertake some lecturing – usually on Westminster Abbey or The First Discovery of America – and he spoke to 4,000 people in the Philadelphia Opera House.

The tour served only to exhaust him further, and when he returned to Westminster he found it possible to preach in the Abbey just once on Sundays. His last sermon there was on Advent Sunday 1874, when he spoke of the many ways in which Christ enters into human life, and concluded, 'Let us say, in utter faith, "Come as thou seest best – but in whatsover way thou comest, – even so come, Lord Jesus."' A few days later he and his wife returned to Eversley, where both became desperately ill, and at first it was thought most likely that she would die first. In the event he succumbed to pneumonia on 23 January 1875 and she lived on long enough to complete in 1877 a two-volume biography of the man for whom her love had always been unbounded.

Burial in the Abbey was offered but declined, since he had often expressed a desire to rest at Eversley. Both the church and the churchyard were crowded for the funeral with people from far and wide. A senior naval officer who had attended several state funerals confessed that he had experienced nothing like it. The service was conducted by the Bishop of Winchester and the Dean of Westminster, his body was carried to the grave by villagers and, in addition to a representative of the Prince of Wales, several generals and a number of colonial governors, there was a group of gypsies from Eversley Common. They called him their 'Patrico-rai' – their Priest-King. A memorial bust of him stands in the St George's Chapel of Westminster Abbey and was said to be a very good likeness of him, though the sculptor curiously omitted his strong side-whiskers on the grounds that they were no more than a fashionable fad. He had in fact worn them for virtually the whole of his adult life. F. D. Maurice, who stands close by, fared somewhat better.

6

The Humorist
Alfred Ainger, Bristol

Alfred Ainger was a canon of Bristol from 1887 until shortly before his death in 1904 and was much admired in that city, but he was mainly occupied at the Temple Church in London's legal enclave off the Strand, where he spent 39 years and enjoyed a considerable reputation as a preacher. He was also a minor literary figure in the capital, writing a biography of Charles Lamb, editing Lamb's works, and producing a biography of George Crabbe, the clerical poet. His own published poetry was unremarkable, but his contributions to various literary reviews were noteworthy, as were those to *Punch*, which marked him out as a humorist.

Appointment to a canonry of Bristol was, initially at least, a disappointment to him. He had coveted a Westminster stall, but as he explained later to a friend, 'Canonries do not come every day and, like jubilees, are to be celebrated.' He was also pleased to know that Sydney Smith had much earlier in the century been a canon of Bristol before moving to St Paul's. Bristol was not in fact an independent cathedral when Ainger became a canon, the diocese having been amalgamated with Bath and Wells in 1836. Neither was the building very grand; work on the nave had been abandoned at sill height in the sixteenth century. By the time Ainger arrived, however, the renewed building of the nave was nearing completion and the great church returned to diocesan cathedral status during his time there.

In common with those of other less well-endowed foundations, the canonry held by Ainger was, in effect, a part-time appointment requiring no more than three months of residence every year and attendance at the quarterly chapter meetings. But Ainger, having elected to live on the heights of Clifton, outside the city, looked forward to his spaced-out visits and in fact made a great deal of them. He repeated the sermons he had preached to crowded congregations at the Temple, where he was first Reader, then Master, and found them no less appreciated in Bristol. The dean was by now in his late eighties and there was little activity in the cathedral apart from the services, so Ainger inaugurated regular series of lectures on literary subjects, together with readings of Shakespeare and other dramatic productions. These proved to be just as popular in Bristol as they were in Hampstead, Edinburgh, Manchester, Sheffield and other cultivated places. Glasgow University rewarded him with an honorary doctorate. Ainger was always ready to preach for neighbouring clergymen, taught in the cathedral school, presented an annual Shakespeare prize, chaired several charitable organizations in the city and, being very good company, with a fund of anecdotes and humorous stores, rarely dined at home. Twice a day he walked down and up the steep Clifton Hill to the cathedral's services and only in his final years did he permit himself to be driven home after Evensong. He became, in fact, greatly loved throughout the city, as a local friend recounted after his resignation, just a few months before his death:

He was a man we could ill spare. His presence counted. We liked to see him moving through our streets. He did not look like other men. A painter, indeed, could hardly have wished for a better subject than Canon Ainger; drawing him, perhaps, as he sat deep in his chair, his hands held up and clasped together as was his manner sometimes, his whole face listening. Or an artist with a feeling for colour might have left us a picture of the preacher bending over his paper in the pulpit, with his beautiful hair, the ivory face, and the full and long white surplice – hopelessly out of ecclesiastical fashion – that he allowed himself to wear. And what was it that gave him his charm as a reader? His voice, if not very strong, was of remarkable beauty and flexibility.

He was also well thought of in Nonconformist circles, and was said to have been a reconciling influence in a city with a long history of unedifying squabbles between Anglicans and members of the other churches. When he sent his resignation letter Ainger declared that 'This is the saddest day of my life' and, after his death, a memorial window was placed in the cathedral, describing him thus: 'As a lecturer on great writers he had few equals – face, voice, gesture and subtle humour each contributing to the charm of his interpretations.'

Alfred Ainger was born in London's West End in 1837. His father, of French Huguenot stock, was a distinguished architect who designed the first Charing Cross Hospital and, controversially, the Palm House at Kew. He was also a Unitarian and nurtured his children in the same faith. When Alfred was only two his mother died and, although his father soon remarried – happily for the whole family – he said later, 'If any excuse will be allowed to a man at the great day of judgement, will it not be to him who can say "Lord, I never knew my mother?"'.

A few years at University College School were followed by entry to a boarding school in Carlton Hill, where he came under the influences that were to determine the course of the rest of his life. The headmaster took him on Sundays to Lincoln's Inn Chapel to hear F. D. Maurice preach. This not only led to his conversion to Anglicanism but also to discipleship of one of the nineteenth century's greatest theologians. Although Ainger did not follow his master in every respect, the influence on his subsequent preaching was unmistakable and in his old age he confessed, 'I owe everything to Maurice.'

The other highly significant schooldays influence was that of Charles Dickens, who had sons at the same school. They sometimes invited Alfred to their home, where Dickens quickly recognized his dramatic gifts. Thus for several years Ainger was, in effect, a pupil of the great novelist – encouraged by him to read widely and to take part in plays staged by him in his home and a local hall. At one time Alfred thought of making a career on the stage and although he abandoned this ambition quite early there was always something of the actor in him and an abiding love of Shakespeare.

When he was 16 he went to the junior department of King's College, London, where F. D. Maurice was Professor of Divinity and English Literature. This encounter proved to be short-lived, as Maurice was soon dismissed for his allegedly unorthodox views on hell and eternal punishment, but Ainger became absorbed in literature and developed a passionate love of music, expressed by a fine singing voice. In 1856 he entered Trinity Hall, Cambridge, with a view to reading Mathematics, but he had no aptitude for the subject and quickly changed to Law, with the intention of pursuing a legal career. In the end this proved impossible, partly because indifferent health got in the way of a good degree and partly because the death of his father meant there was no money available to pay for his articles.

It was also the case that he became a leading light in Cambridge literary circles and devoted much time to acting, dramatic reading of novels and poems, discussion and some writing. He wrote for *The Lion*, a new magazine started by Macmillan's, whose publishing house and bookshop was in Trinity Street. In the event this ran to only two issues, but these were sufficient for Ainger to establish a lifelong friendship with Alexander Macmillan, the head of the firm. Another Cambridge friend described his striking appearance and unusual manner:

His hair was colourless even then, and changed only for the better when it became distinctly white. The face never altered; nor the gait; nor the circular swing of the left arm; nor the tossing back of the lock that would fall forward; nor the quick bird-like turn of the head. Time had no power over the steady blue eyes, nor over their glint of merriment heralding the expressive twitch of the mouth, as it delivered some sportful jest or caustic comment. As for his figure – so strangely convertible, so incorporeal, at one moment altogether fantastic, at another impressively dignified.

The gateway to the law being now barred, he consulted a few friends, including F. D. Maurice, and decided to seek holy orders – a possibility that had for some time been at the back of his mind. In 1860 he became a curate at Alrewas in Staffordshire, where his approach to ministry was that of the older-style non-aggressive Evangelical school. He was not in fact a born parish priest, though he walked cheerfully, often whistling the songs of Schubert, the considerable distances that separated some of the houses of the parish. When he arrived, however, there was no telling whether he would engage in lively conversation or have very little to say. Worship was important to him and he devoted much time to raising the standard of the singing, but he was strongly opposed to Ritualism and, in spite of his friendship with F. D. Maurice, was generally orthodox in his theological opinions. On the other hand, he wrote in his diary soon after the publication of *Essays and Reviews* (1860):

It is because there is some truth in the book that the clergy fear it. They have not the justice to acknowledge the truth or the theological acumen to separate the truth from the error, and think the safest course to try to crush the teaching of the book, good and bad alike. The clergy of the Church of England are not displaying very encouraging signs of enlightenment at this crisis. Like the queen in Hamlet's play 'they protest too much methinks'.

After four years at Alrewas and recognizing perhaps that he was not really cut out for parish work, he moved to Sheffield to join the teaching staff of the Collegiate School. The principal was a good friend from Cambridge days. Two happy years followed during which he developed an abiding love of Sheffield and its people, but when the

Readership of the Temple in London fell vacant in November 1865 he was encouraged by another friend to apply for it. The Benchers were impressed by the beauty of his voice so he entered the service of the Temple Church, where, apart from a very brief interlude, he was to remain for the rest of his life.

The Readership of the Temple, in common with the readerships at some large parish churches, was a Reformation creation designed to provide a place for Puritan preachers in the Church of England's pulpits during the seventeenth century. By Ainger's time the need for such a preaching ministry was long past, but the office remained and the Reader was still responsible for the Sunday afternoon service.

No post in the Church of England could have suited the 29-year-old Ainger better. It gave him a significant London pulpit, little additional work, easy entry into London society and the opportunity to develop his literary interests in a most favourable milieu. He made the best possible use of these opportunities and before long was preaching to a crowded and cultured congregation. He counted himself fortunate, but before long tragedy struck, as it was apt to do in Victorian England. In 1867 his widowed sister, Adeline, who had become a substitute mother to him, died suddenly, leaving two sons and two daughters, the eldest of whom was only ten. This caused Ainger to age prematurely, his hair turning white almost overnight. He became guardian of the children, accepting responsibility for their upbringing until they became independent and, having taken a lease on a house in Hampstead, was joined by two of his nieces, who looked after the domestic arrangements.

Hampstead was still a village separated from central London by fields and farms, but it was already the haunt of writers and intellectuals and had something of the atmosphere of a university town. All of this was greatly to Ainger's liking and before long he was a well-known figure in the community. His work, which included poetry – of a quality some way beneath that of Tennyson, whom he knew and greatly admired – was appearing regularly in *Macmillan's Magazine*; he was on the organizing committee of the popular Hampstead Concerts and translated into English the texts of German operas and songs; he gave literature classes and readings in private houses and played an important part in the founding of a public library. He was also a favourite of the older Hampstead ladies, who vied with each other for his presence at afternoon tea and sometimes plagued him with their letters, ostensibly seeking advice on some matter or other but in reality claiming his attention.

Although Ainger had a very wide circle of women friends, with many of whom he conducted a long-lasting correspondence, there never seemed any likelihood of his being married. He was equally capable of intense friendships with men, one of whom was George du Maurier, also a Hampstead resident and a notable *Punch* artist. The two men had much in common, as well as strong differences, and it was said that while both were wits and humorists, Ainger was more of a wit than a humorist and du Maurier more of a humorist than a wit. Either way, they formed a partnership in the pages of *Punch* in which Ainger provided the jokes and humorous sayings and du Maurier illustrated them. In his entry in *The Dictionary of National Biography* Ainger is described as a 'writer, humorist and divine'. But such is the ephemeral character of humour and the difficulty of translating wit from speech to the written page that to the twenty-first-century mind very little of this material seems amusing and most of it distinctly heavy:

What is the difference between a gardener, a billiards-marker, a gentleman, and a cathedral verger?
The gardener attends to his Peas; the billiards-marker to his Cues; the gentleman to his Peas and Cues; and the Verger to his Pews and Keys.

An anecdote about Bishop Mandell Creighton of London was slightly better:

The Bishop's wife addressed a great Mothers' Meeting in the East End on how to make home attractive and comfortable. At the conclusion one old lady remarked to another, 'Ah! It's all very well – but I should like to know what Mrs. Creighton does when old Mr. Creighton comes home drunk.'

But hardly so a comment in a letter to a friend after the central heating system in the Temple Church had been replaced:

I had thought of preaching from a text good old Bishop Lonsdale used to quote – 'Hot water! Ah! A very good thing in a church, but a very bad thing in a parish.'

He went on to assure his correspondent that he had 'several other side-splitting anecdotes' awaiting their next meeting.
Nonetheless, Ainger was always very good company and he and du Maurier met, over a period of 15 years, at least once, and generally

twice, a day and were a familiar sight in Hampstead every afternoon, walking round the pond with their dogs and engaged in deep conversation. Ainger was also a welcome visitor to du Maurier's happy family home, where the two would sing jolly songs and Ainger would sometimes entertain the company by lying on the floor and suddenly turning into a donkey – assuming its looks, it was said, and rolling over and over, rubbing his back. Or he might become a fly preening its wings; or a parrot drawing a cork with a hissing sound; or a dog in all its moods, preferably in the company of a real dog that would invariably respond as if to a member of its pack. His skill as a ventriloquist would sometimes lead him to drive down Bond Street imitating the loud cry of a cockatoo, causing everyone to look up in quest of the apparently escaped bird while he sat at the back of the carriage quite unconcerned.

He was, however, essentially a very serious man and after his appointment as Master of the Temple abandoned wit on the grounds that it was 'incompatible with kindness or with a sincere religious standard'. If invited by an editor to contribute a light-hearted article to his magazine he would reply, 'No, I cannot write humorous articles for you now that I am Master of the Temple.' He also regarded it as unbecoming for a man of his position to ride on the upper deck of an omnibus. And, in common with many other entertainers, there was a melancholy side to his character and he was known to be moody. Writing from Bristol to a woman friend at Christmas 1889, he recorded:

As my Dean is 90 and my only resident brother Canon, Archdeacon Norris, is disabled with a sprained arm, I am indeed in a poor way – for the whole weight of the interests of this great cathedral rests on my shoulders. I am indeed depressed. I went to a Medical man here, who does not know me by sight, and detailed my sad case – 'Oh!' he said, 'you want rousing – AMUSING – taking out of YOURSELF. I am told that Canon Ainger writes the most amusing letters (especially at Christmas time) – go and see him!'. 'Alas!' I cried, 'I am that unhappy Being!'

Much earlier, not long after he had become Reader of the Temple, the Mastership fell vacant and the appointment went to C. J. Vaughan, who had recently resigned from the Headmastership of Harrow, where he had transformed a small, corrupt institution into one of the country's leading public schools. Vaughan was hugely gifted and destined to become a great bishop, but he declined two episcopal offers –

because, it was said, of a threat from a school parent hanging over him – and, after a spell as Vicar of Doncaster, settled for the Mastership of the Temple, which he later combined with the then non-demanding deanery of Llandaff. He, too, was a fine preacher but is best remembered for his use of the Temple as a place for his personal training of men for ordination – 'Vaughan's Doves', they were called, and their number, over 450 of them, included several future bishops. Vaughan also entered into an intimate friendship with Ainger, allowing him to treat the Master's house as if it were his own home and giving him the free run of the deanery at Llandaff.

Although Ainger's literary work was very important to him, he said in a letter to a friend, written towards the end of his life, 'Do not think me merely professional if I say that I regard my sermons as my chief work in life.' He was undoubtedly a fine preacher – of a certain sort. He did not pretend to be an intellectual or an original thinker and was at his best with moral issues. Some of his congregation said that while he did not kindle a flame, he kept a flame alive and he once averred that he would rather be dull than swerve from strict truth and justice. Certainly the content and style of his sermons was very different from that of F. W. Farrar and other Victorian preachers who packed London churches for a time. Yet he had his own very considerable following, mainly among the well-educated and the thoughtful, who were not looking for fireworks, were suspicious of emotion and extremes, and were attracted by his fastidious use of words and beautiful voice. Lawyers, exhausted by their court battles and their work on briefs, found Sundays at the Temple Church refreshing as well as illuminating, and learned from Ainger that 'The end and aim of religion is not to *admire* what is highest, but to *love* what is highest.'

It was natural, therefore, that when Vaughan resigned from the Mastership in 1894 Ainger should be the leading contender for the succession and, it being a Crown appointment, Lord Rosebery, who had just succeeded Gladstone as prime minister, duly nominated him. Ainger had, in fact, resigned from the position of Reader only 12 months earlier, owing to poor health, and for a few weeks was vicar of the small parish of St Edmund's, Cambridge, where, in the absence of a vicarage, he lived in a couple of rooms above a shop in King's Parade. Once again it became apparent that he was not cut out for parish work and he was ordered by his doctor to take a long holiday abroad, which he did with a young Bristol friend, who was also an invalid.

He returned in time to receive the offer of the Mastership and, having immediately accepted, was flooded with 300 letters of congratulation, all expressing delight. Twelve more happy and fulfilling years at the Temple followed and he was generally able to make his Bristol residences coincide with the legal vacations in London. The Master's House continued to be a place of warm hospitality for lawyers and literary people and he offered much encouragement to his new organist and choirmaster, the young Walford Davies, who 30 years later became Master of the King's Musick. Ainger, for his part, was very proud of his appointment as an honorary chaplain to Queen Victoria in 1895 and was delighted when King Edward VII made him one of his 12 Chaplains in Ordinary. This post was not, however, without its hazards, as he discovered on Sunday, 13 April 1902:

> On arriving at the Chapel Royal about quarter to twelve, I was met by the Sub-Dean with the intelligence that he had only just before had a message from the King that he was coming to the twelve o'clock service. He usually, when he was Prince of Wales, came to Matins at ten. But as he had stayed at Buckingham Palace since his return from his cruise on Saturday, I suppose he found ten rather early. To my horror, the Sub-Dean added – 'You must preach a short sermon, not more than a quarter of an hour; twelve minutes would be better.' Well, what was to be done? I had only one sermon with me (the one I preached at Bristol á propos of Miss Peveril Turnbull) and I could do nothing in the way of rearrangement in a quarter of an hour. However, I saw that I might omit the first two pages – and then saw that I must do the rest by extreme rapidity in delivery. Fortunately, clear articulation at motor-car speed is among my talents. So I did this; and His Majesty stayed till the end. It had been arranged with the Sub-Dean that if the King had left before the sermon, I should be told, so that I need not then hurry.

At the Temple he was known and loved by everyone – porters, vergers, workmen plumbers and servants, as well as by the lawyers – and when in February 1904 the news of his death was conveyed from Darley Abbey in Derbyshire, where he had spent many happy holidays, the newspaper boy from whom he normally bought his evening newspaper said, 'He was my best friend.'

7

The Vice-Chancellor
Arthur Mason, Truro and Canterbury

Arthur Mason was a canon residentiary of Canterbury from 1895 to
1928, a post he combined at various times with important academic
appointments in Cambridge – the Lady Margaret Chair of Divinity,
the Mastership of Pembroke College and finally the Vice-Chancellor-
ship of the University. Earlier he had been one of the first canons of the
newly constructed Truro Cathedral. He owed all his appointments in
the Church to the patronage of Edward White Benson, a great pioneering Master of Wellington College, an outstanding pioneering Bishop
of Truro, and a rather ordinary Archbishop of Canterbury. During
the brief time Mason was on the teaching staff at Wellington, he and
Benson established a close, intimate friendship which *The Dictionary
of National Biography* was bold enough to describe as 'almost romantic', and, once he became a bishop, Benson seemed to need his protégé
close by. It is not difficult to see why.

Mason combined strong intellectual gifts, deep spirituality and a
singularly engaging personality. A. C. Benson, a son of the archbishop,
knew him well and described him during his Truro years as extremely
good-looking, with close wiry curls parted in the middle, and an ethe-
real appearance not unlike that of a figure in a pre-Raphaelite painting.
Add to this an elegant charm and it is perhaps not surprising that his
poetic style was sometimes attributed to affectation. A. C. Benson also
said that he had the quaintest and most characteristic handwriting he
had ever seen. But beneath the apparently delicate exterior there was
a man with a will of iron and, although his always well-dressed body
might have seemed fragile, he had considerable muscular strength and
was known to have leapt over a five-bar gate while wearing a huge
Corsican cloak. Whether he was at the time also wearing his usual
wide-brimmed silk canonical hat is not recorded.

Mason was an uncompromising High Churchman of the Laudian
school who drew heavily on the Church of England's historical

tradition, and valued ancient custom and fine ceremonial in worship. When in 1912, and now in his sixties, he was finding it difficult to combine the mastership of a Cambridge College with the responsibilities of a cathedral canonry, it was the mastership he relinquished, for he loved Canterbury and all that it represented in the history of Christian England. This love was represented in a biography of Thomas Cranmer (1898) and a volume on *The Church of England and Episcopacy* (1912). Earlier he had displayed his Patristic learning in a book on *The Persecution of Diocletian* (1876), followed by a study of *The Five Theological Orations of Gregory of Nazianzus* (1899). Had he been born 50 years later his decision might perhaps have been different. He ministered during what turned out to be the closing years of an era in which it was possible for a distinguished scholar to play his full part in the life of a cathedral and be left with sufficient time to pursue his studies. He was also a great preacher who combined his learning with a burning missionary zeal.

Arthur Mason was born in 1851 in Carmarthenshire, though his father was a well-known Nottinghamshire squire and a sometime high sheriff of that county. Arthur went from Repton School to Trinity College, Cambridge, as a scholar and, in spite of the fact that a lively social life got in the way of much study, he proved to be a natural intellectual and emerged as eighth Classic. On the strength of this he was elected to a fellowship of Trinity, but went off to spend a short time as a master at Wellington College.

The college had only recently been founded as a memorial to the Iron Duke and through the inspired work of its first master, Edward White Benson, was on its way to becoming one of the great public schools of the Victorian age. Benson immediately took to Mason but Mason's stay at Wellington was cut short by the need to earn more money and he returned to Cambridge to take up a tutorship at Trinity College and to become Vicar of St Michael's Church – a responsibility that required little more than a Sunday sermon. Meanwhile, Benson moved to Lincoln, where he exercised a dynamic, albeit relatively short, ministry as Canon Chancellor of the cathedral, and when in 1887 he became the first bishop of the newly constituted diocese of Truro he asked Mason to join him as his chaplain. It was never the intention, however, that Mason should serve merely as a secretary-cum-dogsbody. Benson had great ideas for the exercising of a different type of episcopal ministry and the development of a new sort of cathedral life.

The first task assigned to Mason was to establish a theological college for the training of priests to work in the diocese, there being a serious shortage of adequately educated clergy in the parishes. Within a year 18 students had been recruited and a college and hostel equipped, and Mason, now an honorary canon of the projected cathedral (there was insufficient money to pay residentiary canons), was the warden. His influence over the students was extraordinary, even to the extent that some of them imitated his dress, voice and demeanour, but before long Benson required him for a different post – that of Diocesan Missioner.

This was the first appointment of its kind in the Church of England and eventually the initiative was copied by most other dioceses. The task in Truro was to recruit from among the more able local clergy a company of mission priests who would be trained by the Missioner and led by him on campaigns designed to awaken the sleepy parishes to be found in most parts of Cornwall. Mason was himself a gifted, compelling preacher, and Archbishop Randall Davidson, speaking of him much later in Canterbury Cathedral, recalled:

> the little, spare figure which passed to and fro among the windswept villages of Cornwall as if a mission priest had stepped out from the Celtic centuries into our own.

At one time there seemed the possibility of his founding some sort of missionary society or religious order, but this came to nothing and his work was not sufficiently important to keep him in Cornwall indefinitely once Benson was translated to Canterbury in 1883. In the following year the new archbishop used his patronage to appoint him to the parish of All Hallows, Barking-by-the-Tower in London. The population was tiny, but the living rich and the idea was that Mason would form a college of mission priests for work among London's educated classes. There is no evidence as to how this enterprise developed but Mason himself was more than adequately equipped for the task and was in great demand as a preacher and lecturer. In 1893 Benson made him one of his Examining Chaplains and also an honorary canon of Canterbury Cathedral.

Two years later his scholarly gifts were recognized by election to the Lady Margaret Chair of Divinity at Cambridge and to a professorial fellowship at Jesus College. Benson strengthened his link with Canterbury by appointing him a canon residentiary of the cathedral. This combination of posts was well within Mason's capacity and indeed he had time enough to spare during his residences at Canterbury to fall in love with and marry a daughter of the headmaster of the

King's School – a liaison that occasioned considerable surprise since it was widely believed that the deeply spiritual priest had a celibate vocation. He confirmed that this was not so by fathering two sons and two daughters.

On his appointment as Master of Pembroke College in 1903 Mason resigned from the Lady Margaret Chair while retaining his Canterbury canonry, and from 1908 to 1910 was Vice-Chancellor of the University. He had taught Patristics and was admired as a highly competent scholar, teacher and administrator who was also noted for his generous hospitality. A. C. Benson was a recipient of this in 1904 and, although he immediately recognized 'the old laugh, the old smile', he was somewhat disappointed to observe that 'the old radiance and grace seem to have hardened on to a little knobby core, and not to be the outflow, as I used to think, of a beautiful soul'.

By 1912 Mason was beginning to feel his age and made the decision to serve only Canterbury, where he had another 16 happy years until his death. He served there with three deans of varied temperament and outlook. F. W. Farrar was a notable liberal churchman who had won a national reputation as a great preacher while at Westminster Abbey and St Margaret's, Westminster and was a household name through his authorship of a children's book *Eric, or Little by Little* and a best-selling *Life of Christ*. He and Mason arrived at Canterbury at about the same time and struck up a warm friendship.

A large sum of money was raised for the restoration of the cathedral's severely decayed fabric, close relations were established between the cathedral and the diocese, and church and secular organizations were encouraged to attend the cathedral on special occasions. The Chapter House and Library were in constant use for educational and social work projects. All of which Mason, who had shared Benson's innovative approach at Truro, readily supported. But after four years Farrar was struck with something akin to muscular dystrophy which stopped him from writing and eventually spread to his whole body until, in the end, he had to be carried into the cathedral. Mason played a large part in sustaining Farrar and the life of the cathedral during these difficult years and, following his death in 1903, preached a memorable sermon at the Memorial Service.

Henry Wace, who succeeded him, was a very different character. Already aged 67 and destined to remain at Canterbury until he was 88, he had been a notable Principal of King's College, London, and was known as a man of strong views. As a scholar he had made a special study of the Reformation and was an authority on Luther, but he was himself no twentieth-century reformer, being against any form of innovation, and Farrar's renewing policy came to an abrupt end. He seemed to have little notion as to what cathedrals were about, or might become, and his autocratic style created difficulties at Chapter meetings. The 1914–18 war demanded some changes but, according to Wace, not many. It was agreed to keep safe the colours of the East Kent Regiment 'in case of a raid of the enemy on Canterbury' and also to allow the cathedral to be used as an air raid shelter in the event of bombing. Fortunately, Wace was witty, generous and good company and Mason got on with him very well until 1924 when, aged 87, Wace was knocked down by London traffic and died of his injuries. Five years earlier Mason, in an elegant sonnet, had indicated that capitular bodies are not always at one another's throats:

> Let me recount my comrades gone from hence:—
> Farrar, more admirable when he bore
> His growing palsy, than in years before,
> When London hung upon his eloquence.
> Learn'd Rawlinson, to whose munificence
> This church owes much; to Holland even more;
> Smith's quavering, silvery voice and gather'd store
> Of peaceful wisdom, pure without pretence;
> Walsh, Stuart, Danks, and one whose memory green
> Will never fade, so long as men desire
> To know the mysteries to Dante known;
> And two yet living, but too seldom seen,
> Page Roberts, ruling under Sarum spire
> And you, dear Eden, on your northern throne.

When, following Wace's sudden demise, it was rumoured that the comparatively youthful George Bell, the archbishop's chaplain, would succeed to the deanery, Mason said, 'If it is Bell, I shall kneel down and thank God.' Which, being a devout man, is presumably what he did, as Bell was appointed and the process of cathedral reform started again. The building was opened more frequently to the public, admission fees were abolished, pilgrimages encouraged, a friends' organization (the first of its kind) initiated, and services regularly broadcast on the wireless. For Mason there was the added satisfaction that the new dean had a deep interest in the relationship between religion and the arts, which led to the commissioning of a play by John Masefield, *The Coming of Christ* (1928), with music by Gustav Holst – the first use of drama in an English cathedral since the Middle Ages. Other dramatic productions followed. Mason had himself published a number of books of poetry, and five of his hymns were included in the early editions of *Hymns Ancient and Modern*. These never became popular, however, and did not survive later revisions, though some of his translations of ancient Latin hymns remain in use. He also had a considerable knowledge of stained glass.

Apart from a six-month spell during the 1914–18 war when he was engaged in a preaching mission, mainly to the army, in Alexandria, he never ventured far from Canterbury once he had relinquished his Cambridge responsibilities. He was much involved in the life of the city, as well as in the running of the cathedral, and gave time to its schools and social work. He was also an adviser to successive Archbishops of Canterbury on the Church of England's developing relations with the Lutheran Church of Sweden (he spoke Swedish) and served on commissions dealing with spiritual healing and the ministry of women.

When he died in 1928 the Victorian age in which he had first become a cathedral canon was but a fading memory. Although much remained to be done, the life of most cathedrals was being gradually transformed and Arthur John Mason, first at Truro, then at Canterbury, had played a significant part in this transformation. He was greatly admired at Canterbury and his death, after 33 years of devoted service, inevitably seemed like the end of an era. One of the cathedral's chapels was refurnished in his memory and, appropriately, his friend Archbishop Benson is buried within it.

8

The Mathematician
James Wilson, Worcester

James Wilson, mathematician, classicist, astronomer, schoolmaster, social reformer, antiquarian, parish priest, archdeacon and, from 1905 to 1926, Canon Residentiary of Worcester, lived to be nearly 95 and said that he did his best work after he was 80. He was not ordained until he was 42, this coinciding with his appointment as Headmaster of Clifton College. His religious outlook was, however, essentially that of a layman. He cared nothing for dogma and once declared that his mission was 'to widen orthodoxy'. The Bible must be open to historical investigation and its statements and implications open to question. Belief in the six-day creation and the Fall of Man, together with the doctrine of hell, should be explicitly disavowed from the pulpit and in the religious press.

He did not regard the virgin birth as an essential of faith, but said there was convincing evidence of the continuing spiritual and personal life of Jesus after his death, even though this lay beyond the present power of scientific explanation. The cross was the supreme demonstration of the fact that the divinity in every man was expressed fully in Jesus. This was the essence of Wilson's faith – a faith which he held passionately – and the implication was that the teaching of Jesus provided, for the Christian, the true and only guide to ethical behaviour. In other words he was, in the terminology of the time, a 'Modernist' and once explained that while he did not belong to any section or union in the Church of England he shared the Modernists' view that the ultimate basis of union among Christians was 'the Holy Spirit of God working in man'. He claimed that no scientific discovery could be contrary to religion properly understood.

A man of pronounced opinions, some of them expressing ideas a long way ahead of his time, many of his public utterances found their way into print. Thus the bibliography of his published works consists of no fewer than 131 items. Apart from his Hulsean Lectures on *The*

Gospel of the Atonement (1899), published also in a more popular version as *How Christ Saved Us* (1905), and a new translation of the Acts of the Apostles (1923) in which he also argued for a date much earlier than the one commonly held by New Testament scholars, his work appeared in learned journals, pamphlets, collections of sermons and the like. Their range was remarkable – 'The Forms of Valleys and Lake Basins in Norway', 'On the Velocity of Light', 'Football' (an address to men given in Rochdale), 'The Theory of Inspiration or Why Men Do Not Believe the Bible', 'The Mutual Duties of the Employer, the Employed and the Church' – and there were three school text-books on geometry.

Wilson was warm-hearted, fearless, honest, and of apparently inexhaustible energy and curiosity. A friend said of him, 'He wakes up every morning to a new world', and he was a born teacher with a special ability to explain difficult concepts and to crystallize vague thoughts. From middle age he had a most luxuriant beard. It might be thought that a priest of such unusual, all-round gifts would have been elevated to a position of significant leadership in the Church, but apart from the offer of the bishopric of Sodor and Man, which he wisely declined in 1907, when he had entered his seventies, nothing beyond an archdeaconry ever came his way. This did not appear to trouble him. He recognized that he had not been young when he was ordained and that his initial application for holy orders had been rejected by the Bishop of Worcester because of his 'unusual' beliefs. His lifelong espousal of a liberal understanding of the Christian faith was probably the chief obstacle to his elevation, since it would have seemed odd to hear a bishop regretting that 'the mouths of the "heretics" had been stopped by force, otherwise it would probably have been the case that the heresies contained the real truth, by stripping off the accretions and legends of the past'.

James Maurice Wilson was born, a twin, in the Isle of Man in 1836. His father, a priest of Evangelical convictions, was the first headmaster of King William's College – one of the new nineteenth-century public schools – but the climate of the island was too bleak for his mother, so the family moved to Nocton, near Lincoln, a small rural parish where his father was rector for the next 30 years. Young James was however sent back to King William's College when he was 12 and found the living conditions and the teaching deplorable. 'It was', he recorded, 'a lawless, dirty, degraded life and few survived it without real damage.' F. W. Farrar's best-selling novel *Eric, or Little by Little*, based on the college, indicates that 20 years later the situation had hardly improved.

James was fortunate in being withdrawn when he was 16 to enter the sixth form at Sedburgh School. There he came under an able headmaster, was required to learn by heart the Sunday Bible Lesson, the Thirty-Nine Articles of Religion in Latin, and the texts by which 600 or so dogmatic statements could be 'proved'. In 1855 he went to St John's College, Cambridge, to read Classics and got off to a good start, but at the end of the second term became suddenly and unaccountably ill. There were no physical symptoms, yet he was quite convinced that he would die that night. Soon came a message that four hours earlier his twin brother had died of tuberculosis. James eventually recovered his health, played cricket, did some rowing, and went in for a scholarship of high value which, unfortunately for him, as it seemed, required good knowledge of advanced mathematics. In order to remedy this ignorance, he took a short, intensive course on the subject and, in winning the scholarship, displayed such promise that he was persuaded to read for the Maths Tripos. This he did with such success that he was made Senior Wrangler – first among those securing First Class honours, and a mark of singular brilliance – but soon afterwards he had a breakdown, doubtless the result of overwork, and when he emerged had lost all his higher mathematics. Everything he had learned on the subject at Cambridge was gone and needed relearning from scratch.

Nonetheless, he was elected in 1860 to a fellowship at St John's on the strength of his classics, though he never took up residence at the college. Instead he went to Rugby School to teach maths and there came under the abiding influence of Frederick Temple, one of the great Victorian headmasters, whose work at Rugby was said to be comparable to that of Thomas Arnold. Temple was thought at the time to be dangerously liberal inasmuch as he believed the early chapters of Genesis to be best treated as inspired stories and the findings of science to be treated seriously. He appointed Wilson to organize, for the first time, the teaching of science in the school, though his new master confided to a friend that he was 'impartially and profoundly ignorant of all science, except some parts of astronomy and Newton's *Principia* – all utterly unsuitable for schools'. At first Temple believed he had made a bad bargain in taking him on, but the two men got on very well and Wilson characteristically made up lost ground with astonishing speed, spending a summer vacation learning botany under the direction of the curator of Kew Gardens and another eminent botanist. Before long he was considered something of an authority on scientific education and contributed a chapter to *Essays on a Liberal Education* (1867), which called attention to the inadequacy of science teaching in schools. This proved to be influential and a consequence for Wilson was a lifelong friendship with T. H. Huxley, the distinguished biologist who famously clashed with Bishop Samuel Wilberforce over Darwin's theory of evolution.

In 1863 Wilson became a housemaster and for a time his youthful looks caused parents to mistake him for one of the boys, but his health continued to be far from good. Two insurance companies refused to cover his life, while a third accepted him in the expectation that he would survive no more than three or four years. A surgical operation was needed in 1868 and it was while recovering from this in the Isle of Man that he met Annie Moore, whom he married in December of that year. This coincided more or less with Temple's appointment to the bishopric of Exeter and from this point onwards Rugby went downhill. Anxious about Temple's supposed liberalism, the governing body appointed a more conservative-minded headmaster who turned out to be totally unsuitable and whose eventual dismissal led to a much-publicized High Court case. His replacement also turned out to be a problem for Wilson and they had many disagreements, but besides his teaching and his marriage Wilson had a number of other concerns.

He was instrumental in the founding of the Mathematical Association, which eventually had virtually all the professional mathematicians in the country in its membership, with himself as its president. He also installed a large refracting telescope and an observatory in his garden, with a handbook on double stars, and was elected to the council of the Royal Astronomical Society. Articles by him frequently appeared in scientific journals and he became increasingly concerned about what seemed to him to be the growing and unnecessary gulf between science and religion:

> It cannot long be possible for us to consent to turn out men into the world totally unprepared to meet the problems which will necessarily force themselves on their notice; to turn out men professedly of the highest education, totally unfurnished with true scientific method and knowledge, totally unable to meet the shallowest arguments from false philosophy of nature brought on the side of materialism or atheism; who will talk glibly of the supernatural and yet be ignorant of the natural.

Partly to deal with this, and partly because of his unhappiness with the school situation, he decided to seek holy orders, aspiring to teach Christianity after the manner of Frederick Temple. He was however refused by Bishop Philpott of Worcester after he told him that he had definitely abandoned the theory of the verbal inspiration of the Bible, that he could not accept the general view of miracles, rejecting those of the Old Testament and discriminating among those of the New. What is more, he held the virgin birth to be both unproved and quite irrelevant, and also inconsistent with the perfect humanity of Christ and the significance of the incarnation. Asked about his views on the nature of the resurrection appearances, he said that he had formed none. But the bishop apparently had, and that was that as far as ordination was concerned – at least for a few more years.

In July 1878 Annie died while giving birth to their fourth child, leaving her husband devastated and unable to teach when the school returned from the summer holiday. This led him to abandon the idea of a life spent as a schoolmaster and he applied again for holy orders, this time to Temple of Exeter, who accepted him and arranged that he should become a curate in Devonport. But before he could take this up came news that John Percival, who had once been a colleague on the staff of Rugby and gone on to become a brilliant founding headmaster of Clifton College, was leaving Clifton to become President of Trinity College, Oxford. This was followed by a personal letter from Percival telling him that he had recommended his name to the governing body for the succession and urging him to accept when the offer came. Wilson hesitated, knowing only too well the difficulty of following a man who had raised Clifton from its foundation to become one of England's leading public schools. Furthermore there were known to be serious financial problems, since the original endowment of the school had proved to be inadequate, and he was also conscious of the fact that he had not taught classics for more than 20 years and was only just about to be ordained. He consulted Temple, who more or less ordered him to accept, and Percival delayed his move to Oxford until Easter to give time for Wilson to be ordained and to wind up his affairs at Rugby. There followed what he always regarded as the happiest years of his long life.

He continued Percival's general policy, dealt with the financial situation, returned to classics as his main subject and, more than his predecessor, became involved in the life of the wider Bristol community. There was, however, a nasty incident within the school when in 1882, on the day of his birthday, as it chanced to be, he was stabbed by a pupil. The boy had got himself deeply into debt with a betting agent in Boulogne and when this came to light Wilson, who regarded him as something of a genius, told him that he would need time to consider what action might be appropriate and that it would, in any case, be necessary to inform his father of the problem. The boy presented himself at the headmaster's study the following morning to learn the verdict and, when told that a decision had yet to be made, drew from his waistcoat a large clasp knife with a six-inch blade. 'This then is the only answer,' he declared and rushed at Wilson, who instinctively turned his right shoulder to him and got the blade there, instead of in the chest. He seized his assailant by the wrist and pinned him to a bookcase, at the same time shouting for assistance, and although he suffered some loss of blood, as well as shock, and had to have his arm in a sling for a time, there was no serious injury. The boy turned out to have a history of mental illness, unknown to the school, and later, after a period of incarceration in an asylum, committed suicide.

Soon after this incident Wilson's housekeeper, who was his half-sister, announced that she was to marry the curate of the college mission in Bristol, leaving the widower headmaster responsible for four children with, as he put it, 'only one solution to the problem'. He must himself remarry and, never one to shilly-shally over decisions, he convened a meeting the next morning of the mother and sister of the 29-year-old Georgina Talbot, currently engaged in work among friendless girls in the city, whom he thought might be suitable. On the following day he proposed to her, was accepted and by the end of the same month they were married. Three more children were added to his brood, and the marriage proved to be extremely happy. They were on the same intellectual wavelength and, as the years went by, he came to rely heavily on her understanding and support. But the excitement of the initial decision and engagement was a little too much for him and the school doctor ordered him away for a week to compose his nerves.

The college mission served by the enterprising curate had been founded by Percival in one of the poorest parts of Bristol but after a period of good work was, by the time Wilson arrived on the scene, more or less moribund. Within ten years, however, Wilson developed from the mission a men's clubroom, a billiards room, a parish room, a small park with a house for a keeper, and finally a very fine church, complete with a vicarage and a Church Commissioners' endowment to enable it to become a parish. Wilson had a strong social conscience and a firm conviction that education should have a social dimension. To this end he was the first headmaster to start a summer camp to enable public school and working-class boys to share an active holiday – a project subsequently copied by many other public schools.

Preaching and lecturing was another of his high priorities and a former Clifton pupil recorded:

It would be impossible to overrate the influence of his sermons in Chapel, both on the Sixth and on the School as a whole. They were looked forward to beforehand and discussed afterwards. Fresh, stimulating, thought provoking, they were yet couched in simple language that the youngest boy could follow; and the verdict of a Junior School boy, 'Another ripping sermon from Jimmy this afternoon!' would express the feelings of many of his fellows. But it was above all the solemn earnestness of the preacher which riveted the attention of his hearers; he spoke with power, and his words sank in and were remembered.

Another pupil, describing the 'Headmaster's Hour' attended by the Sixth, Classical and Modern forms, wrote:

One sees him again standing there in the Old Sixth School, at the plain desk where Percival had taught before him, a tall, gaunt figure with sweeping beard and shaggy eyebrows, like some Old Testament prophet; using few gesticulations, only the head flung suddenly back as he launched a question, or brought emphatically down to enforce some weighty conclusion. The striking figure, the sonorous voice, the sweep of the eye, counted for much, besides the infectious enthusiasm of the speaker, and the gift of lucid explanation which he possessed in a supreme degree; but there was something greater, something which could be felt, though not seen, the power of a rare personality.

Nor was his influence confined to schoolboys. He was in constant demand for sermons and addresses at church congresses, educational meetings and social work consultations as well as preaching once a year at St Paul's and Westminster Abbey. Present at one of his St Paul's sermons was a young barrister, with a distinguished Oxford career behind him, who was helped to see that there was room for a man who, without becoming involved in the life of the Church or taking holy orders, might use his intelligence to explore religious faith in terms compatible with intellectual honesty. That man was Cosmo Gordon Lang, who later remembered it as 'a psychological moment in his career', though it did not prevent him from becoming Archbishop of York, then of Canterbury.

Another influential sermon, preached long after Wilson had left Clifton and become a canon of Worcester, was given before the University of Cambridge. This raised a number of questions about the historical basis of the belief that only the episcopal churches – Roman, Greek, Anglican and others – are branches of the one Catholic Church. Are we justified in claiming exclusive privileges – that sacramental grace is given only through episcopal orders? And what about the history of the prophetic order in the Church of the first two centuries, which, apparently, performed all the offices of the ministry, including the celebration of the Eucharist, without the sanctity of ordination? Wilson concluded that the time was ripe for a re-examination of the subject of the apostolic succession and the development of the dogmas connected with it. These were posed as the questions of a genuine enquirer who, like most others in the Church, lacked the historical and theological skill to find the answers. Given Wilson's general religious outlook, it seems likely that he had at least a strong suspicion that the traditional Catholic position on these, and many other divisive matters, was not well founded. But the sermon, published in a church newspaper, was noticed by Archbishop Randall Davidson, who took it seriously enough to write to H. B. Swete, a distinguished Cambridge scholar, suggesting that it would be opportune to collect and state in as concise a form as possible the latest results of scholarly research on the subject.

The response to what Swete regarded as an order was hardly concise, consisting as it did of a volume of almost 450 pages. Neither was the matter regarded as urgent, since the book took some eight years to produce, and its elderly editor died shortly before its publication in 1918. But no one could doubt that its contents were weighty. Swete recruited some of the leading scholars of the day – including A. J. Mason, J. Armitage Robinson, W. H. Frere and F. E. Brightman – who examined as much of the historical evidence as could at the time be located, and Swete edited their contributions to form *Essays on The Early History of the Church and the Ministry*. Described as a book by scholars for scholars, it nonetheless made a considerable impact. A second edition was soon required and for 30 or more years it was regarded as a standard work for students of theology. Wilson was always proud to have been the instigator of such an important enterprise, even though the scholars did not on the whole tell him what he wanted to hear and, in any event, it made no difference to his own outlook and his attitude to England's non-episcopal churches. He did not live to see a later generation of scholars seriously questioning the basis on which their predecessors had erected their doctrine of apostolic succession.

More modest in scope, but not less important in its subject, was a course of lectures given by Wilson in Bristol in 1883 on 'The Bible and Modern Science'. The course was originally designed to answer a group of secularists who were active in the city but at the end of the first lecture, given by a lay fellow of Trinity College, Oxford, the secularists present tore him to pieces, whereupon the majority of the 400-strong audience called for him to be stood down and replaced by Wilson for the remaining lectures. After consulting the city clergy later that week he agreed and gave three lectures, dealt adroitly with the secularist opposition, and earned for the SPCK the congratulations of *The Spectator*, who said that their publication of the lectures was the boldest and wisest thing they ever did. But the Bishop of Bristol, the learned C. J. Ellicott, who was also Bishop of Bristol and Gloucester and had chaired one of the meetings, took fright when he was bombarded with critical letters and an adverse vote in his diocesan conference. A member of the governing body of the school also attempted to get Wilson to withdraw the opinions expressed in the lectures or to resign, but backed down when told that the headmaster had letters of support from the Archbishop of Canterbury and the Bishop of Winchester.

After 11 years at Clifton, the question arose as to what he was to do next, and this was given a degree of urgency by the fact that he had at the beginning of his headmastership resolved to stay for no more than 12 years and also that he had become increasingly interested in social work, at the expense of education. The Bishop of Manchester, James Moorhouse, who was a close friend, came to the rescue with the combined posts of Vicar of Rochdale and Archdeacon of Manchester. This was by no means an easy assignment. The archdeaconry was reasonably straightforward, since archdeacons were still a long way from being given a mini-episcopal role and their official duties were largely confined to matters of church law. True, he was expected to attend many parish functions – opening bazaars, prize-givings and the like – but there were also opportunities for lecturing on such subjects as Joan of Arc, Care of the Feeble-Minded, Astronomy, Erasmus, and Switzerland, all which he enjoyed.

Rochdale was the problem. The Church of England's record there was abysmal, its finances scandalous. The medieval parish had been endowed with more than 300 acres of land. Towards the end of the eighteenth century and during the first half of the nineteenth, the growth of the cotton industry required this to be developed and blocks of 99-year leases brought the annual benefice income to something in the region of £10,000 – a massive sum in today's values. An Act of Parliament requiring the transfer of the estates to the Ecclesiastical Commission was passed in 1866 but this needed the consent of the then vicar as freeholder. He drove the hardest of bargains, demanding £4,000 a year for life and the patronage of the four new parishes that were to be endowed. He had already been in the parish for 27 years by this time, and remained for another 11 until his death. Meanwhile the Nonconformists had prospered by the Church of England's pastoral neglect and become the largest Christian body in the town. Relations between Church and Chapel were antagonistic and for more than half a century the Free Churches had regarded the parish church as, in the words of one of their number, 'a sort of fortress, in an enemy's country, equally detestable and impregnable'.

This situation had hardly changed when Wilson arrived on the scene in 1890. The value of the living had been reduced to £1,500 per annum, but that left it still one of the richest in the country, and there was resentment in the diocese that this 'plum' had gone to a public school headmaster with little or no parish experience. Apart from the obvious task of creating confidence among the diocesan clergy and leading laymen, Wilson saw his chief task, initially, as building better relations with the Free Churches, with whom he had considerably more sympathy than any of his predecessors. But this was not easy, partly because the hurts and scandals of the past were too well remembered, but mainly because the conflict was now embedded in a battle for the future of church schools and for positive influence in the new Board schools. Wilson fought hard to retain the church schools, maintaining that their influence ensured a place for the Bible and religious teaching in secular education, and there was some improvement in relations with the Free Churches but nothing like as great as he hoped for. There was, however, much else to keep him occupied and at the end of ten years he was able to report that five new parishes had been created and endowed in the town, together with several new schools and replacements for old ones, and Mission Rooms accommodating just over 800 people – all at a total cost of over £50,000. Within the rural deanery the laity had been given some responsibility and there was a flourishing Lay Helpers' Association which enjoyed annual outings to Oxford, Cambridge, Durham and as far afield as Belgium, the Rhine and Switzerland.

Yet Wilson and his wife never felt really at home in Lancashire.

Their style, though warm-hearted and generous, was different and his liberal ideas were a long way from welcome. It was not like Clifton and Bristol; the intellectual and social climate, as well as the weather, was different and there were times when he felt a failure and became deeply depressed. Then his wife's sympathetic support became especially important, and there were a multitude of rewarding diversions in writing and lecturing, including the important Hulsean Lectures at Cambridge, and a speech to the National Society for Women's Suffrage. An opportunity to return to schoolmastering as Headmaster of Rugby had been declined in 1895, but the offer of a canonry of Worcester by the Crown in 1905 was too good to miss and he accepted. Just a few weeks before the letter came from the prime minister, A. J. Balfour, Wilson and his wife were returning to Rochdale after a short break in Malvern and the train chanced to pass through Worcester. The sight of the cathedral and close houses caused him to confess that this was just the kind of place in which he would like to spend the final phase of his ministry. The sudden death of one of the canons made this possible. He was now 69 and, as it turned out, had another quarter of a century of life before him. The Bishop of Worcester candidly expressed his disappointment at the Crown's selection, but welcomed him and remained on friendly terms. The dean also welcomed him and assured him that there was nothing to do and nothing that ever wanted doing. All that was necessary was the performance of the three months of residence.

But Wilson was not looking for such an assurance; neither was he ready then – or ever – for a life of idleness. His first commitment was to take over the Governorship of the local College for the Blind – a cause for which he had considerable sympathy, having worked among the blind in Manchester. Next came the discovery, resulting from a housing survey being carried out by the mayor, that some of the worst property in the city belonged to the dean and chapter. After inspecting it for himself, he asked for the matter to be placed on the agenda of the next chapter. The timing of this was unfortunate, inasmuch as he was himself unable to attend the meeting and instead sent a strongly worded document in which he declared the property to be a scandal to the cathedral. This was not well received. The dean and the other canons had all been at Worcester for 20 years or more and were not ready for criticism by their newly arrived junior colleague. Furthermore, he had no business to be visiting the property without the chapter's consent and his presence among the tenants was bound to agitate them. Wilson responded by correcting his assumption that his colleagues were aware of the state of the property, but pointed out that the City Council were certainly in no doubt as to its deficiencies and urged speedy action. The Receiver General, an office held by one of the canons, quickly did a deal with the Ecclesiastical Commissioners whereby they took over the property and put it in good repair, in exchange for two houses they owned in the close. Soon afterwards the Receiver General resigned and Wilson was elected in his place.

The new broom immediately took over the accounts – previously kept by the chapter clerk for a small fee – and made them more easily intelligible. Three stables and four coach houses, held by himself and two other canons but unused and in poor repair, were released to the chapter, which became responsible for their upkeep and in due course made them available for extensions to the Choir School and the King's School. Next, Wilson sought and was gladly given the office of Librarian. The printed books were in good order but he had heard rumours of boxes and drawers full of old manuscripts stored in the cathedral's Edgar Tower. These were retrieved and on examination turned out to contain almost 6,000 unclassified items, some of the greatest importance. From the Anglo-Saxon period there were three leaves from an eighth-century manuscript of the Vulgate Bible, together with some leaves of St Jerome's commentary on St Matthew, and fragments showing the state of learning in an eighth-century college at Worcester. A massive volume of 49 vellum leaves comprising the letters and minutes book of the prior and convent belonged to the fourteenth and fifteenth centuries, while a copy of Cranmer's visitation of the monastery in the sixteenth century threw new light on the problems of the pre-Reformation era. There was also a large collection of fragments of music, including the Worcester Antiphons – the finest example in England of Benedictine antiphons. All of this was far too much for Wilson to handle unaided, so he recruited expert advisers and competent assistants, but taught himself how to read medieval scripts and undertook a great deal of the transcription and publication with commentaries – a task he continued until almost the end of his life, when his sight began to fail.

There was however a temporary diversion from this when in 1908 the headmaster of the King's School, on the edge of a serious breakdown, had to be given a term's leave for recovery. Wilson gladly stepped into his shoes, moved into the headmaster's house, sacked a Sixth Form master and appointed a replacement, raised £400 for the conversion of the coach houses into a Sixth Form room and library, and after a considerable battle secured for the school an annual grant of £400 from the Ecclesiastical Commissioners. This was not bad for a Lent term's work and when the headmaster returned after Easter Wilson resumed his labours on the archives and an extraordinary programme of preaching, lecturing and writing. No fewer than 46 of his published works belong to the Worcester years.

The interest in social reform which had led him to abandon his career as a schoolmaster was also carried from Rochdale to Worcester and he became much involved in the life of the city, coining the maxim, 'If you see something that ought to be done, you must give a very good excuse why you should not do it yourself.' The high rate of infant mortality was of special concern to him and, after persuading the mayor to convene a public meeting on the subject, he was elected active president of an Infant Health, Nurse and Milk Supply which, over a period of six years, helped to reduce Worcester's infant death rate from 147 to 76 per thousand births. The city health committee then took over responsibility for the scheme. Playgrounds and open spaces were another of his interests and, following another public meeting, he joined a committee to deal with the existing spaces and find new ones. He and his wife bought a substantial piece of land and gave it to the city as a small park and playground for children. The council added further land and there were few days when he was not supervising the park's development. His wife was chairman of a newly founded Christian Social Service Union, which concerned itself with almost the entire range of social reform in the poorer quarter of the city, ranging from refuse collection to street lighting and licensing laws.

Wilson was not, however, very interested in politics – at least not directly – though his speeches and writings often expressed egalitarian ideals. He was a keen supporter of the Co-operative movement, which had begun in Rochdale, and in a speech at Bolton in 1894 on 'The Ethical Basis of the Labour Movement' warned that 'a more Socialistic form of government will make greater demands on human virtue and those who desire it must bend the members to the task of training men in every virtue'. In the same speech he turned to the 'drink issue' and told his audience:

There is nothing, I believe, which would do more to further your ethical aims than the elimination of private capital and profits from the trade of the publican, and the creation of a new and improved class of *public* public house and refreshment and recreation rooms, under the Municipality and the State.

The Manchester Diocesan Conference was given a paper on 'The extent to which aspirations and efforts after greater equality are a vital and reasonable part of the religion of the people'. The answer for him was 'a very considerable extent'.

At Worcester retirement and death brought changes in the chapter that made Wilson's life altogether happier. After 15 years he was no longer the new, junior canon, though he was now deaf and it was a sign of the admiration and affection in which he was held by his colleagues that his wife was permitted to attend chapter meetings to take notes and interpret the proceedings to him. By 1921, however, there were serious problems with his sight and, having reached the age of 85, he thought it expedient to retire. This presented a diffiulty inasmuch as he and his wife had, over the course of their marriage, given away most of their money and, there being no Church of England Pension Board, he could only be paid a pension from the income of his canonry. The chapter were willing to accommodate him by keeping his stall vacant for a few years but the bishop was required to certify that Wilson was 'too incapacitated in body or mind to perform his duties'.

For some strange reason he was unwilling to do this, so Wilson soldiered on for four more years. It became impossible for him to read lessons or other parts of the service except under strong light and failing memory made him insecure at services. His wife's health also began to fail and at the end of a winter stay in the small house they had bought in Steep, near Petersfield in Hampshire, it was apparent that he could never return to Worcester. His resignation took effect at the end of May 1926, but he lived on for almost another five years, played a full part in the life of the village, was always a welcome visitor to nearby Bedales School, and during the final months of his life had electric light installed in his house – the first house in which he had had such a luxury. After attending the 8 o'clock Holy Communion on the morning of Easter Day 1931, he noted in his diary 'My last Easter Day, I think.' And so it turned out to be. On the Monday he had a severe stroke and died a few days later, leaving strict instructions that only his children were to attend the funeral and burial in Steep churchyard. His final published work – a correspondence between himself and Bishop Hensley Henson on the subject of disestablishment – appeared in the February 1931 issue of the *Modern Churchman*. His wife died in July of the same year.

9

The Social Reformer
Samuel Barnett, Bristol and Westminster

At the end of a visit to England in 1884 the French statesman Georges Clemenceau said that among the three really great men that he had met was Samuel Augustus Barnett – the vicar of St Jude's, Whitechapel, in London's East End. This assessment was shared by Queen Victoria, who wrote nine years later:

> The appointment of the Revd. Samuel Barnett of St Jude's, Whitechapel to a Canonry at Bristol is eminently satisfactory. One says 'At last!' Here is a man who for a quarter of a century has been doing the greatest possible work for the Church of England, reconciling the Church to a class long estranged from it – showing the people the Church in daily life – placing the Church before them as never before they saw it – not pushing and driving and pulling and bribing them to attend the Church services, but letting the services be the ever-present and visible centre of the work they could see going on all around them – a work of self-sacrifice and never-ending toil. Nowhere can be found a parish whose history is more remarkable for this long period than that of St Jude's. But to the man who did it all, who created that history with his own hand, nothing had hitherto been given – no honour; no dignity; no public recognition. As elsewhere, so it is in the Church – *tulit alter honores* – the other fellow gets the honours. The Revd. Samuel Barnett is now a Canon of Bristol. But he has worked in the Diocese of London. What about St Paul's? What about Westminster? Bristol, however, is getting on. They already have Canon Ainger. They are aiming perhaps at the laudable ambition of giving their Canonries to the clergy of distinction.

Another 13 years were to pass before this great priest became a canon of Westminster, where he remained until his death, aged 69, in 1913. But his most important work was carried out in a parish described by the Bishop of London as the most difficult in his diocese. He was in Whitechapel from 1873 to 1894 and remained Warden of Toynbee Hall, the educational and social work centre he had founded there, until 1906. He was among the greater social reformers of the Victorian age, combining vision, compassion, courage, originality, power of persuasion, administrative skill, remarkable energy and a faith that sustained him during more than two decades of labour amid deprivation and suffering now to be found only in the developing world.

Barnett saw much more clearly than most that relief work among the poorest of the poor, whether provided by charities or from municipal funds, did not answer their long-term need and was, except in very special circumstances, a hindrance to true social progress. Extensive change was needed in local communities and as a social innovator he was without peer in the fields of housing, education, child care and medical service, as well as in the use of the visual arts and music to inspire the oppressed. At the same time, the aim of social action must always be to lift individuals from dependence to independence by enabling them to work for their living and make provision for their families. Only so would their human dignity be realized and the massive problems created by the new industrial towns and cities solved.

Increasingly, however, he came to recognize that certain improvements in their lot could be effected only by the creation of a fairer society and a degree of intervention by local or national government. 'God loveth a cheerful tax payer,' he once declared. He was among the first advocates of the municipalization of hospitals, and unemployment pay and a universal old-age pension. He played a large part in the formulation of a parliamentary Artisans' Housing Act and in the language, of the time, he was a socialist. His most influential book, *Practical Socialism* (1894), extended to three volumes and consisted mainly of a collection of his writings on social questions. These made powerful pleas for greater justice and fair dealings. But, in common with F. D. Maurice, Charles Kingsley and other Victorian social reformers, he did not recognize the need for radical political change to create a more egalitarian society.

Barnett's ideal for the artisan was a pleasant cottage, a living wage, an annual holiday, a faithful, thrifty wife and a brood of happy children attending a well-run, enlightened school. Politically he was a Liberal and, although no great admirer of Gladstone, was a friend of H. H. Asquith and associated with many other leading politicians, educa-

tionists and artists who were committed to social reform. All of this
was undergirded by the faith of a liberal churchman. His religion ran
deep and coloured everything he did, though he rarely talked about it,
except in church. He had little time for dogma, believing that God's
love was experienced and expressed in loving, pure and truthful lives.
Such lives demanded a constant battle against sin, and an acknowledgement of the need for repentance. Hence the urgent need for church
reform, so that its worship and teaching might be shared more readily
with the poor, illiterate people among whom he ministered.

Most remarkable of all was the partnership he shared with his wife,
Henrietta, in virtually everything he undertook. They came from very
different social backgrounds and met when he was a curate in a slum
area of a London West End parish and she, the 21-year-old daughter
of a wealthy Kent family, came to undertake social work under the
supervision of Octavia Hill, the pioneer social worker and housing
reformer. They married shortly before his appointment as Vicar of
St Jude's, Whitechapel and had 40 years together in the contrasting
circumstances of a turbulent slum and the privileged tranquillity of
Westminster Abbey's Little Cloister. Their personalities were comple-
mentary. He was a sensitive man of quiet speech, somewhat diffident
and careless of dress, not physically strong, and sometimes depressed.
She was bold and assertive, tirelessly energetic, and had immense
organizing ability. At the age of 72 she began to paint and was good
enough to exhibit in the Royal Academy. He used to say that he was
but the mouthpiece of his wife and had the courage of her opinions,
but she attributed this to his humility.

They shared the same vision, even if they sometimes differed on
the detail of its translation into action, and they were deeply devoted to each other. Without children, they had the emotional freedom
and the time to give themselves without limit to the service of others.
Soon after he became prime minister in 1908, Asquith described her
as 'The custodian of the State's children'. She brought to the marriage sufficient money to enable them to live without financial anxiety
and to make possible generous hospitality, charitable gifts, and good
holidays. It is virtually impossible to disentangle the contribution that
each of them made to a unique joint ministry. Even his sermons were
combined efforts, and it is safest to assume that everything they undertook was in some way shared. His living memorial is Toynbee Hall,
hers is Hampstead Garden Suburb. He was honoured with an Oxford
DCL; she was made a dame.

Samuel Augustus Barnett was born in Bristol in 1844. His father, an ironfounder, was the first manufacturer of iron bedsteads and a selfish, somewhat unpleasant character who had little time for either books or education. In marked contrast, his mother was of a generous, loving disposition and Samuel was devoted to her. Until he was 16 he was educated at home by tutors and, to the displeasure of his father, he always felt drawn to holy orders, which required entry to Oxford or Cambridge. At Wadham College, Oxford – chosen by his father because the warden was a Tory and a noted Protestant – he worked very hard, squeezing into three years the contents of the four-year Honour Schools, for which his father was unwilling to pay. On coming down from Oxford he spent two years as a don at Winchester College, simply to earn sufficient money to finance a visit to America, where the memory of the Civil War was still fresh and where the experience led him to say later, 'Born and bred in an atmosphere of Toryism, what I saw and heard knocked all the Toryism out of me.'

Returning to England, Barnett combined studying for ordination with work as a lay helper in the parish of St Mary, Bryanston Square in London's West End. He was ordained to a curacy there in 1867 and, although the parish had a number of fine houses occupied by the rich, work in its slums had a profound effect on the rest of his life and ministry, as also did the influence of Octavia Hill, who was also working in the parish and with whom he established a lifelong friendship. There were those in the parish who believed, and hoped, that they might one day marry, but this was never really on the cards and Barnett's personal life took a different turn when, at a birthday party for Octavia Hill, he met Henrietta Rowland, whose second Christian name also chanced to be Octavia. She, too, began social work in the parish under Barnett's admiring eye and in 1872 he wrote to ask her to marry him. She felt flattered, but was not immediately attracted by his offer. Her parents lived in Champion Hall, Kent, where she was used to hunting, gardening and other outdoor pursuits, as well as extravagant parties, so the prospect of a life spent in slum parishes with an impecunious parson needed some consideration. But in June 1872 she accepted him. 'I realized that his gift of love was too holy to refuse,' she explained.

Shortly before they were married in St Mary's, Bryanston Square, Barnett was offered a country living near Oxford, but this was not the direction in which either he or his fiancée felt drawn and Octavia Hill contrived to get him offered instead St Jude's, Whitechapel. In his letter the Bishop of London told him that there was no hurry for a reply, since it was 'the worst parish in my diocese, inhabited mainly

by a criminal population, and one which has, I fear, been much cor-
rupted by doles'. But Barnett was not deterred and, accepting in 1873,
stayed for 21 years – 33 years if his time as Warden of Toynbee Hall
is counted. The population of the parish was 6,270, housed in only
675 dwellings, many of them lodging houses in which each room,
furnished with a sack of hay, a table and a chair, was let to one or
more families for eightpence a night. Packed together in squalid court-
yards and alleys, with unmade roads, some of the buildings were three
storeys high, with pits in their cellars for sanitation purposes. In some
alleys each inhabitant had only four square yards of space. Lower
buildings were usually made of wood and soon became dilapidated.
Broken windows everywhere were repaired with paper or rags. Stand-
pipes provided water, but the people were dirty and bedraggled. Most
buildings were infested with vermin. One-fifth of the inhabitants were
without adequate food or clothing and, with fever and other afflic-
tions never far away, the annual death rate was 40 per thousand.

This was also 'Jack the Ripper' territory, where murder and other
forms of violence were commonplace. Along the main streets cattle
and sheep were driven every day to unhygienic slaughterhouses, which
added to the general squalor. The only decent housing took the form
of three rows of cottages, occupied exclusively by Jews, and even the
vicarage was small and dark, with an underground kitchen and no
bathroom. When the Barnetts moved into Whitechapel this needed
a good deal of renovation before it was fit for occupation and they
lodged with a grim landlady for several months. St Jude's Church had
been built of cheap common brick in the Gothic revival style and with
a substantial tower – all now discoloured by grime and already showing signs of decay. Inside it was equally unattractive, its huge galleries
blocking the windows and making it very dark. The parish was run
down and on his first Sunday Barnett had a congregation of six old
women who had come in the expectation of receiving a dole when the
worship ended.

This was the challenge faced by the Barnetts – and tackled gladly.
But although no one did more to improve the lot of the poor in Victorian England, he always said that his chief task was not to overcome
suffering but to overcome sin. His aim in Whitechapel was 'That everyone may know God as Father', and over the next two decades he
laboured heroically in his attempt to make this vision come true. He
declared 'Nothing short of the best is good enough for this parish.' At
the end of his first year the Sunday morning congregation had grown
to 30 and at Evensong there were 100 to 150.

The church was opened every day, the ugly galleries were removed, heating was installed, and later the east end of the building was decorated by William Morris in various shades of red and green, embellished by gold. In due course the artist G. F. Watts loaned four of his paintings and another artist contributed huge drawings of angels. Flowers and plants played their part in making the whole of the interior strikingly attractive. Although he was well aware that the three Prayer Book services on Sundays did not meet the needs of the people of Whitechapel, Barnett did not feel able to break the law by modifying them in any significant way, but his wife, who never liked the traditional services, often pressed him to do so. In the end he agreed that she might organize on Sunday evenings at 8.30 what she called a 'Worship Hour'. Normally conducted by the curate, this consisted of a mixture of hymns, readings, anthems, solos and prayers on a particular theme – but with no sermon – and attracted large congregations, assisted by 'chuckers-in' who went round the streets and alleys urging people to give it a try and assuring them that there were dark corners where they could sit if they felt ashamed of their clothes.

Barnett was not himself musical, but he recognized the religious dimension of great music and, aided by his many friends and admirers in the musical world, he arranged on weekdays at fortnightly intervals throughout the winter months performances of oratorios – *Messiah, Elijah, The Creation* and so on. These were treated as acts of worship, ending with the singing of a hymn and the Blessing. The church was always crowded, but less so in the intervening weeks, which were given to lectures on the lives of great historical figures such as Milton, Savonarola, Marcus Aurelius, Epictetus and Spinoza. A parish library was started with 638 books – Scott, George Eliot, Dickens, Trollope and the like – which were handed out on Tuesdays to those who could be encouraged to read. Volunteer librarians were always on hand to offer advice. Within five years the number of books had risen to 1,000 and parcels of them were regularly despatched to the social clubs recently established in the area. From this small beginning grew the Whitechapel Public Library – masterminded by the Barnetts – which was opened in 1892 and soon had over 6,000 borrowers.

At a different educational level the ill-designed and more or less derelict church schools were reopened. On completion of the repairs the interior walls were decorated with coloured illustrations of Aesop's fables, the cloakrooms were equipped with soap, towels and mirrors, and during the summer months the classrooms were filled with flowers. An early experiment in co-education had to be abandoned when the girls rebelled, but regular meetings of parents and managers were held and it was decided that parents should individually decide what fees it was appropriate for them to pay.

Barnett had many conflicts with the education authorities over his methods and in 1884 formed the Education Reform League to 'enlist the co-operation of the working classes in the effort to infuse more life into the dry bones of State-aided Elementary Education'. Several of its aims were a very long way ahead of their time and included education to be compulsory, and free to the age of 15 or 16, with continuation colleges, again compulsory to 18 or 19; staggered summer holidays; free breakfasts; school premises to be available for use by the wider community; school journeys; university education for primary school teachers; and equal opportunities for all children to attain their highest capability – technical, intellectual and physical. Barnett recognized that the achievement of all this would be a long haul – one that has not yet ended – but the League, which was never large, became influential, some of its members attaining high positions in the world of education.

Visiting the homes of parishioners was always a high priority for the Barnetts and during their first year in Whitechapel they often went incognito in order to meet families on their own terms. At one point Henrietta proposed that they should move out of the vicarage and identify themselves more closely with the poor by living in a slum house, but Barnett would not agree to this as he needed more, not less, domestic space to develop his work. Eventually the inadequate vicarage they had inherited was replaced by a more spacious house. Hospitality was a central feature of their shared ministry and Barnett once claimed that all his important strategic decisions had been made at his wife's tea-table.

The vicarage saw the beginning of another of their major projects which, again, achieved spectacular success. Some of the interesting and beautiful objects acquired during an extended visit to Egypt were displayed and explained at their Sunday afternoon tea-parties. This proved to be so popular that more items were borrowed from friends and museums and displayed in the church schools, making them remarkable oases of beauty. Barnett was firmly convinced of the religious value of great art but the opening of the exhibitions on Sunday afternoons soon incurred the wrath of the Lord's Day Observance Society, who sent men to patrol the nearby streets and to threaten with eternal punishment any who entered the schools. The Bishop of London also expressed his unease, but Barnett told him that, having lived close to the people of Whitechapel for eight years, he believed that he had a better right than most to say what means would hasten their knowledge of the Kingdom of God. Sunday opening continued and such was the popularity of the exhibitions that Barnett convened a committee which raised sufficient money to build a permanent Whitechapel Art Gallery. This was opened in 1901 and its first director was subsequently appointed director of the Tate Gallery.

Remarkable and heroic though his ministry in Whitechapel undoubtedly was, Barnett went through periods of deep depression when he doubted his suitability for the work and blamed himself for the fact that attendance at St Jude's for worship was often small. His ideals were high, he longed to save the souls of his parishioners from sin, he worked himself too hard, he was humble and his physical health was often far from good, but Henrietta saw him through another 30 years of ministry that was never other than sacrificial and always highly innovative.

Soon after their arrival in Whitechapel they arranged for nine ailing children to go on a country holiday and within seven years this initiative had become the national Children's Country Holiday Fund, which, over the ensuing years, benefited some hundreds of thousands of children. Henrietta also served on a national departmental committee to enquire into the condition of Poor Law children, and this led to the formation of a State Children's Association, of which she became the secretary. Other work for young people arose from concern for the plight of girls whose parents were for the most part beggars or criminals, who had no home training and little education, and whose future was bleak. These were recruited for service in West End homes, where they received friendship and training, and through Barnett's involvement in the Metropolitan Association for Befriending Young Servants, of which he was the chairman, places were found for several thousand girls. The needs of boys were different and the chief objective was to find them some means of employment locally or to facilitate their going to sea. Others lived in a home – which Barnett turned into a self-governing hotel – from which they went out every morning to work as shoe-blacks on the London streets, returning in the evening to give an account of their earnings, to buy their food, and in their time off to participate in social and educational activities.

Housing was always a major concern to the Barnetts and they worked closely with Octavia Hill, who had acquired specialist knowledge of how to replace slums with decent flats and houses. At a meeting in the vicarage the East End Dwellings Company was formed to build homes

for unskilled labourers, day workers at the docks and the many men
and women who lived by casual employment – none of whom was
eligible for assistance by the main housing charities. Barnett gave evidence before a House of Commons committee on housing, after which
the Home Secretary, together with various officials, spent a day with
him in Whitechapel. New legislation to speed the demolition of slums
and the erection of replacement housing quickly followed.

Immediately after becoming a ratepayer he was recruited to the
Board of Guardians of the Whitechapel Union, which was responsible
for the administration of the Poor Law and the local workhouses. The
treatment of those seeking relief had been inhumane in the extreme
and he did much to change this, but with just under 4,000 supplicants
on the books there were frequent protests from ratepayers who were
financing the relief. Severe restrictions were applied and by 1877 the
number of relief recepients had been reduced to a mere 122, causing
great suffering. Barnett supported this policy in a general way, but not
for the same reasons as his fellow Guardians and ratepayers. He was
firmly convinced that the system of relief did more harm than good:

> Indiscriminate charity is among the curses of London. The poor
> starve because of the alms they receive . . . The people never learn to
> work or to save. Relief from the House, or the dole of the charitable,
> has stood in the way of providing what God their Father would
> have taught them.

He, Henrietta, Octavia Hill and a few others formed the Charity
Organisation Society (COS) to counteract what a century later would
be known as 'a culture of dependence'. The Society, which eventually
had 40 district committees, provided an agency through which charities and philanthropists could constructively help the poor. But this
approach was by no means easy, at least not in the early stages of its
adoption. Refusal of 'handouts' to people in deep distress tested the
consciences of the sensitive and the Barnetts often felt unable to eat
their own suppers while the hungry lay on the doorstep of the vicarage. Refusal also created anger and, even though toughened glass was
installed in their windows, these were sometimes broken by riotous
mobs. Some donors to charities were worried lest unrest among the
poor might lead to revolution.

The long-term benefits of the COS's approach were, however, considerable and the lives of many hundreds of Whitechapel people were
transformed. Yet Barnett eventually came into conflict with some

of his COS friends over what seemed to them to be a breach of the 'principles' on his part. His advocacy of state intervention in certain areas of need would, they believed, be as discouraging of self-help and thrift as the 'doles' had been. Barnett responded by accusing the COS leadership of inflexibility and dogmatism and when agreement became impossible he gradually withdrew from the central leadership while always remaining a member of his local committee.

During the 1870s there was growing concern at Oxford and Cambridge about the plight of the poor and a desire to do something about it. A few colleges established missions which aimed to strengthen the evangelistic work of the Church and to help create new parishes. But Barnett was firmly against this and in 1875 took the opportunity, while enjoying 'Eights Week' at Oxford, to speak to some undergraduates about poverty. Thereafter he went to Oxford every year to talk about social problems and to invite members of his audience to share in his Whitechapel work in their vacations. In a paper given at St John's College, Oxford, in 1883 he argued that East London's need was not for evangelists but for bridges between social classes, and added, 'Little can be done *for* which is not done *with* the people.' This, he suggested, could be best achieved by the founding of what he called 'settlements' – small communities of graduates and undergraduates living together, with a permanent group consisting of curates and professional men, these being augmented in vacations by others who were still studying or working elsewhere. All would collaborate with the local clergy and others in the running of clubs, local government work and charities. Such settlements would have a religious basis, but no religious tests for their members since, said Barnett, 'The true religious teacher is he who makes known God to man. God is manifest to every age by that which is the Best of every age.'

Soon after this meeting a number of undergraduates met in the rooms of Cosmo Gordon Lang, the future Archbishop of Canterbury, in Balliol College and pledged themselves to support Barnett in the founding of a settlement. By February 1884 they had raised enough money to purchase an old school in Whitechapel, and by the end of the year 15 residents had moved in, with Barnett as the first warden – a post he held for the next 22 years, always without pay. A Cambridge committee was also formed, with B. F. Westcott, a future Bishop of Durham, among its members, and five years later 54 men had at different times been in residence. About 500 associates, who for one reason or another could not reside in the settlement, were also involved in the work.

This work involved the Charity Organisation Society, the Children's Country Holiday Fund, Poor Law Guardians, Legal Aid for the Poor and a new Society for the Relief of Distress. A business strike was organized, embryonic trades unions were fostered, and Barnett was frequently called upon to mediate in local industrial disputes. From the outset education, with its 'cleansing and uplifting power', was always a priority and in 1895 one hundred and thirty subjects were being taught, often by distinguished scholars, to over 3,000 students. The process was two-way inasmuch as Barnett intended that those who came to the East End to teach should also learn about the way in which many of their fellow human beings were condemned to live. William Beveridge, the architect of the post-1945 welfare state, Clement Attlee, the Labour prime minister, who inaugurated the welfare state, and R. H. Tawney, an economic historian who for many years presided over the Workers' Educational Association, were among the many residents deeply influenced by the experience. Arnold Toynbee, a brilliant young economic historian and reformer at Oxford who had often visited Whitechapel to work with Barnett and was much involved in the planning of the settlement, died a year before the opening and the name Toynbee Hall was a tribute to his memory.

It was hardly surprising that when in 1893 the Master of Balliol stayed with Barnett in Whitechapel he found him looking very tired. Twenty years of incessant labour had taken their toll. Shortly afterwards the Lord Chancellor chanced to be staying at Balliol and as a result Barnett was offered a residentiary canonry of Bristol, it being understood that he would remain as Warden of Toynbee Hall. The prospect of returning to the city where he had spent his early years and where his brother and his family, and some elderly aunts, still lived was attractive and he accepted. His appointment was widely applauded, though was naturally much regretted in Whitechapel in spite of his assurance that he would continue his work at Toynbee Hall. The Bristol newspapers expressed some anxieties about his informal dress, his attitude to Sunday opening of art galleries, and extraordinary rumours of his 'atheism'. The arrangement was that he would be in Bristol to carry out his residence duties in three consecutive summer months, and return for the monthly chapter meetings and for any other events requiring the presence of the whole chapter.

During his first residence in 1894 he quickly declared his hand with a course of lectures in the chapter house on 'Christ and Workmen's Problems'. These included Wages and Work, Short Hours and Leisure, Educational Ladders, Women's Position, the Sick and the Old, and the

Unemployed. The large audiences included trade unionists and Labour candidates for the City Council, but not everyone was pleased by what they heard. Some of the local newspapers were distinctly lukewarm, with one remarking:

> Many secular subjects having a bearing on the work of the Church, or on her usefulness, are rightly and properly discussed. Even foolishness like that of Canon Barnett is not altogether out of place, though his is an extreme case.

The London papers, who thought the lectures worth covering, were however more favourable and the dean demonstrated his support by attending all of them.

Before long Barnett was investigating Bristol's social conditions and in the course of his first two periods of residence visited every elementary school in the city, as well as most of the charitable and philanthropic bodies. He also got to know the members of the city council and the leaders of the Labour Party and the trades unions, and thus became well acquainted with the problems they were facing. As a result of this investigation the Barnetts came to the conclusion that, because of the scale of Bristol's needs, it was their duty to devote the greater part of their social concerns to East London. But when he was in Bristol he was sometimes called upon to act as a mediator in labour disputes, and he often spoke about the evil of indiscriminate distribution of charity among the poor – an opinion that caused anger, since Bristol was proud of its charities. He responded with the prediction that:

> co-operation and trade-unionism are the two forces which will make the 20th century. It will be the working men's century, and they must take their place in it.

The Barnetts greatly enjoyed their periods of residence in Bristol. They gave dinner parties and became very much part of the city's social circuit, though they did not neglect to invite workers from East London to stay. They cycled around the countryside, picked wild flowers and found refreshment after nine months of labour at Toynbee Hall. Barnett also appreciated the cathedral's daily services and got on well with the dean and the other canons, but was often annoyed by chapter meetings. Having travelled from London, he would find that there had been little preparation for the meeting and, in the absence of facts and figures, it was difficult to make decisions. Often it seemed a waste of time. The church reformer found much to do and he regarded the lack of a tranquil close of the Salisbury or Wells type a positive advantage inasmuch as it challenged the cathedral to relate more closely to the life of the industrial city and to the concerns of its workers. Most Saturday afternoons he invited about 25 of these to a personal tour of the building, Evensong for those who were disposed to attend, and a generous tea provided by Henrietta in their home.

Barnett's preaching, on 13 consecutive Sundays each year, was generally regarded as controversial, since he often spoke on subjects such as housing reform, free trade, strikes, class divisions, Sunday observance, war and poverty. 'We come to church to be comforted,' some complained, 'whereas you think it proper to make us uncomfortable.' Whenever he was in the pulpit the press were never far away, but he did not attract large congregations, since his quiet style was unfashionable at a time when orators drew the crowds. The sermons were always prepared in Whitechapel, lest they became unduly influenced by the more privileged ethos of Bristol.

The cathedral building itself was of considerable interest to him and he was there when the nave, which had been left unfinished at windowsill height, was finally completed. He thought that something less dated than the Gothic revival style adopted by G. W. Street and J. L. Pearson would have been preferable, though it is not apparent what this might have been at the end of the nineteenth century. Being fanatically keen on light and air, his own contribution to the building was to pay for an extra external door. But his final contribution to Bristol's life was a pamphlet, *The Ideal City* (1905), in which he once more deplored the slum housing as a disgrace to the city and offered a picture of Bristol as it might be, 'where there shall be nothing to offend, everything to help'.

When he had been at Bristol for 13 years the prime minister, Campbell Bannerman, offered him a deanery, but he declined on the grounds that he did not feel it right to leave his work at Toynbee Hall. In 1906 Asquith offered him another deanery, by which time he had already decided to leave Whitechapel, but again he declined, this time on the grounds that he ought to remain in London. 'If you won't have this, what will you have?', enquired Asquith, to which Barnett replied that when next a canonry of Westminster fell vacant he would feel honoured by the offer of this. There was not long to wait, for within three months Bishop Welldon had left the Abbey to become Dean of Manchester and in August 1906 Barnett was installed in his place.

The early days at Westminster were not auspicious. He was too ill to appreciate the solemnity and joy of the installation ceremony. Moreover, he did not care for the somewhat gloomy house in the Little Cloister which had been allocated to him, and doubtless he would have been pleased to know that it was completely destroyed by wartime bombing in 1940. While waiting for the house to be restored and redecorated in their own time the Barnetts stayed in the huge deanery with Joseph Armitage Robinson, which led to a lasting friendship. But Barnett's first chapter meeting was not encouraging and he recorded in his diary:

I had my first Chapter, very uneventful. I thought the Dean really ill and felt very tender towards him as a bit of fine china among rather coarse pots.

In fact, Robinson's autocratic style, which Barnett himself would soon experience and regret, was playing havoc with the chapter's fraternal life. Barnett was also beginning to miss Toynbee Hall, where men of high intelligence were united in their determination to improve the world, whereas at the Abbey the chief concern seemed to be with maintaining a tradition of privilege and exchanging ecclesiastical gossip. His decision to include Henrietta's name, as well as his own, on the front-door plate of their new home caused more than raised eyebrows, while the introduction of a telephone was said to be 'intrusive'. But he soon came to value the life of the Abbey. The daily services nourished his (but not his wife's) spirit and he was endlessly fascinated by its history and place in the life of the nation. On Saturdays and Sundays groups from Toynbee Hall came for conducted tours and tea, and on bank holidays, when the Abbey was crowded, he gave informal talks about its history to those who quickly gathered around him. He was, as always, particularly good with schoolchildren and persuaded the Education Department to regard visits to the Abbey as part of the curriculum. He wrote a penny guide, *A Walk through Westminster Abbey* (1908), which remained in print for many years and sold in huge numbers.

When Barnett moved to Westminster he announced that he intended to devote the remainder of his life to 'spiritual matters', rather than to social reform. But although he took the Abbey's worship and witness very seriously, there was no realistic possibility of his turning his back on concerns to which he had been personally committed for most of his life. A course of Advent addresses on 'Charity, Law and Living' set the ball rolling and over the next 16 years there were many references in his sermons to the plight of the poor, the homeless, the ignorant and the handicapped. Sometimes there was support for strikes, for trade union action, and for claims for women's rights. All of this annoyed his chapter colleagues, who accused him of 'socialism', and from time to time his wife, who still helped with his sermons, suggested that he leave out the more controversial passages. 'No,' he would reply; 'Everyone else leaves them out, or if they don't they talk sentimental patronage. You and I *know* and must tell the truth.'

The church reformer in him found ample scope in the life of the Abbey and no less cause of frustration. He pleaded for greater use of music outside the services – oratorios, organ recitals and the like – and, drawing on his Whitechapel experience, asked, 'Is not music one of God's voices? It can do its own work.' Applying this also to cathedrals, he added:

> It is not hard to imagine our cathedrals rescued from the tradition which leaves them to be the hunting ground of antiquarians and the practising place of choirs, to offer instead the music whose greatness and beauty would make hard hearts soften, proud knees bend, and dumb lips speak.

He admired the dean's flair for the devising of special services, but thought that these should be extended to include trades unions, teachers' associations, co-operatives, settlement workers and other non-Establishment bodies. The vergers and guides should, he thought, be trained and minor canons chosen for their ability to teach as well as to sing.

Barnett demonstrated once more his ability for being many years ahead of his time by proposing the creation of a shop for the selling of picture postcards, guidebooks and other educational material. But, like virtually all his other ideas, this did not win approval and he complained, 'If a proposal had not been provided for by some ancient document, or still more antiquated usage, the Chapter would count it sacrilegious and find it their duty to forbid it.' His frequent complaints that doles were offered to the poor without even a semblance of friendship also went unheeded. More successful was his scheme for the building of a new choir school that would provide the choristers with a residential education related to 'the development of their devotional and artistic instincts'. The plans for this were well advanced at the time of his death and came to fruition a few years later. Shortly before he died he drew up a 'Memorandum of Financial Policy' which surveyed the organizational and business aspects of the Abbey's life and went on to make a number of proposals. Among them were: to use the accumulated income in the Ornaments Fund to enable the Royal Chapels to be opened free on Saturdays; to finance additional services for special occasions such as the meeting of national congresses, whether of workmen or men of science; more frequent lectures on theological and other subjects, by which it would be more possible than in the regular sermons to show the presence of the Divine Spirit in modern as in past times; and great musical performances at stated intervals in the afternoons and evenings, to which working people should be invited and be provided with books such as would help them to understand the music.

His prophetic vision extended once again to the cathedrals which, he wrote:

> seem to be waiting to be used by the new spiritual force which, amid the wreck of so much that is old, is surely appearing. There is a widespread consciousness of their value – an unexpressed instinct of respect which is not satisfied by the disquisitions of antiquarians or the praises of artists. People feel that the cathedrals must be preserved and beautified, that the teaching and music they offer must be of the best, offered at frequent and suitable times, and that they must be used for the service of the great secular and religious corporations of the diocese.

That was in about 1910; a half-century would pass before his vision was widely realized.

During these Abbey years Barnett's health remained a problem and in 1913 he became seriously ill with some sort of cardiac failure. After spending eight weeks in bed, he died on 17 June, leaving instructions that his funeral should be as simple as possible, and that he should be buried in St Jude's Church, rather than in the Abbey. A memorial service was in fact held in the Abbey at the same time as the funeral in Whitechapel and later a fine memorial to him was erected on a south choir aisle wall of the Abbey. Henrietta's name was added, but not for another 23 years, during which she wrote a two-volume biography of her husband and did much more innovative social work, and completed the planning and development of Hampstead Garden Suburb – said to be one of the most remarkable achievements of humane urban planning. So remarkable and so humane was it that what was intended to provide the best of housing for the poor of East London is now, by an irony of social history, one of the most expensive areas in the capital.

10

The Master of Ceremonies
Percy Dearmer, Westminster

No canon – and arguably no other clergyman – had a greater influence on the life of the Church of England during the twentieth century than Percy Dearmer, who was at Westminster Abbey briefly from 1931 to 1936. But his chief work was accomplished long before the prime minister, Ramsay MacDonald, under strong pressure from within and without the Church, recognized his gifts with an appointment that was generally regarded as long overdue.

Dearmer's influence owed everything to his concern for that which lies at the heart of the Church's life, namely its regular round of worship. He, more than anyone else, perceived the extent to which this had become impoverished through the unimaginative and often careless ordering of services in parish churches and cathedrals, the failure to grasp the importance of good music, and the readiness to accept the dreary and the ugly in the setting of worship. His *The Parson's Handbook*, published in 1899 when he was still a curate, became an instant best-seller, ran to many editions, and set a challenging standard for the ordering of worship to which many in successive generations of clergy felt moved to respond. Even more influential was his responsibility for the compilation of two new hymnbooks – *The English Hymnal* and to a lesser extent *Songs of Praise* – which, until the arrival of much banal new hymnody in the closing decades of the twentieth century, raised the standard of hymn singing in most churches.

His influence was due to two related factors. He was not primarily a scholar concerned with the fine detail of ancient liturgical texts; rather was he an artist for whom beauty, as well as truth and goodness, was an integral part of religious experience and an essential ingredient in worship. And that this was no theoretical concept was demonstrated by his years as Vicar of St Mary's, Primrose Hill in North London, from 1901 to 1915, where his insights were put into practice and the church became a mecca for artists and for a multitude of clergy who wished to raise standards in their own parishes. His friendship and close collaboration with some of the leading writers and musicians of his time – G. K. Chesterton, Ralph Vaughan Williams, Laurence Housman, Laurence Binyon, Gustav Holst, Sybil Thorndike – promised the opening of a renewed, creative relationship between the Church and the world of the arts, but this proved to be a false dawn and after his death was seriously pursued by only a few.

Dearmer's appointment to Westminster was not only long overdue, but came too late, when he was 64 and had, as it turned out, only another five years to live. By the time of his installation, appropriately on May Day 1931, severe rheumatism was already affecting his heart and, although he much enjoyed living in the Little Cloister and made good use of his beautiful official house, he lacked the energy and dynamism that had enabled him to achieve so much when he was younger. The dean, Foxley Norris, had opposed his appointment, ostensibly on the grounds of his age and health, though more likely because he disagreed with most of his views, but Dearmer was given the warmest of welcomes by Jocelyn Perkins, who had become a Minor Canon and Sacrist of the Abbey in 1899. This was the year of publication of *The Parson's Handbook* and Perkins had been converted to its ideals. By 1931 (with still another 27 years to go) he had managed, by dint of determination, cunning and obstinacy, and sometimes the indifference or inertia of the dean and chapter, to rescue the royal church from the liturgical depths into which it had sunk during the eighteenth and nineteenth centuries. The services and ceremonial were well on the way to exhibiting the beauty and dignity for which the Abbey eventually became world-famous. For the moment, however, the insights and especially the support of Dearmer promised powerful reinforcement of reforming effort, and this he readily provided over the next five years.

Dearmer also pressed the chapter into initiating a series of commemorative sermons on great figures in English history, and St George's Day was marked by the clergy and choir wearing a red rose. His own sermons were often devoted to social issues, such as birth control and capital punishment, and on several occasions he made a plea for federal union:

The only hope for the world is the spread of federation, which combines liberty with order and co-operation . . . Both the British Empire and the United States are examples of the federal principle producing real unity without loss of freedom. The continent of Europe must follow the same method or it will succumb.

In a course of lectures on 'The Bible as Poetry' he described the Bible as 'the worst printed book in the world'. As a preacher and lecturer, however, the quality of his utterances was uneven and, although he always had a strong following, it was left to his second wife to be candid enough to admit that he did not always rise to the great occasion. What was true of his preaching was no less so of his writing. He published over 30 books on a variety of subjects and, inevitably perhaps, these proved to be of ephemeral rather than lasting value, though much of what he proposed is now taken for granted.

Dearmer was always diligent in contributing to the administration of the Abbey and soon after he became librarian a grant from the Pilgrim Trust enabled the library to be considerably enlarged and Laurence Tanner to start what became a long and distinguished career as Sub-Librarian and Keeper of the Muniments. As Steward with responsibility for the gardens, Dearmer brought life and colour to hitherto neglected flowerbeds and opened them to members of the Westminster community besides the dean and chapter.

Many of the activities which had occupied him during the years when he was without a church appointment and living in Chelsea were continued at Westminster and a new initiative, 'Club', brought forward-looking, generally liberal clergy and some laymen – 60 to 70 strong – to the Little Cloister three or four times a year for a cold lunch and a longish discussion. At the beginning of 1934 he accepted an invitation from the BBC to conduct a series of Sunday afternoon broadcasts for children. These consisted of informal half-hour services, broadcast live from a studio, with his own children and their friends forming the congregation, and a quartet of professional singers assisting with the music. Dearmer used his great teaching gifts, usually to expound one or other of the parables, and these broadcasts were deemed so successful that they continued until virtually the time of his death.

Percy Dearmer was born in London – in the area bordering on St John's Wood and Kilburn – in 1867. His father was at the time a bank clerk but gave this up to become a painter. He was also a talented amateur flautist and, although he died when Percy was only ten, it seems more than likely that a deep love of the arts passed from father to son. Soon after his death the family moved to Streatham Common, but Percy's mother, a fervent Evangelical, lacked any affection for him and this may explain the somewhat shy and reserved elements in his personality. After a spell at Streatham School, he went to Westminster, then a tough and boisterous school, which did not really suit him, and he was soon moved to a school run by Lutherans at Vevey, on

Lake Geneva. This he greatly enjoyed and he learned to speak French fluently.

On his return to London in 1885 he took the opportunity to make frequent visits to the Victoria and Albert Museum, then in the early stages of its development and building its collection. Already his attraction to art was showing itself and this continued at Christ Church, Oxford, where he came under the influence of his tutor, York Powell, who introduced him to the work of John Ruskin and William Morris. This led to what became another lifelong concern – the social implications of art. The beauty and harmony expressed in art demanded extension to the circumstances and lives of the whole human race, which meant a special concern for the plight of the poor. Dearmer entered the cause of Christian socialism, pioneered in 1848 by J. M. F. Ludlow, F. D. Maurice and Charles Kingsley and then undergoing something of a revival in the Guild of St Matthew, of which he became the Oxford secretary. Before long, however, this small organization became too left-wing in its outlook to stand much of a chance of attracting wider support and real influence. A split ensued and under the leadership of Henry Scott Holland, later to become a notable canon of St Paul's, the more moderate Christian Social Union was formed. Dearmer identified himself with this and was its London secretary from 1891 to 1912.

Membership of the Oxford University Drama Society also claimed some of his time and, given the extent of his extra-mural activity, it was not surprising that he managed to achieve only a Third in Modern History. His visual impact was far greater. He wore odd clothes, loud checks, bright blue shirts, and extravagant ties. There was something of the Bohemian about him, and he also had striking facial features, accompanied by a highly individual personal style and way of speaking. F. R. Barry, who knew him as a friend and later as a colleague at Westminster, described his face and his attire as exquisite.

For most of his time at Oxford Dearmer aspired to become an architect but during his final year felt drawn to holy orders. There was, however, the problem of how his training was to be financed, since his mother, who was entirely unsympathetic to his intention, refused to provide any money. Fortunately he discovered that his father had left him a small income, payable when he became 23, and Charles Gore, the great theologian and future Bishop of Oxford, provided the rest by making him his secretary at Pusey House, Oxford – an Anglo-Catholic institution where he was at the same time able to prepare for ordination. He also began to use his gift as a writer by contributing to the

Church Reformer and acting as a reviewer and drama critic for the
Daily Chronicle.

Most important at this stage of his life was the influence of Charles
Gore. The two men were later to have sharp disagreements, particularly over the theological aspects of certain hymns contained in *The
English Hymnal*, but Dearmer emerged from Pusey House as a convinced High Churchman and with his commitment to Christian socialism considerably reinforced by Gore's teaching. He also went with
Gore on a visit to Italy to see some of the country's art treasures and
when, round about the time of his ordination, he became engaged to
Mabel White, it was Gore who persuaded her reluctant parents to
consent to the marriage.

In 1891 Dearmer became a curate at St Anne's, South Lambeth – a
small church erected amid factories and poor housing near Vauxhall
railway station. This was a tough parish with a no less tough vicar
– W. A. Morris, a socialist and labour leader who played a leading part
in strikes and other industrial disputes. He and Dearmer got on well
enough and the young curate and his wife – an artist who later turned
to writing novels – settled in a small house furnished with William
Morris wallpaper and other manifestations of the developing Arts and
Crafts Movement. The only difficulty lay in the fact that Dearmer
became so involved in extra-parochial work, with the Christian Social
Union, the Fabian Society, journalism and lectures on socialism, that
eventually his vicar complained to the bishop that this was being
undertaken at the expense of parish work.

It was therefore arranged, in 1894, that Dearmer should move to
a part-time curacy at St John's, Great Marlborough Street, in London's West End. There he worked among the many poor in the parish,
visited the workhouse, gave lantern-slide lectures on religion and art,
and organized colourful church processions through the streets. He
added the Independent Labour Party to his external commitments and
became, with Henry Scott Holland and James Adderley (a socialist
priest of aristocratic background), a joint editor of a new magazine,
Commonwealth, designed to propagate the Church's social teaching.
W. R. Inge, in no sense a socialist, and Ramsay MacDonald, the future
Labour prime minister, were among the early contributors. Dearmer
was responsible for the arts section. During this time he established
what was to become a lifelong and influential friendship with Conrad
Noel – a colourful priest who introduced much pageantry into his
church at Thaxted, in Essex, and also flew from its tower the Red Flag
and that of Sinn Fein.

Again, there was conflict between Dearmer's parish responsibilities and his other commitments and, after accepting an invitation from Adderley to assist him briefly at the Berkeley Chapel in Mayfair, he moved to St Mark's, Marylebone Road. All the time he was devoting more and more time to writing, and his combination of decided opinions and an easy, flowing and often witty style made for good reading. This contributed to the huge success of *The Parson's Handbook*.

Its publication was timely. The Church of England was in turmoil over its rites and ceremonies. The Tractarian movement, the basis of which was deeply theological, had spawned in the latter part of the nineteenth century a ritualistic movement. The Eucharist having now been established in a significant number of parishes as the central act of worship, the need was felt for robes and ceremonies that would help to emphasize its importance. In the absence of any guidance on this some priests had turned to continental Roman Catholicism, believing they would find there a living example of the style of worship normal in pre-Reformation England. What they found and, lacking knowledge of liturgical history, embraced were rites and ceremonies which had been considerably developed since the sixteenth century and were difficult, if not actually impossible, to square with the rubrics of the Book of Common Prayer. This had led to a series of unedifying legal disputes and even the committal of a handful of clergy to prison. Yet the overwhelming majority of the parishes were far removed from the conflict, being still under the influence of the dull and often careless approach to public worship that characterized the Hanoverian era.

Dearmer sought to deal with both problems by appealing to the Book of Common Prayer, and in particular the following rubric:

And here it is to be noted that such ornaments of the church, and of the Ministers thereof, at all times of their ministration, shall be retained and be in use as were in this Church of England, by the authority of Parliament, in the second year of the reign of King Edward the Sixth.

The critical question, then, was: what were the ornaments of the Church and the ministers in use in 1549? The answer was, and remains, one of considerable complexity. Dearmer was not an academic liturgiologist – there were very few of those in the Church of England at that time – but he had the mind of a scholar as well as the temperament of an artist and chose to popularize the work of Wickham Legg and a few other scholars who had formed the Alcuin Club to promote the study of the history of Anglican worship. The only information available concerning the robes, ornaments and furnishings in use during the reign of King Edward VI was to be found in surviving inventories, usually of cathedrals, and in illustrations and paintings of sixteeth century church services. There was good evidence for the customs of Salisbury Cathedral and for the so-called Sarum rite, which had been widely adopted throughout the country.

Painstaking study of these sources by Dearmer and his Alcuin Club colleagues led to the compilation of what they called 'the English Use'. Their critics denounced it as 'the British Museum Use' and later studies revealed that the rites and ceremonies in use at sixteenth-century Salisbury were in fact common to the Church throughout Western Europe at that time But it could not be denied that *The Parson's Handbook*, which offered detailed guidance for the adoption of the late medieval tradition, provided a colourful and dignified accompaniment to the forms of worship prescribed by the authorized Book of Common Prayer. The *Handbook* ran to many editions during the first half of the twentieth century (it was substantially enlarged in 1905) and a revised and largely rewritten version of it appeared under the imprint of the Oxford University Press as late as 1965.

In February 1901 came the opportunity to put precept into practice when Dearmer was appointed Vicar of St Mary's, Primrose Hill, just south of Hampstead. This proved to be an ideal place for his pioneering ministry. Church life was already flourishing and known for its High Church worship and social work. The building was in the nineteenth-century French Gothic-revival style, of red brick, good of its kind and fortunate enough to have a lofty triptych reredos by the noted architect G. F. Bodley. The parish itself, easily accessible from central London, was not large, consisting of about 350 respectable villas, housing just over 2,000 people.

Dearmer's first move was to have whitewashed the interior brick walls and vault of the chancel, and the walls of the side chapel. Later this was extended to the remainder of the building, thus conforming its appearance to that of a medieval church interior and providing an appropriate background for colourful ornaments and vestments. These were always specially designed and he and a few collaborators founded the Warham Guild with the dual aim of producing items of high quality and of paying craftsmen decent wages – linking art with social justice, in marked contrast to the common ugly items made by sweated labour. His use of colour also broke new ground, or at least returned to old territory. He condemned the use of garish

colour, copied from continental churches, and prescribed more sub-
dued blues, reds and golds, as portrayed in medieval pictures. Black
and white also found favour, and the robes themselves were to be full
and flowing – all in the best possible taste. Altars should not be clut-
tered with flower vases, book rests and a multiplicity of candlesticks,
but reduced to a longish table, covered with a decent-coloured textile,
accommodating no more than two candlesticks and surrounded on
three sides by coloured hangings supported by gilded posts.

The Parson's Handbook prescribed for every Prayer Book service
and extended to the outdoor garb of the clergy. Dearmer was never to
be seen out in his parish in a suit, but always in a cassock and gown
and often with a square velvet cap. Even at the beginning of the twentieth century this made a curious sight and G. K. Chesterton related
how, when he was walking with him from a meeting thus clad, little
boys called out 'No popery' and 'To hell with the Pope', only to be
asked by their learned vicar, 'Are you aware that this is the precise
costume in which Latimer went to the stake?'

On the subject of music at church services the Book of Common
Prayer was singularly unhelpful, prescribing no more than the possibility of an anthem at Mattins and Evensong in 'Quires and places where
they sing'. Returning therefore to the repertory of the early sixteenth
century, Dearmer embraced plainsong as the most appropriate music
for his own and other parish churches. One of the leading authorities on medieval plainsong was recruited as organist of St Mary's and
practices were held on Friday evenings to drill the congregation in its
tones and inflections. The result was impressive but unfortunately the
congregation did not care for so spartan a musical diet every Sunday
and asked to be allowed to sing some more recently created hymns.
This presented Dearmer with a major problem, for while he was
prepared to recognize merit in the work of some eighteenth-century
hymn-writers and composers, he loathed the torrent of sentimental
hymnody which had poured out during the Victorian era and had
found a home and an increasingly wide outlet in *Hymns Ancient and
Modern*. Robert Bridges, the Poet Laureate, had sought to improve
matters with the publication of the *Yattenden Hymnal*, but this was
too small to meet wide parochial need. Dearmer, with characteristic
boldness and flair, decided that the only solution was the production of
another hymnbook of high poetic and musical quality and more closely related to the liturgical pattern of the Book of Common Prayer.

He formed a small committee, with himself as General Editor, and
in 1906, after three years of intensive work, *The English Hymnal* was

published. The securing of Ralph Vaughan Williams as Musical Editor was a master-stroke and guaranteed the high quality of the tunes. The book provided hymns not only for Sundays, but also for the other holy days of the Christian year. Translations of 'office' hymns from the ancient choir services of the English church were included, as was a fair amount of plainsong for no less ancient processionals, introits, litanies and the like. All of this presupposed, or at least hoped for, parish churches with a liturgical tradition as precisely ordered as that of a Benedictine abbey. It was in practice the main body of the hymns that came into use, chiefly in Anglo-Catholic churches, and brought lasting success for the book. For the first time a church hymnal included John Bunyan's 'He who would valiant be', John Milton's 'Let us with a gladsome mind', George Herbert's 'The God of love' and Christina Rossetti's 'In the bleak mid-winter' – and among contemporary authors, G. K. Chesterton's 'O God of earth and altar', Henry Scott Holland's 'Judge eternal, throned in splendour' and Dearmer's own 'Jesu, good above all other' and 'A brighter dawn is breaking'. A new edition appeared in 1933 and a thoroughly revised edition, the *New English Hymnal* (1986), is very widely used and generally thought to be the best hymnal in the English language.

After the 1914–18 war, however, Dearmer felt the need for a different sort of hymnbook that would cross denominational boundaries, improve further the literary quality of the words, and include many poems that were songs, rather than hymns, and that would express a non-dogmatic form of Christianity, with a strong emphasis on the natural order and the need for social action. This resulted in the publication in 1925 of *Songs of Praise*. Once again Dearmer was the General Editor and once more Vaughan Williams – assisted this time by Martin Shaw, who had been the organist at St Mary's, Primrose Hill – was responsible for the music. The theologically liberal character of the collection was unmistakable and this became even more pronounced when an enlarged edition was published in 1931. The words of many of the hymns had been altered. In some instances hymns were entirely rewritten to eliminate 'difficult' doctrinal concepts such as the atonement, or 'demanding' requirements such as penitence and fasting. It was anticipated that *Songs of Praise* would be specially popular in schools, which it proved to be, and F. R. Barry, who was not normally given to extravagance, went as far as to write that any parish which adopted the book would double its congregation in twelve months. But liberal theology and churchmanship was already on the wane and after a brief success in a limited number of churches the hymnal went virtually out of use, its only legacy being Eleanor Farjeon's 'Morning has broken, Blackbird has spoken'. This, thanks to its conversion into a pop song by Cat Stevens in the 1970s, is now a popular choice at the weddings of brides recalling their schooldays. Dearmer contributed 23 items but, with a handful of notable exceptions, these were of an embarrassingly poor quality and have not survived.

Altogether more successful was his editorship, again with Vaughan Williams and Martin Shaw, of *The Oxford Book of Carols*, the appearance of which in 1928 marked a turning point in the understanding of the significance of the carol in musical life generally, and not simply in the celebration of Christmas.

Dearmer was very fond of children and a gifted teacher who painted wonderful word-pictures, drew examples from the world of animals and flowers, and made his lessons vivid and memorable. Drawing on a method he had encountered at St Sulpice in Paris, he instituted at St Mary's a Sunday afternoon catechism which was actually a children's service, lasting one hour and with a much more formal structure than would be thought appropriate today. But this proved to be extraordinarily attractive: the church was filled to capacity, a Little Catechism and a kindergarten were started for the younger children, and some other churches adopted the same pattern, though the lack of Dearmer's 'magic' brought less dramatic results. Later on, Sunday afternoon tea at the vicarage became a popular institution. This provided Dearmer with an opportunity to spend time with his two younger sons, Christopher and Geoffrey, but other friends and parishioners were also invited and the warmth and jollity of the occasion was long remembered. Mabel Dearmer was herself a noted author of children's books and plays and became also a successful novelist. She shared her husband's artistic interests and the vicarage was a meeting place for writers, artists and scholars, many of whom valued the form and quality of the worship offered in the parish church. A branch of the Christian Social Union reassured those who feared that the life of the church was in danger of becoming too exclusive.

The character of the local community in fact began to change, as the attractive villas gave way to boarding houses and maisonettes, and the number of children in the parish decreased. By 1911 Dearmer was feeling discontented and restless, and his spirits were further depressed by his discovery that, while he was enjoying a fortnight's holiday in Devon, the churchwardens had closed the church, without his authorization. But he had plenty of admirers and Oxford recognized his scholarship with the award, on the same day, of a BD, and a

DD. Yet he felt undervalued by those with patronage at their disposal, believed that after ten years he had little more to give to St Mary's, and lamented the fact that cathedral appointments seemed to go to 70-year-olds as a form of pension rather than to younger men like himself who might actually put some life into these great churches. Nevertheless he soldiered on for a few more years, unaware of the double family tragedy that awaited him.

This came not long after the outbreak of the 1914–18 war. In April 1915 he responded to an appeal for a priest to minister to the nursing units serving in Serbia. Mabel decided to accompany him and to join the nurses. For the next three months he conducted services and visited the hospital units, where the problem was typhus rather than war wounds. There was also an outbreak of enteric fever, which claimed Mabel's life in July. Devastated, he returned to Primrose Hill in September only to receive news in October that his son, Christopher, a Royal Fusilier officer, had been killed in the Dardanelles. Totally disorientated by the double loss he resigned from St Mary's at the end of the year and went to France in January with the YMCA, lecturing and preaching, and serving tea and cigarettes to the troops. In August of that year he married Nancy Knowles, another gifted woman, who would write his biography, and who had for some years attended St Mary's. They were married, quietly, at St James's, Piccadilly, by William Temple, the future archbishop, another of Dearmer's friends and supporters. Soon afterwards they embarked for India, where he carried out a number of lecture tours, conducted missions to army units, and in the end became a lecturer in English at St Stephen's College, Delhi. In September 1918, with the end of the war in sight, he accepted an invitation to teach liturgy and theology at the Berkeley Divinity School, Connecticut, and played an important part in establishing the School as a centre of the Liturgical Movement in America, as well as an exemplar of Anglican ceremonial principles.

Dearmer returned to England in February 1919 with no prospect of a significant appointment in the Church of England, and this remained the situation for the next 12 years. The reasons for this neglect of such a talent are impossible to pin down. After the family tragedies of 1915 the Bishop of London, Arthur Foley Winnington-Ingram, paused from promoting the war and asked Dearmer what he would like to do. Dearmer replied that he would like to try to make something more of St Martin-in-the-Fields, but this appointement went instead to Dick Sheppard and neither Dearmer nor anyone else could ever complain about that. There seemed no point in sending him to an ordinary run-of-the-mill parish to repeat the Primrose Hill pioneering work, but unfortunately, he did not get on well with bishops. Some of them tried to forbid the use of *The English Hymnal* or *Songs of Praise* in their dioceses – the one because its contents were too high church, the other because it was too liberal – and his response to this was to describe them as scoundrels. Then there was the matter of his socialism, which was romantic rather than politically revolutionary, but may have been a problem for some, though this did not prevent the promotion of others of his stamp. The most likely explanation seems to be that among those with important patronage at their disposal there was a singular lack of the imagination necessary for the appointment of a somewhat odd rebel like Dearmer to a position of wider influence.

The consequence of this was a dozen years of more or less freelance ministry, which was by no means wasted and may, arguably, have been far more creative than anything he might have achieved had he been tied to an ossified cathedral. On his return from America Dearmer was immediately offered a newly created chair of ecclesiastical art at King's College, London. This was the bright idea of an old friend, Ronald Burrows, who had become principal of the college and hoped also to create a chair of church music. Money, however, was short and it was fortunate that Dearmer had a wife with private means, and a useful income of his own from hymnbook royalties. The college provided an honorarium and some expenses for the part-time post, which he occupied until the end of his life. He took it seriously – never repeating any course of lectures – and attracted such large audiences that the venue had to be transferred to the Great Hall of the college. From 1924 to 1933 he was also Lecturer in Classical and Mediaeval Art, another new post, this time on the secular side of the college. Appointment as an honorary associate of the Royal Institute of British Architects was an indication of his standing in the realms of art and design. From 1920 until his death he was first honorary secretary, then chairman, of the League of Arts. The League attracted strong support and organized performances in Hyde Park, and during the winter in the lecture hall of the Victoria and Albert Museum, of operas such as Edward German's *Merrie England* and Purcell's *Fairy Queen*. The first performance of Gustav Holst's choral ballet *The Golden Goose* (1926) was also promoted.

Closely associated with the League was the Guildhouse. Maud Royden, a remarkable woman who attended St Mary's, Primrose Hill, and usually had lunch at the vicarage afterwards, felt drawn to ordination but found no response from the Church of England. She

was, however, taken on as an assistant minister of the City Temple
– London's chief Congregational shrine – where her preaching created
something of a sensation, and much controversy in Anglican circles.
At one point Dearmer suggested to her that she really needed a preaching place of her own, so when the minister of the City Temple left for
another appointment she decided to pursue this possibility.

In 1920 Kensington Town Hall was hired for a Sunday evening 'Fellowship Service', with Royden as minister and Dearmer as her assistant, and to emphasize that the venture was designed to complement,
rather than rival, the work of the established churches it was called
'The Guildhouse'. Ecumenical in its spread, it soon attracted large congregations and in June 1921 the redundant Eccleston Square Congregational Church, with a main hall holding 1,000 people together with
a smaller hall and ancillary rooms, became available to provide an
independent home. An afternoon service was started under Dearmer's
leadership, to give scope for the use of poetry, orchestral pieces and
solos, as well as an address. The aims of the project had been clearly
outlined in a lengthy statement issued at its beginning in the Town
Hall, the opening paragraph declaring:

> Our feeling is that the Church of England, like other churches in
> this country, is at present appealing to that minority of English peo-
> ple who go to church on Sunday – a minority which appears to be
> decreasing. She ought to appeal to the public at large, by means of
> addresses and informal gatherings for discussion, and to speak to
> the great body of people who are not at home in church, or who
> do not even know their way about the Prayer Book. Very probably
> there should be a centre of this sort in every district of our great cit-
> ies, and certainly several in London.

This was a noble aim and large numbers attended, especially when
Maud Royden was preaching on Sunday evenings, and by 1924 the
Guildhouse was sufficiently well established to allow Dearmer to
leave and give more time to his other interests. It went on until 1936
but never succeeded in attracting the intellectuals, artists and young
people for whom it had been designed. The building was packed almost
entirely by women, who regarded Maud Royden as a great champion
of the feminist cause both inside and outside the Church – something
to which Dearmer was also firmly committed – and, while this had its
own importance, it was not the real intention.

Dearmer's other interests included the Life and Liberty Movement, concerned with church reform – which he joined some while after its wartime foundation – church unity, psychical research, healing (he had helped to found the Guild of Health) and, naturally, Prayer Book revision, in which he was not officially involved but to the discussion of which he made a largely unheeded contribution. All of this he carried out from a rented house in Chelsea's Embankment Gardens. By this time he had a daughter, Gillian, and a son, Anthony, both from his second marriage, and the family enjoyed a degree of comfort, facilitated by the combined incomes of husband and wife, employing a governess and maids. They made fairly frequent visits to the Continent, especially to Venice, Florence and Rome, and the house replaced the Primrose Hill vicarage as a meeting place for artists, musicians and writers. 'At Homes' for students attracted 50 to 60 from London's art colleges, who valued the opportunity to meet leading artists and to hear Dearmer's views on art's ultimate aims and the relation of art to life.

This was not a way of life or a form of Christian ministry about which a priest of Dearmer's gifts could reasonably complain. But as the years passed, he was in serious danger of becoming embittered. He assisted at St Luke's, Chelsea, and at one time preached regularly at Holy Trinity, Sloane Street – sometimes described as 'the Cathedral of the Arts and Crafts Movement' because of its furnishings and stained glass. But he longed for recognition by the Church that his work was significant and when this came in 1931, with his appointment to a canonry of Westminster, his time was running out.

For four years he accomplished a great deal there, but in July 1935 he had a serious breakdown in his health and he struggled through the following winter, unable to do much work. By April 1936 he had sufficiently recovered to be able to preach two more Sunday sermons, one on immortality, the other on unity, and during the afternoon of 29 May he took a group of King's College students on a tour of the Abbey. But later that day he suddenly died while working on what was to be his final book, *Man and His Maker* (published posthumously in 1936). He once said, 'I know perfectly well why I personally became a Christian. It was because I felt that the world is extremely beautiful, but eminently unsatisfactory.' His subsequent life was devoted to trying to lessen this dichotomy.

11

The Liberal Evangelical
Vernon Faithfull Storr,
Winchester and Westminster

Vernon Faithfull Storr, who was a canon of Winchester from 1907 to 1916 and of Westminster from 1920 until his death in 1940, was one of the most highly regarded churchmen of the first half of the twentieth century. He belonged to, and for much of this time was the acknowledged leader of, the liberal Evangelicals – a school of thought in the Church of England now defunct and, except among the very old, almost entirely forgotten. In vain can its origins and influence be sought in histories of the modern church, though in the 1930s its organization, the Anglican Evangelical Group Movement, had over 1,500 clergy, including several bishops, on its books and as many as 1,000 clergy and laity attended its annual conventions in Cromer. There were also 61 local clergy groups.

In order to grasp the significance of this movement it is necessary to disassociate its use of the name 'Evangelical' from that of the revivalist or charismatic Evangelicalism now active in many parts of the Church of England. True, it emphasized the vital importance of the Bible, the centrality of redemption through the cross, and sanctification through the Holy Spirit. But there the common ground ends, and for the rest it had much more in common with the liberalism of the Modern Churchman's Union, of which Storr was a vice-president until the end of his life. He was the link between the two movements.

Two biblical texts were of special importance to the liberal Evangelicals – 'the truth shall set you free' and 'the mind of Christ'. Christian truth, as Storr explained in his *Spiritual Liberty* (1934), which was the textbook of the movement, and in its earlier, shorter version, *My Faith* (1927), sold over 25,000 copies in several languages, was not something static, confined to biblical revelation, but a moving and growing body of knowledge for which human beings must search, and be ready to follow. New knowledge must always be welcomed, no matter from what quarter it comes, and followed wherever it leads. The application of this new knowledge must, however, always be subject to the discerned mind of Christ. Here for the liberal Evangelical was the supreme authority and in a later book, *Freedom and Tradition* (1940), Storr asserted:

> This is his standard in testing developments in theology or ecclesiastical organisation, thus going back to the creative source of Christianity . . . The liberal evangelical will constantly remind himself that the mind of Christ was larger than some of the interpretations which have been given of it. Few will deny that Christ's interest was ethical and religious rather than ecclesiastical and that what counted most in his scale of values were the spiritual issues concerned with character and men's relation to God and the Kingdom . . . The Founder of the Church must be greater than the Church.

As a preacher and teacher Storr attracted large and grateful audiences but there was nothing flamboyant about his style, nor did he seek to exploit the emotional. Rather were his sermons and lectures statements of personal faith, carefully crafted and expressed with the profound simplicity available only to the true scholar. Someone who heard him often in the pulpit of Westminster Abbey said, after his death, 'Forgiveness and redemption and the grace of God were realities which that good man, with his pale, ascetic and beautiful face, proclaimed with clear and simple conviction.' Towards the end of his life, by which time he was preaching almost weekly in St Margaret's, Westminster, he said in one of his sermons:

> I think as one grows older one grows simpler in one's religious faith. I become more and more aware of the profound mystery of life, and of how little we really know. And I am content to put a query in the margin about my beliefs, even theological beliefs. But a reverent agnosticism is compatible with a glowing faith in the great things that really matter, and of those incomparably the greatest is Jesus Christ. What I do not know I leave to him.

Storr also had the gift of a true pastor and, although his spells as a parish priest in Hampshire were brief, he was the kind of priest who, snail-like, always carried a parish on his back wherever he went. At both Winchester and Westminster he was always available to the multitudes who came to him for counsel and made a lasting impression on the lay staffs, who came to regard him as a friend as well as their employer.

Vernon Faithfull Storr was born in 1869 in India, where his father was in the Madras Civil Service. His mother, whose maiden name was Faithfull, was the daughter of a parish priest in Hertfordshire and his great-grandfather was a notable Evangelical priest in Kent. As a child Vernon was baptized by a chaplain of the Dutch Reformed Church in Madras but within a few years his father had been invalided back to England and he attended private schools in Sussex and Kent before going to Clifton College. There he came under what turned out to be the lasting influence of a remarkable headmaster and liberal thinker, the Reverend J. M. Wilson, and he later described his schooldays as some of the happiest of his life.

At Queen's College, Oxford, to which he went as a scholar, his health was generally poor and he suffered a knee injury while taking part in the high jump, which left him with a weakness of which he never ceased to be aware. Nonetheless, he took a Second in Mods and a very good First in Greats, and stayed on for a fifth year to attend a course of biology lectures, having by this time become interested in the relationship between religion and science, especially Darwinism.

Having been brought up as an Evangelical Storr was now keen to be freed from its intellectual constraints and this led to a period of unsettlement. So he postponed his planned ordination and became, instead, a fellow of University College, Oxford, and a tutor in philosophy. He was now greatly influenced by the master of the college, James Bright, whose liberal theological views had caused the Bishop of Oxford to forbid him to preach in his diocese, though the bishop could not prevent him from preaching in the college chapel. Storr collaborated with Hastings Rashdall, a liberal theologian and future Dean of Carlisle, in the organizing of fortnightly meetings of philosophical scholars for the discussion of philosophical and theological problems, but after two further breakdowns in health he was driven to resign his fellowship. During this time he had also become a friend of Charles Gore, the Anglo-Catholic theologian and future bishop, and although differences of opinion never damaged their friendship, he remarked on 'the absolute divergence between the Christianity of Christ and the perversions and extravagances of Catholicism'. This opinion never left him, though his tolerant spirit permitted friendships with other Anglo-Catholics and with Roman Catholics.

By 1900 Storr was ready for ordination and became a curate of the

Surrey parish of Haslemere, then in the diocese of Winchester, where the bishop, and later Archbishop of Canterbury, Randall Davidson, became a lifelong friend and admirer. At Haselmere he was given charge of a mission church – an iron structure near the railway station – which served a mainly artisan population. He learned a great deal about parish work from the gifted rector and was planning to replace the iron church with a permanent brick building, but shortly before he was due to be ordained priest he was offered by Queen's College, Oxford, the rectory of Bramshott, a few miles away in Hampshire. The bishop, who had already made him one of his examining chaplains, agreed that he could accept, since he was older than most of his curate contemporaries.

The next five years were spent in what was then a largely rural parish, covering about 35 square miles and only sparsely populated, except at Liphook – a growing town where there was a temporary mission church. Besides the parish church there was another church in a neighbouring village and services were also held in the schoolroom at a nearby hamlet. The rectory was in need of major repairs and could not be inhabited and Storr envisaged that when these were completed the house should be sold and a new rectory erected at Liphook. This scheme was, however, rejected by the patrons and from the restored house he exercised a preaching and pastoral ministry that was long remembered. While there he also became the first holder of a new Stanton Lectureship in the Philosophy of Religion at Cambridge. His first course, on 'Development and Divine Purpose' attracted a lot of attention, as did the published version in 1906.

He now felt the need of more time for study and writing, and University College, Oxford, obligingly presented him to Headbourne Worthy, near Winchester, one of the smallest parishes in the country: this appointment to be combined with a college research fellowship. The mainly Saxon church was in urgent need of repair and it was necessary to raise £3,000 for this. He also recovered a fine Elizabethan chalice and paten which his predecessor had sold and which turned up in Cornwall. In 1907, however, Herbert Edward Ryle, who had succeeded Randall Davidson at Winchester, asked Storr to become a canon residentiary of the cathedral, explaining that he believed it ought to become a centre of inspiration, organization, theological teaching and religious study, and that he would provide the necessary elements of 'youthful energy and keen intellectual sympathy.'

There was a problem, though, inasmuch as Storr was committed to the church restoration project, so it was agreed that he should stay at Headbourne Worthy until 1910 and meanwhile combine the two posts. A major restoration was also on hand at the cathedral, for it had been discovered in 1905 that the whole of the east end of the building was in a state of near collapse. The medieval builders, having discovered the water-table to be unusually high, erected the retrochoir and the Lady Chapel on a platform of wooden logs which had now decayed. The walls had begun to lean alarmingly and large, threatening cracks appeared throughout the great building. Since the remains of the eastern foundations were submerged in water, it was decided that the only solution was to employ a diver who would descend into its depths, remove all the decayed material and replace this with brick and concrete. Thus over a period of several years William Walker, who became one of Winchester Cathedral's great heroes and was rewarded by King George V with an MVO, handled 25,800 bags of concrete, 114,900 concrete blocks, and some 900,000 bricks.

Inevitably this and the repair of the entire building cost a huge amount of money, £113,000, and although most of this was raised by the dean and the bishop in the City of London, Storr and his colleagues were necessarily involved in the mammoth undertaking. He was in fact the youngest canon residentiary in the Church of England and, together with one of his colleagues and the headmaster of Winchester College, he became involved in a scheme for promoting higher education in the diocese through courses of lectures for both clergy and laity. A good deal of his time was also devoted to a book, which he had started writing while at Headbourne Worthy. *The Development of English Theology in the Nineteenth Century* (1913) covered the period 1800 to 1860 and is a learned study, severely critical of the Tractarian Movement. It was intended to be the first of two volumes, but the second was never written owing to health problems.

During his Winchester years, where his fine preaching and sensitive pastoral work were greatly valued, he began to suffer disabling attacks of insomnia, so when the prime minister, H. H. Asquith, offered him the rectory of St Margaret's, Westminster, annexed to a canonry of the Abbey, in 1912 he felt obliged to decline on the grounds that the dual responsibility would be too taxing. Ryle, who had by this time left Winchester to become Dean of Westminster, was particularly keen for Storr to join him, describing St Margaret's as 'the finest preaching platform in London', but it was just as well that Storr turned it down, since in the spring of 1913 he had a serious breakdown. A long recuperative sea voyage that took him all the way round Africa saw him back in Winchester, much restored in health, a few days before the outbreak of war in 1914, but he was never robust enough to serve as a forces chaplain.

Instead he did much work among the soldiers who were stationed in and around Winchester, usually prior to their embarkation at Southampton for the front, and as chaplain of the local hospital, which was always full of war casualties. He was, however, becoming unsettled at the cathedral since the new bishop, E. S. Talbot, a High Churchman, began to press for more Catholic forms of devotion and ceremonial. Storr told one of his colleagues, A. G. Robinson, who was also Archdeacon of Surrey, that he was minded to return to parish life and shortly after this, when the parish of Bentley in north Hampshire, of which the archdeacon was the patron, fell vacant Robinson offered it to him. Storr was on holiday in the Lake District at the time and Robinson thought that the offer would help him to clear his mind and resolve to stay at Winchester but, to the great surprise of the chapter, he accepted.

Bentley was a rural parish with two churches and Storr threw himself into pastoral work, went about on a bicycle and became much improved in health. The rectory, which he described as 'one of the ugliest houses in England', needed extensive repair. There was no main water supply, so he had a well dug, but all drinking water had to be boiled. In the 'flu epidemic of 1918 almost half the parishioners were affected, though Storr escaped and worked ceaselessly among its victims. During the hop-picking season he gave a lot of time to the gypsies who moved into the area to lend a hand. As an honorary canon of the cathedral, he also continued to preach there from time to time and a course of lectures, repeated at Aldershot and Southampton, was published under the title *Christianity and Immortality* (1918).

Two years later came another offer, this time from Lloyd George, of a Westminster canonry, but without the attachment of St Margaret's. The dean was still Ryle and he and the canons urged Storr to accept, which he did. The sub-dean was William Carnegie, who was also rector of St Margaret's and lived in considerable style, employing a butler, a couple of footmen, and several maids as well as a cook and a pantry boy. He was, however, outshone by Basil Wilberforce, the rector of St John's, Smith Square, who also held a canonry and whose house in Dean's Yard became, it was said, 'the scene of a brilliant and varied hospitality, to which nothing else in London exactly corresponded'. R. H. Charles, a staunch Protestant and preacher of lengthy sermons, was a leading authority on apocalyptic literature and once welcomed a very late visitor from Oxford with the comment, 'I am delighted to see you as I've been longing for some intelligent conversation.' Others who came later included C. S. Woodward, who left to become Bishop of Bristol, and F. R. Barry, a liberal churchman and close friend, who left to become Bishop of Southwell when both St John's, Smith Square, and his house were bombed in 1941. Lewis Donaldson, a Christian Socialist, had led a march of striking Leicester textile workers and owed his appointment to Ramsay MacDonald. He arrived not long after Storr in 1924 and stayed until his death in 1950, becoming sub-dean at the age of 82. Percy Dearmer was a colleague from 1931 to 1936.

Storr felt very much at home at the Abbey and, in spite of sharp differences of opinion, got on well with all his colleagues. The style of worship suited him and although he cared little for ceremonial, believing it to be a distraction from God-centred worship, the 'English use' introduced by Jocelyn Perkins, who was Sacrist for 60 years, was not over-elaborate. Beyond the Abbey, Storr was one of the leading opponents of the 1928 revision of the Prayer Book, not because he was opposed to change, but because he feared that some of the proposals would encourage a less rational understanding of faith.

Initially, Storr was Steward, responsible for hospitality and over-sight of the gardens, and for a time also Keeper of the Muniments. From 1926 to 1931 he was Treasurer, the most demanding office on the chapter, and in the absence of a developed administration spent much time on business affairs. He was glad to exchange this for the archdeaconry of Westminster – a sinecure office, since there was no archdeaconry, and his responsibilities were largely confined to the pas-toral care of the residents in the precincts. He used this to build closer relations with Westminster School – always sensitive territory – and, as chairman of the Choir School Committee, was responsible for add-ing 25 to 30 day boys to the 34 boarders. This was to enable the Abbey to have, in effect, two choirs and to offer choral services during August and September, when most visitors were present. Five years later this was abandoned in favour of a 40-strong boarding school still able to support a reserve choir.

Storr's presence in London made him immediately accessible to a variety of people and causes needing the benefit of his gifts. 'Never in my whole life', he once wrote, '(and I have always been a hard worker) have I had so many demands made on my time and energy as at West-minster.' His small study was always overcrowded with papers, books and letters, and he generally chose to work in an armchair by the fire-side, rather than at his desk, which served as an additional table. He worked from early morning until late at night, yet if anyone called on him he was always ready to lay down whatever he was doing and give the visitor his undivided attention. For his first five years at Westminster he was without secretarial support and dealt with his considerable correspondence unaided and promptly. He was one of Archbishop Davidson's trusted advisers and at the times of bishops' meetings and the Church Assembly the flow of callers increased very considerably, as church leaders sought his counsel. There was always time, too, for unknown visitors who might have been struck by one of his sermons and wished to discuss its implications.

Efforts were soon made to draw him more closely into the Church's leadership. He had declined the offer of the Regius Chair of Divinity at Oxford not long after his arrival at the Abbey and did the same when he was offered the bishoprics of Peterborough and Worcester. On three separate occasions he said 'No' to the deanery of Canterbury, which must constitute some sort of record, and following the third refusal he had a personal interview with the prime minister, Stanley Baldwin, to explain his position. Baldwin responded with a letter in which he promised, 'I won't worry you again until you want to be worried.' Storr simply did not wish to be involved in the administrative chores that were already hampering the effective ministry of the bishops; neither did he wish to be deeply immersed in the affairs of a cathedral. He believed that he could do far more good remaining in London, and exercising his own distinctive ministry of writing, preaching and teaching. The leadership of the Anglican Evangelical Group Movement, of which he was the executive president, was also of some importance. His decision to stay put was widely regretted in the Church, but Archbishop Davidson came to recognize, albeit reluctantly, that he had 'acted rightly'.

His literary output during the Westminster years was in fact considerable – 14 books in all. Not all of them were large tomes but, rather, readable essays on what he believed to be the urgent issues facing the Church at the time, such as *The Missionary Genius of the Bible* (1924), *God in the Modern Mind* (1931) and *Do Dead Men Live Again?* (1932). He also edited a series of 53 pamphlets on the liberal Evangelical approach to various issues, and from 1932 onwards was one of a small team of writers who anonymously contributed religious articles for the Saturday edition of *The Times*.

From 1922 until the publication of its report in 1937, Storr was a member of a distinguished Archbishop's Commission on Christian Doctrine, which met under the chairmanship of William Temple. The report, when it finally appeared, was recognized as an important piece of work, and Temple said of Storr's contribution to the Commission, 'He seemed very little interested in theological discussion as a scientific enterprise, but profoundly concerned about the devotional and ethical values involved, to which his rather infrequent interventions recalled us.' Someone also said that if the other members of the Commission had embraced Storr's disciplined approach to discussion the report would have been completed in half the time. The truth is that he did not really care for meetings of this sort and although Archbishop Cosmo Gordon Lang persuaded him, much against his own inclinations, to join a Church and State Commission in 1932, he refused to join another on relations between the Church of England and the Church of Scotland.

A piece of additional work he greatly enjoyed was that of Preacher to Lincoln's Inn. He first became associated with this company of lawyers in 1923 when he became the Warburton Lecturer – the first series of which, on 'The Development of the Theism of the Old Testament', was published under the title *From Abraham to Christ* (1928). In 1926 he was appointed Preacher, which involved a Sunday sermon during the legal terms, but he also regarded himself as the Inn's pastor, staying for lunch with the Benchers after the service, visiting members who were ill, and generally making himself available as a counsellor. His influence became considerable.

In November 1936, however, he accepted the Crown's offer of a sideways move to the Abbey canonry annexed to St Margaret's, following the death of Canon Carnegie. After 16 years at the Abbey Storr was ready for change and fresh opportunities for preaching and teaching. It was also the case that his relations with Dean Foxley Norris ('Old Bill'), who had succeeded Dean Ryle in 1925, were less cordial than either of them might have wished. They often had disagreements about the Abbey's finances and Storr always staunchly defended the changes instituted by Ryle, but the real problem was marked differences of temperament. So Storr was glad to be given an independent sphere within the Westminster community, but the first four months of 1937 were occupied mainly with preparations for the coronation of King George VI, which involved the transfer of all the Abbey's services to St Margaret's. When, shortly after the coronation, Foxley Norris died, Storr found himself responsible, as sub-dean, for the running of the Abbey's affairs as well as those of St Margaret's. It was, therefore, not surprising that he once again became seriously ill and in the spring of 1938 had to take a four-month break, spent with one of his sons, who lived in South Africa. In the event, he was able to give only just over two years to St Margaret's, and there was much to do and to be endured.

Although the parish had at the end of the nineteenth century a very large, and mainly poor, resident population, slum clearance and other developments had reduced this considerably, and new parishes had been formed by the time Storr took over. The practice of the wealthy leaving Westminster for the country at weekends had also started, and MPs were tending to return to their constituencies. Nevertheless, St Margaret's remained the parish church of the House of Commons, though Storr was never Speaker's Chaplain, and it was still one of the prime churches in London for fashionable weddings and memorial services for the great and the good. The number of each was huge and, although the memorial services normally consisted of a simple standard form, without an address, both provided the conscientious Storr and his curate with a taxing pastoral ministry.

The church fabric was also in urgent need of repair and the bells, having become a danger to the stability of the tower, needed to be overhauled and rehung. All of this Storr financed out of the personal fees for weddings, memorial services and other special services. He started lunchtime lectures in Advent and Lent, and his Sunday morning sermons attracted large congregations from all parts of London and beyond. Missionaries home on furlough often took the opportunity to sit at his feet.

The outbreak of war in 1939 brought a further increase in the number of worshippers at St Margaret's and the Abbey, and increased concern for the safety of the two buildings as the German blitz got under way during the summer of 1940. In July Storr became ill again with what turned out to be a particularly painful form of cancer, and on 13 September, when the Battle of Britain was reaching its climax and bombs were falling all around in Westminster, he was admitted to a nursing home in Vincent Square. One of the bombs – an oil bomb – fell on St Margaret's, causing considerable damage which required the church to be closed for 12 months. Another, which fell in Dean's Yard, blew out some of the windows in his home.

At the end of September he was moved to Matfield, in Sussex, to stay with cousins, but soon had to go into Tunbridge Wells Hospital and died there on 25 October. The dean, Paul de Labilliere, was away on the following Sunday and it was left to Jocelyn Perkins, never an easy man to please, to say in his sermon,

Since the foundation of this collegiate church by Queen Elizabeth in the year 1560 twenty-nine Deans and two hundred and thirty-two Canons have held office therein. Three have been enthroned in the chair of St Augustine – Bancroft, Laud, Hutton – seven others have been appointed to the Northern Primacy, while scores of the remainder have made solid contributions to the life of church and nation. In that large and goodly company the name of Vernon Faithfull Storr will ever occupy a high position, as a great Canon of Westminster, a great Churchman, a great Christian.

With his death the liberal Evangelical movement in the Church of England, in common with its Modernist counterpart, went into terminal decline. Neither had bred a succession of strong, inspiring leaders, but more significantly the uncertainties created by the war brought a climate more favourable to a Biblical Theology movement, which had gathered support in academic circles in the 1930s and in its neo-orthodoxy provided what seemed to be a more solid basis for faith. These foundations proved in the not-so-long run to be much less secure than their constructors had suggested, and by the end of the century the philosophy and faith of Storr and his followers appeared strikingly relevant to those who were aware of their existence.

12

The Parish Priest
Peter Green, Manchester

Peter Green was one of the twentieth century's greatest parish priests. He ministered for 49 years in two of Salford's roughest slum parishes and for 40 of these was also a canon residentiary of Manchester Cathedral. And not only this: he wrote 38 books, had a weekly column in the *Manchester Guardian* – becoming one of the paper's institutions – and was in constant demand for the conducting of missions in parishes far away from his own. It was a unique and unrepeatable achievement made possible only by the combination in one priest of extraordinary physical stamina, a deep and highly disciplined spirituality, unusual gifts as a communicator, and a total commitment and dedication that went with his celibate vocation.

It is also the case that although his Manchester canonry had, by the beginning of the twentieth century, ceased to be the near-sinecure office of times past, it was far less demanding of its occupant than cathedral canonries were to become not so long after his retirement in 1954, when he was in his eighty-fourth year. Even so, the three other members of his chapter who, because of a Manchester arrangement that beggared belief, had also been required to serve as rectors of large city parishes, were relieved of their parochial responsibilities in 1926. Green refused this opportunity and said that if required to choose between the cathedral and his parish he would opt for the latter. But such was his reputation by this time that no one would have dared demand such a choice.

Peter Green, the son of a highly respected Southampton solicitor, was born in 1871. His father was a member of the Hackney Phalanx – a High Church group founded before the Tractarian movement which had produced Keble, Pusey, Hurrell Froude and others of its leaders. His mother, a devout woman, had by contrast been brought up in the Clapham Sect – an Evangelical group whose number included William Wilberforce – but as she grew older she was attracted by the Oxford

Movement and for the remainder of her life was a Tractarian. Her influence on young Peter, which he always acknowledged, was profound.

When only 11 he, in company with his brother, witnessed a foreign sailor being stabbed to death in a sleazy area of the city, near the docks, and this had a lasting effect, expressed in a concern for ethical questions and the effect of environment on character. As a boy he was taken by his father to a Tory meeting and had to be ejected for his persistence in calling attention to the Liberal gains in a recent general election. 'Will someone take that damn boy out and break his neck?' cried the chairman. Thereafter Green was a committed Liberal.

At Cranleigh, then a fairly new public school, his Christian commitment also developed and later he wrote in one of his books, 'I believed whole-heartedly in God, and said my prayers, and enjoyed the services in the school chapel or in church during the holidays, and found my Communions a help.' He won a scholarship to St John's College, Cambridge, where one of his fellow undergraduates was Bertrand Russell. The two strongly disliked each other. He rowed for the college, did some boxing and in his final year was elected President of the Cambridge Union – none of which got in the way of his gaining a brilliant First in Moral Sciences, having switched to this subject after achieving only a disappointing Third in Mathematics.

It is not clear what prompted him to seek holy orders but later in life he said, 'Had I nine lives like a cat, I should have been a parish priest every time.' Those who knew him found it impossible to believe that he could have been anything else, and in counselling young men who were considering the possibility of ordination he always insisted on the need for an imperative interior calling. As late as 1894 it was still possible to be ordained without resort to a theological college and, after some directed reading, Green was ordained by Bishop Randall Davidson of Rochester to a curacy at Lady Margaret Church, Walworth. This was the St John's College mission in one of the toughest areas of South London, where the social conditions were appalling.

He was in no way daunted by the challenge, which he later came to regard as having been the best possible preparation for his future ministry in Salford. His work among young people in Walworth was not hindered by his readiness to take on a prizefighter in a local boxing booth and winning a prize for standing up to him for five minutes. He said, however, that the prize was not worth it. He described this and many other Walworth experiences in his first book, *Our Kid* (1910), and his reflections on them in *How to Deal with Lads* (1920), which for many years was a widely used guide on the subject.

His four years in Walworth were not, however, entirely happy. The vicar, an eccentric, difficult man, took a dislike to Green – possibly because of his great success with the boys of the parish and his more general popularity – and this eventually reached a crisis point requiring the intervention of the bishop. Edward Stuart Talbot, who had by this time succeeded Randall Davidson at Rochester, solved the problem by arranging for Green to join the large team of curates at Leeds Parish Church, where he had himself exercised a notable ministry as vicar. This was an inspired move. Green was assigned to the roughest and most disorderly area of the town, where he was soon joined by another new curate, O. G. Mackie – a rugby international – who also had a special gift for ministry to boys. Between them they founded the Market Street Club, which became outstandingly successful. Members were offered games and a wide variety of other activities, including religious teaching which led invariably to confirmation. Besides the satisfaction derived from this work, Green greatly appreciated the dignified worship in the cathedral-scale parish church and the supervision of the scholar-vicar, E. C. S. Gibson, who went on to become Bishop of Gloucester. Gibson in turn recognized Green's qualities and whenever a notable clergyman was invited to occupy the pulpit in the parish church Green was despatched to take the visitor's place in his own church. The news that the Bishop of Shanghai would be coming to preach in a few months' time led Green to enquire, pointedly, if he ought to be booking his passage.

In 1902 Green was appointed Rector of Sacred Trinity Church, Salford, an appointment not unrelated to the fact that the parish was said to be the most difficult in Manchester Diocese. Close to the cathedral and just over the Salford border, it consisted almost entirely of back-to-back houses, with not a blade of grass to be seen anywhere. Dirt and gloom prevailed and it was inhabited by the most deprived, dysfunctional and lawless families in the area. At night the police never patrolled alone. The church was poorly attended, generally run down, and kept locked to avoid vandalism and desecration. Yet Green said that he fell in love with Salford at first sight. It reminded him of Walworth and he never expected to be given such a chance so early in his ministry. The appointment of a 30-year-old priest to so large a parish was certainly unusual, and even more so to a living worth £1,400 a year – four or five times the national average at the time. The income had probably been inflated by the sale of expensive leases on benefice land for industrial and housing development, and the rector was required to meet from his stipend the salaries of any curates he might employ, as well as many of the parish's overheads.

The Bishop of Manchester was Edmund Knox, a leading Evangelical, who agreed that Green might have two curates, and these were soon augmented by a local ordinand who served as a paid lay reader. Frock coats were worn. The life of the church was gradually transformed by a combination of well-ordered worship, fine preaching and intensive pastoral care of all who lived in the parish. Before long worshippers from outside the parish were being attracted, among them Nurse Edith Cavell, who worked in a local hospital until she went to France on the outbreak of war and was executed by the Germans in 1915 for assisting the escape of British soldiers from occupied Belgium. Another extra-parochial worshipper was Ronald Knox, son of the bishop, who later became a notable Monsignor in the Roman Catholic Church.

Green described his approach in *The Town Parson* (1919), which was based on lectures given at King's College, London, and Cambridge in 1914 and became a classic of pastoral ministry. Designed to aid newly ordained curates and with a final chapter for newly appointed vicars, it dealt in the most minute detail with every aspect of parish life – The Ordering of One's Day, Parochial Visiting, The Conduct of Services, The Ministry of the Word, Work with Special Classes and The Management of a Parish. The highest standards were expected of the priest and also, by implication, the extraordinary degree of energy displayed by Green himself and the same depth of spirituality. On examination almost a hundred years later, the volume offers a fascinating insight into the methods employed in the best parishes during the first half of the twentieth century. For Green was by no means alone in his approach and practice. What sets him apart is the length of his ministry in just two difficult inner-city parishes and the fact that he was able to combine this for 40 years with the residentiary canonry of a cathedral.

Much of his method is still applicable today, though social change requires a very different approach to work among children and young people. Systematic house-to-house visiting is also an altogether different proposition in the modern inner-city parish, though Green deplored its all-too-frequent neglect in his own day. The most significant changes, however, have been in the retreat of the Church to the margins of British society and a consequent serious reduction in the number of clergy available for parish ministry. The church of the nineteenth and early twentieth centuries could not claim the active allegiance of most of the population, but it was still valued and used on family and other significant community occasions. Thus the clergy had a widely acknowledged position in society and it was still possible to attract to the ordained ministry men of high calibre who could find in an inner-city area work that seemed to them infinitely worthwhile and immensely satisfying. Green was ahead of his time in recognizing the importance of the laity in the Church's ministry, but the clergy dominated the pastoral scene and believed it to be right to do so.

Green was only 40 when in 1911 he was made a canon residentiary of Manchester Cathedral, and at the time there were those who believed him to be far too young for so senior an appointment. Others feared that a great parish priest would become distracted by the temptations and demands of cathedral life and that his special gifts would be lost to the Church. In fact, it is impossible to believe that he would have accepted the offer of the canonry had it not been annexed to St Philip's, the largest parish in Salford and only a short walk from the Church of the Sacred Trinity.

The Church of England was disastrously slow in responding to the radical social and economic changes brought about by the Industrial Revolution, and nowhere was it more dilatory than in Manchester. While the future great city was developing into the cotton textiles capital of the world it remained within the diocese of Chester and until well into the nineteenth century the ancient collegiate church of Manchester was virtually the only building in which Anglican worship was offered and from which some sort of ministry was exercised. A measure of progress was made in 1825 when, with money provided from a government fund established to commemorate the victory at the Battle of Waterloo, St Philip's Church was built in Salford. Designed to seat 2,000 people, this was intended to serve a wealthy, fashionable parish, consisting of large terrace houses and the country houses occupied by rich cotton merchants in the rural area that still surrounded Salford. The extensive galleries were intended for soldiers from a nearby barracks.

Meanwhile, the collegiate church was coming under increasing pressure. The Warden and Fellows, as the clergy were then titled, were enjoying large and ever-increasing incomes in return for no more than three months' formal residence every year – and this often discharged only perfunctorily. The creation of new parishes was resisted, even when the population of the city reached one million, and it was necessary to hold mass weddings and baptisms, often with unedifying results. The registers indicate that one member of the chapter alone conducted during his time at the cathedral 33,211 baptisms, 13,196 weddings and 9,996 funerals. When in 1846, however, one of their number accepted the headship of a college this aroused so much local indignation that a petition signed by 400 parishioners demanded that he should either devote his whole time to the service of the church in Manchester or resign. This led, in the following year, to the forming of an Association for Promoting a Reform in the Ecclesiastical Provisions of the Parish of Manchester – an initiative that coincided with the creation of a new diocese of Manchester and the designation of the collegiate church as its cathedral, to be served by a dean and four canons. Then, in 1850, came the Manchester Parish Provisions Act, which, in reaction to the scandalous inactivity of the previous order, decreed that to each of the canons should be attached one of the largest and poorest parishes in the city.

It was recognized that this would inevitably present the canons with some conflicting claims on their time, but it was evidently believed that the cathedral's claims would not be unduly heavy and that the problem could be solved by a minor readjustment of the calendar of residences. What was not foreseen was that further increases in the populations of the four parishes, creating even more social problems, would be quite beyond the capacity of many of the elderly clergymen likely to be appointed to the canonries. Neglect could hardly be avoided, not least at St Philip's, Salford, whose parish soon ceased to be a leafy suburb, as slum housing was inserted into its open spaces and the wealthy fled to more salubrious havens. Almost half of the population consisted of Irish immigrant labourers and their families. When Green became rector of St Philip's he had, however, one distinct advantage. His predecessor, the liberal and learned Edward Lee Hicks, had for the previous 18 years managed successfully to combine with the canonry an outstanding parish ministry – so outstanding that he was deemed an appropriate successor to the saintly Edward King as Bishop of Lincoln.

Green was more of a High Churchman than Hicks could ever have been but, although he started a daily Eucharist in both his parishes, he was not interested in vestments and ceremonial and was always faithful to the Book of Common Prayer. There was also something of the Evangelical in him, represented by his belief that people needed to be converted by a personal encounter with Christ, this leading to what he called 'vital religion'. Such a transformation might take a long time but it was always to be the objective. He was tall and sparely built, with a thin, ascetic face, adorned by steel-rimmed spectacles that suggested an intellectual. By the time he was 40 it was difficult to believe that he had ever been a college oarsman, much less a boxer, but he protected himself against the ever-present danger of exhaustion through over-work by installing a couch in his study, and in his cathedral room, on which he would take an occasional nap. In 1908 he declined the bishopric of New Guinea on medical grounds, as he had a constant throat problem and was also discovered to have a weak heart.

There could be no doubting of his pastoral heart and he was greatly loved and admired, but he was also quick-tempered and could make cutting remarks. When a leading businessman tried to make a butt of him at a public dinner, only to have the laugh turned against himself, he wrote to complain that he had been made to look a fool in public. To which Green replied:

> Dear Sir,
> You are mistaken. I merely called attention to the fact.

He was, however, generally quick to apologize when he recognized that he had caused hurt, though almost certainly not on this occasion. His highly disciplined way of life also made him intolerant of unpunctuality and, in spite of the appalling social conditions in which he ministered, he always insisted – at least until the outbreak of war in 1914 – that his curates should emulate him by wearing tall hat and frock coat on Sundays. On weekdays he wore in the parish a Norfolk jacket and baggy trousers.

When Green accepted the canonry it was suggested to him that St Philip's parish could safely be left to a curate, but he was unwilling even to consider this, though he took with him the two curates from Sacred Trinity. The senior of these had already served with him for six years and had become something of a specialist in inner-city ministry. The rectory was turned into a centre for women and girls supervised by a full-time woman church worker, while an ordinand at Manchester University was recruited to work part-time in the parish. Thus the impressive ministry of Edmund Lee Hicks was continued and developed. Every afternoon, at 2.30 precisely, Green and his staff started house-to-house visiting, which continued until the evening organizations required their presence. If he had been away, usually conducting a mission in another parish, on his return he would walk the streets for a time, talking to the people he met and popping into houses to greet their families. In *The Man of God* (1935) he explained:

> One thing is certain. No time is wasted that you spend with your people. The time a man spends in the Lads' Club or with the Scouts, the time he spends on rambles with his young people of both sexes,

the hours devoted to meetings of a purely social character, such as
Mothers' Meeting teas or excursions, Sunday School parties, in a
word, the time he spends in friendly intercourse with his people
so that he gets to know them and they get to know him, is never
time wasted. And the closer and more intimate the relationship
into which he enters with his people, the more spiritual fruit it will
yield . . . One thing remains to be said, of all the places in which a
clergyman can get to know his people, incomparably the best is the
people's own homes.

During the 1914–18 war he never took a day off and maintained the
closest contact with the homes of those with men in the armed forces,
who all too often became casualties. Letters were written to those who
were away and individual memorial services were held for those who
were killed. Four to five hours were spent every day in the local hospital, which received large numbers of the wounded. In his wartime
sermons Green, who was never afraid to court controversy, said that
it was wrong to hate the Germans, since others shared responsibility
for the war and there was a need for a wider repentance. It was hardly
surprising that the end of the war left him exhausted and in need of a
period of recuperation.

Four years later he wrote an article for the *Church Times* after its
correspondence column had for several weeks included letters criticiz-
ing the clergy for their alleged laziness. It was at a time when he was
working single-handed at St Philip's, and he described a typical day in
his own ministry:

Sunday began at 6.45 a.m. when I went into the church to get things
ready for the 7 o'clock Mass, and ended at 9.45 p.m. when, having
closed the Vicarage door on a parishioner who insisted on coming in
after Evensong to discuss some troubles he was having with his wife,
I turned to the supper I was too tired to eat. The day had included, in
parish church, mission church and hospital, eight services and five
addresses. Monday began with a ward Celebration in the hospital,
followed by another in church. It closed when, at 9.15 p.m., I got
in from my last sick case to attack the day's correspondence. I actually had 40 minutes for breakfast, but against that must be set that
dinner was taken in 15 minutes in a restaurant, between a meeting
of the school trustees and hearing confessions in church. And when
I got in to tea at 7.10 I found (I declare before heaven I am writing
the truth):

(a) A man with passport papers to be filled up;
(b) A day school teacher with a grievance;
(c) Two women with pension papers to be filled up and signed;
(d) Three boys wanting swimming-bath tickets;
(e) One man and one lad wanting letters to possible employers, as both were out of work;
(f) A boy with a Convalescent Home letter to be filled up.

And Evensong with missionary intercessions was at 7.30 p.m. Tuesday began with Mattins at 7.00 a.m. followed by a Celebration. It ended when I got in at 11.15 p.m. from speaking for the Anglo-Catholic Movement in a neighbouring town. And so it goes on, day after day.'

Shortly before the outbreak of the war he had, to his very great pleasure, been appointed a chaplain to King George V and although the duties of this office did not claim much of his time it was not quite the sinecure it later became. The King obviously took a great liking to Green and valued the simplicity of his preaching. On the occasions when he was due to preach at the Chapel Royal he would be summoned to preach first at Buckingham Palace, where the King and Queen normally worshipped, and found that sermons previously preached in the Barrow Street Mission were very acceptable. He was not afraid, however, to be controversial and during a coal strike, about which he knew the King to be annoyed, he put before him the miners' case. Other controversial public utterances led to his exclusion from the official party that welcomed the King on a wartime visit to Manchester, but his absence was immediately noticed and the King gave instructions that whenever in future he visited the city he expected his chaplain to be present. Preaching assignments at Sandringham provided opportunities for longer conversations with the King about social and parish matters, and also with Queen Mary, who had a special affection for him and a particular interest in his Lads' Club. She presented it with an autographed photograph of herself and wrote personal letters to some of its members. Green was allowed to make a choice of furniture for himself from the royal workshops. He found relations with the Prince of Wales, the future King Edward VIII, less easy, and a resolution not to leave his parish during the 1939–45 war inhibited contact with King George VI.

The outbreak of another world war in 1939 found Green still at his Salford post but faced with new and unprecedented problems. He resumed his practice of corresponding with the men who were away in the forces, but from 1940 onwards Salford itself was in the front line as a target of German bombing. The crypt of St Philip's Church became an air-raid shelter, visited every night by the rector, who said prayers before going to the wards of the nearby hospital. During 1941 and 1942 the bombing was severe and Salford, in common with much of central Manchester, sustained very considerable damage. Now his task was to offer comfort and help to those who had suffered the trauma of losing their homes and often members of their families. No one could have been more effective in such testing pastoral work and he was himself shattered when his curate, John Hussey, was killed while walking from the hospital to the church. Earlier, the Dean of Manchester had more than once begged Green to resign from the parish and confine himself to his cathedral duties (he was now 70) but he always replied that, quite apart from his own wishes, which were to stay in the place he loved, he thought it best that he should not leave the parish in wartime. In the event he stayed until 1954.

Although the parish was his first love, Green was always very much at home in the cathedral. He appreciated the dignity and formality of its worship, and the opportunity it presented for preaching to large congregations – sometimes as many as 2,000 in the broad nave. As a preacher, he tended to speak conversationally, without histrionics or extravagant gestures, and this established a close rapport with his audiences. In preaching the gospel his method was to take biblical incidents, develop these by means of logical argument, and spice the resulting discourse with personal anecdotes. This was highly effective and although he was more of a teacher than an evangelist, as this description is commonly understood, he conducted innumerable missions in other parishes and became a national authority on the subject. He took part in an annual beach mission at Blackpool until almost the end of his life.

The Dean of Manchester at the time of Green's appointment to the canonry was J. E. C. Welldon, who had been an outstanding headmaster of Harrow School, though a less than satisfactory Bishop of Calcutta, and who moved to Manchester after a few recuperative years as a canon of Westminster. He was a larger-than-life figure who easily assumed the historic role of Rector of Manchester and became a very popular figure in the city. Green supported his efforts to open the cathedral to the multitudes who would not dream of attending Mattins or Evensong and a 100-strong voluntary choir led the worship at a Sunday evening nave service over which Welldon himself normally presided. Others, requiring stronger fare, looked forward to Green's periods in residence and he, too, developed a considerable following. At the beginning of the 1914–18 war he started a lunchtime Service of Intercession which continued for many years afterwards and, as late as 1950, Bishop Leonard Wilson, who had become dean following his Second World War suffering in Singapore, commented on the care he took over its preparation. The Fraser Chapel of the cathedral became known as the place where Green heard confessions and this brought many penitents. During his residence he was present, as required, at the daily choral Mattins and Evensong, but also said Mattins in St Philip's with his curates and any parishioners who came.

Bishop Welldon's extrovert personality and love of the limelight did not make him the easiest of colleagues, but he and Green got on well enough, chiefly because Green was preoccupied with his parish and they shared a deep hatred of alcohol and gambling. In Green's case this hatred was brought about by his experience of their effects on the lives of his parishioners. For many years he held the office of bursar, which, in the absence of a lay administration, was demanding. He was normally impatient with administration but kept a very close watch on the cathedral's finances and the dean and chapter's still considerable estates. Although these and other substantial endowments were normally more than adequate, the financial position was less good during the inter-war economic recessions, requiring careful stewardship of resources.

Green, perhaps surprisingly, was conservative over many aspects of the cathedral's life, especially over its textiles and furnishings, so during his reign as bursar the interior retained the somewhat bleak appearance it had inherited from a more Protestant past. This situation was, however, dramatically altered when the cathedral was hit by wartime bombs. The east end was severely damaged and had to be boarded up, leaving only the nave available for worship. By this time he had ceased to be the bursar, but when the war was over he joined the recently appointed dean, Garfield Williams, in raising the money required for the restoration. He was now sub-dean.

Another project on which he was specially keen and which he kept going through two world wars was the cathedral's country home at Tarden in Cheshire. This provided holidays for people too poor to make their own arrangements and who were ministered to from a lay mission in the slums. Green was its enthusiastic chairman for all his years at the cathedral.

Various attempts were made to attract him to wider responsibility.

In the 1920s he was offered the bishopric of Lincoln in succession to Edward Lee Hicks, and strongly pressed by Archbishop Randall Davidson to accept. He declined on the grounds that he had no experience of rural life but admitted later that he believed bishops should divest themselves of the trappings of their office in order to exercise a more apostle-like ministry, and he considered Lincoln to be too conservative a diocese to understand and accept this. Faced with his explanation Davidson confessed that he had never thought of such a possibility. When the new diocese of Blackburn was created in 1926 Green was again pressed, not least by the Bishop of Manchester, William Temple, to accept the bishopric and once again declined. Had he ever been offered Manchester, however, he would probably have found this irresistible.

In 1926 two of the canons residentiary resigned from their parishes and the third soon followed, leaving only Green, with his huge responsibilities in Salford. But he made it clear that if a division became compulsory he would resign from his canonry, rather than forsake St Philip's. It was not until January 1951, when he was 80, that he was driven by ill-health to resign from St Philip's, but he then moved into two rooms not far from the rectory and, to everyone's pleasure, continued to attend the services as a member of the congregation. He retained his canonry for another three years, but became increasingly frail and resigned in 1954. He lived on for seven more years, becoming more and more removed from reality by the onset of dementia, and died in a church nursing home in Surrey in November 1961. A former parishioner, who chanced to live nearby and whom he had not seen for 20 years, went to visit him a few days before his death and was immediately recognized. After a brief conversation about the past, Peter Green took him by the hand and said, 'Goodbye, dearest friend. May God bless you.' These words expressed the basis of a very remarkable ministry, and appointment earlier as a Freeman of the City of Manchester demonstrated a great community's recognition of this.

13

The Broadcaster
W. H. Elliott, St Paul's

Some priests should never become residentiary canons and Wallace Elliott, who went to St Paul's in 1929, was certainly one of these. Unlike most cathedral misfits, however, he recognized his mistake and after 18 months resigned in order to return to parish life as vicar of St Michael's, Chester Square in London's Belgravia. This he also regarded as a mistake, though he stayed for nearly ten years and during his time there established a national reputation as the foremost among religious broadcasters, commanding huge radio audiences which have never been surpassed. The cost of this to his health – and, many felt, to the quality of religious broadcasting – was heavy and when eventually his programme was brought to an end the BBC decreed that never again must a broadcaster be permitted to win such a personal following.

Although the offer of a St Paul's canonry came as a surprise, he confessed that he had 'felt for years that the pulpit of St Paul's was somehow meant for me'. But he had not reckoned with the fact that the guardians of his pulpit were a dean and chapter whose vocabulary did not include the word 'change' and whose outlook and understanding of the Christian faith were light-years removed from his own. The dean, W. R. Inge, a Platonist philosopher, was nearing the end of his time and had felt for the past 18 years that his position was akin to that of a mouse watched by four cats. The vacancy that led to Elliott's appointment, the first to be created for 17 years, was occasioned by the appointment of Canon Simpson to the deanery of Peterborough. He had failed to attend a chapter meeting for 18 months after authorization had been given in 1917 for prayers for the dead – these being mainly soldiers killed in France and Flanders. His preferment to Peterborough was engineered by Inge, whose tolerance had by 1928 reached breaking point. There was to be no relief from Canon Sidney Alexander, however, who was no less awkward, albeit with a valuable flair for fund-raising, and who, having arrived at St Paul's shortly before Inge, stayed for 39 years.

It was to Alexander, who chanced to be canon in residence at the time, that Elliott despatched a telegram requesting an interview following the offer of the canonry from the prime minister, Stanley Baldwin. Neither Alexander nor, more importantly, Inge was aware that Elliott's name was even under consideration and when presented with the Downing Street letter Alexander's only response was 'indecent haste'. It was hardly the warmest of welcomes and 45-year-old Elliott felt from the outset that his appointment was regarded by the chapter with resentment. He was installed on the feast of the Conversion of St Paul in 1929 and began what he described as 'one of the most miserable and wretched times of my life'. The cathedral had, he believed, stagnated and was now 'dead, *very* dead'.

This was undoubtedly true. But Elliott was essentially a performer and, like most of his sort, a loner and there was never the remotest possibility that he would manage, even with patience and cunning, to persuade his colleagues of the need for change. The fact that he, whose preaching was his chief gift, could occupy the St Paul's pulpit on only 13 occasions a year – at Sunday afternoon Evensong – caused him acute frustration. And his claim that, given greater freedom, he could fill St Paul's every week was not such as to win the glad support of his colleagues. Inge was well aware of Elliott's unhappiness and made what many would have regarded as the wise and helpful suggestion that he should regard St Paul's as the centre, rather than the circumference, of his activities and Elliott did in fact preach in some other, more hospitable churches. He also augmented his income by giving lectures on Dr Johnson. Inge believed he was exaggerating the chapter's hostility to him, and the closure of the cathedral for several months for extensive repairs was not helpful, but by the early part of 1930 Elliott was speaking of resignation. Arthur Foley Winnington-Ingram, the Bishop of London, who had much in common with Elliott and sympathized with his plight, tried to persuade him to persevere a little longer, and Ramsay MacDonald, who had succeeded Baldwin as prime minister, also attempted to get him to stay, but the July chapter meeting was his last. His only happy memory of the place was of his visits to the choir school, made in his capacity as precentor, where he lectured to the choristers on prehistoric animals. Otherwise the atmosphere was, as he put it, 'all wrong'.

Wallace Harold Elliott (he always hated his Christian names) was born at Horsham in 1884. His paternal grandfather, an alcoholic, had been a jobbing gardener, while both his parents worked long hours to make a success of their butcher's shop. There was never much money about and this led Elliott to exclaim when grown up, 'You who have lived in great houses, you who have ridden to hounds, you who have steered your yachts in summer's shimmering seas, you who have toured with House Party cricket teams in August – what can you know of the humble waiting of the poor for the left-overs of meat on Saturday evenings?' This, however, never stood in the way of his enjoying their company and hospitality. When only five he went down with meningitis and was not expected to live. The doctor said it was a miracle he did, and when recovered he announced that he wanted to be a parson. It seems that he was attracted by the clerical robes, and from this early intention he never swerved.

When he was nine a new grammar school was about to be opened in Horsham and he was among the first 40 boys to be entered. His father struggled to pay the £3. 6s. 8d. per term fees and must sometimes have wondered if it was worth it, since Wallace hated science, maths and Latin, and his health would not permit him to play games. He was often away ill and, following a severe attack of tonsillitis, was off school for seven months. Nonetheless the teaching was exceptionally good – nearly all the Sixth Form of his year won open scholarships to Oxford or Cambridge – and he managed to win an Exhibition in Theology to Brasenose College, Oxford. He had earlier been confirmed by Bishop Samuel Wilberforce.

Elliott's introduction to university life was not auspicious. During his first night his room was raided by drunken undergraduates who threw the furnishings about and jeered at him in bed. The following evening he went home, causing his father and headmaster to write letters of protest to the principal of Brasenose College. An apology was forthcoming, so he went back and it was arranged that he should live out of college. This had the effect of making him always feel an outsider and his Oxford years were on the whole a miserable time. He went for solitary walks, attended the daily services in his college chapel and was drawn by the music to Christ Church, New College and Magdalen. Diligent study brought him a Second Class in Theology. He was also greatly affected by Oxford's architecture and said later that if he could relive his life he would, in spite of all the unhappiness, still go to Oxford.

It was towards the end of his time there that he was greatly impressed by a sermon in the university church preached by the Bishop of Ripon, William Boyd Carpenter, and he attended a meeting afterwards when the bishop talked about the theological college he had established at Ripon. As a consequence of this Elliott went there in 1906 and had a happy preparation for holy orders, largely under the direction of the vice-principal, H. D. A. Major, one of the leading modern churchmen of the time, who became principal of the college when it moved to Oxford.

Elliott was ordained in York Minster in 1907 at the last ordination to be carried out by 81-year-old Archbishop William Maclagan, whose advanced dementia required him to be guided through the service by his chaplains. Yet the new deacon felt that 'No better hands than his could have set my little craft a-sailing, with storm clouds fast gathering, across the uncharted seas.' The style of his future broadcasts was already forming – ominously. But first there had to be a curacy at Guisborough, in North Yorkshire, where his ministry made a good start. The once-small market town had expanded to accommodate the miners who were extracting iron ore from the nearby Cleveland Hills, provoking Elliott to anger when he discovered the appalling conditions under which they were required to work. 'Downright devilry' was how he described it and when the miners went on strike he ran a soup-kitchen for them and their families. He also formed a branch of the Church of England Men's Society – a new organization that flourished nationally for half a century before going into decline, then extinction, after the 1939–45 war.

Elliott was bold enough to invite the new Archbishop of York, Cosmo Gordon Lang, to speak at the first meeting of the branch, at the end of which he was asked to leave Guisborough to become CEMS Organising Secretary in the Northern Province. Agreement to this proved to be the first of what he came to regard as the 'great mistakes' of his life. For one thing he was a poor organizer and he soon tired of speaking at five or more services and meetings a week across the North of England. His heart was not really in the cause and after three years he had the first of many breakdowns. A chaplaincy at St Raphaël in the south of France was suggested as a possible cure, but this proved to be too exacting an assignment. He spoke to no one and his services were said to be 'childish'. Recovery came after spending several months with his parents in Horsham.

Then came a letter from the vicar of Leeds Parish Church wondering if he might be well enough to lend a hand there during the summer when several of the dozen curates were on holiday. Elliott had been an honorary curate at the church during his CEMS years and liked the set-up. So he returned in 1913 for a possible four to six weeks and stayed for five years, eventually becoming senior curate and holding the fort for seven months when the vicar left to become a canon of Canterbury. Life in the clergy house suited him and kept him cheerful; he enjoyed the fine music and did a good deal of pastoral work, especially in the hospitals, and his preaching at Sunday Evensong attracted crowded congregations – 'Going home to tea I saw the queues beginning to form.'

His sermons were always delivered extempore, which may account for the fact that they seldom lasted less than 35 minutes, and he strongly condemned preachers who used notes or, worst of all, a full script. His advice to them was to use mnemonics as an aid to memory or to condense a rather complicated paragraph into a short memorable sentence – 'the sillier the sentence the better'. As an example of this he offered 'Abraham's father jumped over the moon with a cow under each arm.' Unfortunately, the content of the resulting sermon has not been preserved. During the early part of 1918 he once again became ill and required several months of rest. The cause of his recurring health problem is not altogether clear. He came to believe, towards the end of his life, that it was due to a misdiagnosed thyroid problem, but it seems more likely that the emotional intensity that characterized his ministry, particularly his preaching, led to periods of nervous exhaustion. His depressive personality demanded the approval of crowds for the raising of his spirits, yet the multitudes exacted their own emotional price.

Once recovered, the question arose as to his next move and, believing that he would probably be happier in the south of England than in the north, Archbishop Lang, who always thought a great deal of him, commended him to Archbishop Randall Davidson of Canterbury. This resulted in the offer of the parish of Holy Trinity, Folkestone, which he gladly accepted and where he stayed for the next 11 years. On his arrival in June 1918 he found that most of the population had been evacuated and that the hotels and boarding houses were all occupied by soldiers awaiting embarkation for France and the Front. But the war soon ended and he was on hand to welcome back the resident population and help rebuild community life.

His sermons again attracted very large congregations, though he came to believe that Folkestone had heard his worst sermons, accounting for this by the fact that he was still very ill, suffering from insomnia and claustrophobia. But he soldiered on, started a very successful children's church and a very remarkable literary society which met on Tuesday evenings and sometimes attracted as many as 1,500 people to

hear a lecture by a notable literary figure. There were many invitations
to preach elsewhere and he was made a Six-Preacher of Canterbury
Cathedral – an office founded by Henry VIII to enable the new theological learning to be spread abroad in Canterbury diocese by a team
of itinerant preachers. This was now reduced to one sermon a year in
the cathedral, for which a welcome allowance of £40 was payable.
In 1926 Elliott was summoned to preach before King George V, who
took a liking to his style and made him a royal chaplain – an office he
was to hold, and make much of, for the rest of his life. Next came an
invitation to become provost of Newcastle Cathedral – he had recently
taken part in a mission there – but when he consulted Archbishop
Davidson he was told to delay his decision for a week since 'something
else' might be coming. This turned out to be the offer of a St Paul's
canonry, and not a sensible one.

After 18 months St Michael's, Chester Square offered an escape
route. Dean Inge strongly advised against it, as did Archbishop Lang,
but Elliott went and lived to regret it. He described his first year as 'Hell'
and later said that he should have refused the offer. But St Michael's
was in fact the church where he exercised his greatest influence and if
success is to be reckoned in numbers (which were not unimportant to
him) his ministry there was phenomenal in its achievement. True, the
very large building was down at heel when he arrived. The galleries
were empty and, being a stronghold of Protestantism, the lay leadership was exceedingly suspicious of the young man who had left St
Paul's after the briefest of encounters. Many of the malcontents left
before his arrival, and the fears of those who remained were quickly
realized when Elliott proposed that a cross and two candlesticks
should be placed on the altar. An almighty row broke out, leaving
him thoroughly miserable, finding consolation only in the existence of
a large church school, from which he recruited boys to form a much
larger choir. In the end the choir procession at Evensong numbered
70 to 80.

Then in 1931, when he had been at St Michael's for about a year,
came a telephone call from Sir John Reith, the founding Director-
General of the BBC, inviting him to a meeting to discuss the possibility
of a late midweek service from the church. Broadcasting was still in
its infancy, and religious broadcasting not yet out of its cradle. The
attitude of the Church of England ranged from suspicion to open hostility, fearing that broadcast services would reduce further the dwin-
dling congregations or that holy things would be transmitted into
unholy surroundings. Dick Sheppard would, however, have none of

this and was broadcasting a very popular Sunday evening service from St Martin-in-the Fields once a month.

The idea of a midweek service arose from the concern of Reith and other Establishment figures, including the prime minister, Ramsay MacDonald, over the deteriorating morale of a nation facing an unprecedented economic recession. The number of unemployed was approaching three million of the insured population, large sections of industry were lying idle, no one seemed to know how to solve the problems and there was a sense of hopelessness and despair, especially in the north of England. Reith was no churchman but he believed Christianity to be 'a good thing', not least for its usefulness in cementing the social fabric of the nation. Might not a short service, consisting of a couple of hymns, a Bible reading and a prayer, broadcast midweek at 10.15 p.m., cheer up depressed listeners and send them to bed with a glimmer of hope? It would be worth trying for a few weeks. Elliott had already done a few broadcasts from the Savoy Hill studio and his church in Folkestone, and was brought to Reith's notice by one Sir Basil Peto, who had been greatly impressed by a sermon in St Michael's and put it to the prime minister that Elliott should be allowed to broadcast it all over the country. MacDonald passed the letter to Reith.

A six-week trial schedule of Tuesday evening services was arranged and Elliott, having secured Reith's permission to give a brief introduction to the Bible reading, took the opportunity to give a six- to seven-minute address. The services were held in St Michael's Church, with a congregation involved, but for the address Elliott, who was a consummate broadcaster, turned away to speak quietly to the microphone as if to an old friend sitting with him by a fireside. His words were no less cosy. He spoke of God as the eternal comforter, the bestower of the courage and hope necessary for getting through the current crisis, and indeed life itself. This required honesty, kindness and consideration for others – all illustrated by personal anecdotes, of which Elliott had an endless store.

Although there were at the time no scientific listener-research figures to prove it, the initial response to the broadcasts was highly favourable and since at the end of six weeks the national crisis was still very serious, it was decided to continue them until the summer, when a favourable break would provide an opportunity for further assessment. In the last service before the break Elliott, cunningly it might be thought, asked his listeners if they would like the broadcasts to be resumed in September and to indicate their wishes on a postcard to the BBC.

Over 10,000 postcards were received and, since the number of people owning a wireless set was still relatively small, further assessment was deemed unnecessary. The services, later moved to Thursday evenings, continued for another eight years and became a national institution. Elliott, a household name, was engaged to write a weekly article for the *Sunday Pictorial* and his broadcast talks were best-sellers. The BBC provided him with a paid secretary to deal with a mountain of listeners' letters.

The effect at St Michael's soon became evident. As many as 500 people joined the congregation for the broadcasts and on Sunday attendances of 2,000 became normal, with every seat in the church occupied – by the fashionable in the morning and the normal in the evening. All were treated, as at Leeds, to a sermon of no less than 35 minutes, and those who glanced at their watches were told that the preacher still had important things to tell them about the meaning of life. A curate ran a very successful Sunday afternoon children's service.

In December 1938 Elliott gave a heart-rending broadcast address on 'Sally in our Alley' – a fictitious poor child who would have no presents at Christmas. He then described a Christmas tree in St Michael's from which donated gifts were distributed to a host of 'poor Sallys'. Listeners responded with 212,000 gifts, requiring vans for their delivery and an army of helpers to organize their distribution to all parts of the country. Elliott assured the donors that 'Sally and Jimmy, her brother, together with many other Sallys and Jimmys would be pleased'. Officially he was not allowed to make direct appeals to listeners, but he knew how to drop pointed hints, and broadcast talks in June on the plight of children who had never been taken to the seaside brought in thousands of pounds. A loud clap of thunder which fortuitously occurred at the beginning of one of those live broadcasts was quickly exploited to illustrate the place of ill-luck in the stunted lives of poor children. That was a specially good year for the holiday fund.

By 1935 there were signs in the country of economic recovery, but these were soon replaced by the threat of another European war. In the following year Elliott announced the launching of a League of Prayer and Service to join an existing St Michael's Prayer Movement. Members were required simply to pray for peace, using a prayer on a provided card, which they signed. Again, there was an immediate response and by 1939 five and a half million had signed their cards. Mail was now being delivered by the sackful and 70 helpers were needed to handle it. Elliott raised a large sum of money to cover the not inconsiderable cost of postage. Two leading Free Church ministers joined him in his leadership of the League and mass meetings were held in London's Albert Hall, the Free Trade Hall in Manchester and other regional venues. Elliott came to believe that if only it had been possible to flood Germany with the prayer cards, war might have been averted.

But not everyone was pleased with his broadcasting success. An address on temperance which began, 'Look here, old boy – you sitting there alone – you had better put away that bottle. You have had quite enough. You are terribly worried, I know, but really that bottle won't help,' brought angry protests from a number of alcoholics who were convinced that the BBC was bugging their homes. Among the sober there were a substantial number who found Elliott's deep rich voice uttering homely platitudes cringe-making. Most significantly, the BBC's Head of Religious Broadcasting, F. A. Iremonger, was horrified by what he heard and even more by the fact that he was generally regarded as having some responsibility for the programme. He had been closely involved with William Temple in the Life and Liberty Movement and shared Temple's understanding of the social aspects of the Christian faith. By the time Iremonger became Head of Religious Broadcasting in 1933, Elliott's Thursday evening service was firmly established in the BBC's schedule. He complained that the addresses offered only comfort, with no challenge. There was no analysis of the desperate social crisis in which the nation was engulfed, only exhortations to be brave. The hymns were sentimental and often tear-jerking. There was no prophetic element and later, when the Nazi menace had reached the national agenda, Iremonger accused Elliott of 'talking about crocuses when the world is going up in flames'. But there was nothing Iremonger could do about it. Elliott was strongly supported by Reith, who did not despise large radio audiences, and by others in high places. It was known that King George V and Queen Mary listened to the service and liked what they heard. Far from bringing it to an end, Iremonger was chastened by the news that it was also to be broadcast once a month on the BBC's World Service.

A second world war was needed to get Elliott off the air. In April 1939 Iremonger was succeeded by another Anglican clergyman, James Welch, who had been Principal of St John's College of Education in York. Welch shared his predecessor's assessment of the service and when war broke out in September of that year he determined that Elliott must go. This view was not shared by Archbishop Lang, who believed that Elliott's style might be specially valuable in wartime and, as he put it, 'help to steady the people'. Reith's successor, F. W. Ogilvie, was of the same opinion. But the BBC was restricted to a single channel and the fact that for 15 minutes on Thursday evenings there could be no escaping Elliott became more widely regarded as intolerable. Furthermore, his simplistic use of phrases such as 'Blessed are the peacemakers' disturbed the military, who feared that the readiness of the millions of listeners to stand up against Hitler was being undermined. The decisive moment came in 1940 when the Religious Broadcasting Department, along with other sections of the BBC, moved to Bristol, and, with bombs falling in London, it was no longer possible to transmit a regular live broadcast from Chester Square. Elliott was asked to conduct his service once a month from the Lady Chapel of Bristol Cathedral, which he did for a time, but there was a growing feeling in the BBC that he was now a spent force. It was decided therefore to discontinue the service and he was invited instead to contribute to the new early morning 'Lift Up Your Hearts' programme. But a four- to five-minute slot at breakfast time, to be shared with other contributors, was not to his liking and he declined – devastated by the loss of a national role which had taken control of his life and ministry.

That he should have suffered another collapse at the end of 1940 was hardly surprising. Although the weekly broadcast had for eight years fed some of his own needs and by its momentum kept him going, it inevitably drained him emotionally and, when it ended, left him cruelly exposed to his old enemy – depression. It was also the case that listener response had for most of his time required his mail to be delivered by the Post Office in sacks. There was not the remotest possibility of his being able to deal with the immense number and variety of pastoral problems that came to him by this route. Every morning of the week apart from Sunday he devoted to 30-minute interviews with some of his correspondents; others were farmed out to collaborating Harley Street psychiatrists, but they were touching only a tiny fraction of the hundreds of thousands who sought help.

Within St Michael's parish, where he had built a clubhouse for young people, organized seaside holidays for children from the poorest streets, and spent a good deal of time in the school – visiting it weekly even after it had been evacuated to Windsor – the German bombing made life hazardous and many sleepless nights were spent in air-raid shelters. Following his collapse he had a thyroid operation, then spent two years convalescing in Banbury. These were for him, once again, 'sheer hell' and culminated, shortly before Christmas 1942, in the death of his 16-year-old son, Robin, in a road accident.

This might have seemed the last straw but the effect of the shocking news was to lift him out of his acute depression and set him on the way to a quick recovery.

He was soon ready for light work and this was offered to him in the form of the precentorship of the Chapels Royal, for which he had been recommended by Archbishop Lang. There followed what he regarded as the six happiest years of his life. There was not much to do, since the Sunday morning preaching at St James's was shared with the 36 other royal chaplains, and the sub-dean (an office to which he was promoted in 1945) had overall responsibility. Nonetheless, he made good use of his time, commuting from Little Bookham in Surrey, where he had bought a house. King George VI liked him, as did his mother, Queen Mary, while Queen Elizabeth took a close interest in the restoration of the war-damaged Chapel Royal. He enjoyed being a member of the Court and mixing with its celebrities, and involvement in the Distribution of the Royal Maundy was one of the highlights of his year. He also conducted quiet days in the chapel for people who had been bereaved, when he spoke about his belief in life after death, aided – or possibly hindered – by accounts of his paranormal experiences, a subject in which he became increasingly interested.

By 1948 Elliott's health was once more deteriorating and, feeling unable to cope with the modest demands of the Chapel Royal, he wrote to 25 bishops and about the same number of other influential people to see if a small country parish might be found for him. Only a tiny village in Kent was forthcoming, one look at which convinced him that 'once again we had gone a long way and arrived nowhere'. But then came the offer from the Lord Chancellor of the Collegiate Church of St Mary in Warwick. This glorious church, once a cathedral, could hardly have been less suitable for a priest with ailing health, but it was too flattering an offer to decline. He stayed for 18 months, preaching twice every Sunday to large congregations and became an honorary canon of Coventry Cathedral. But it was all too much and in 1951 he retired to the Sussex village of Compton, not far from his birthplace. There he continued to work – his total output of books, which included many collections of broadcast addresses, was nearly 50 – and completed an autobiography, *Undiscovered Ends* (1951), which some found nauseating. In 1951, however, the memory of his broadcasts was still alive and the book required reprinting just a month after its publication. He died in 1957.

14

The Naturalist
Charles Raven, Liverpool and Ely

Charles Raven, a canon of Liverpool from 1924 to 1932, then of Ely from 1932 to 1938, was a brilliant scholar who backed unfashionable causes. His liberal theology ran counter to the Neo-Orthodoxy of Karl Barth, which spread like wildfire in academic circles in the 1930s and 1940s. His ways of reconciling religion and science, evolution and faith, were some years ahead of his time. And his passionate pacifism attracted little sympathy during the dark years of the Second World War. He was nonetheless recognized as one of the great preachers and orators of his time, and a considerable figure in Cambridge, where he was Regius Professor of Divinity, Master of Christ's College, and for a time Vice-Chancellor. A tall, impressive figure, his mind worked very quickly and hardly ever seemed still and, brilliant scholar though he was, his interests were perhaps too broad and practical for his colleagues to regard him as a true academic.

His interest in scientific matters was by no means theoretical, since he was a distinguished ornithologist and had considerable expertise in botany. From his earliest years he was, as he put it, madly interested in birds. This took him on special expeditions to Ireland, the Netherlands and America, and between engagements in various parts of Britain or while attending conferences he snatched time to study local bird life. Shore birds were of particular interest to him and after a visit to Textel, in the Netherlands, he declared, 'Heaven for me must surely have its avocets'.

His study of birds and plants was, however, conducted in the context of their total environment. He believed that they revealed much about the evolutionary process, which led to the emergence of human beings, and that in the natural order lay the secret of human existence:

Where sea meets earth under an ever-changing, ever changeless sky, here, if anywhere, is the mystery that will reveal to us the mystery of our being. Even a day at Blackpool is some sort of initiation.

This quotation from *Ramblings of a Bird-Lover* (1927), one of several of his books on this subject – all beautifully illustrated by his own paintings – provides both a summary of his basic religious faith and an example of his lyrical style. It is hardly surprising that his views were often regarded with considerable suspicion in orthodox circles, and for most of his life he felt lonely and isolated. It was not until the 1960s, just a few years before his death, that he learned how the great Roman Catholic theologian Pierre Teilhard de Chardin had been working along lines similar to his own – and in even greater isolation. Raven wrote the first English-language biography of Teilhard.

His experiences of cathedral life were extreme. He was fortunate to be appointed to Liverpool just a few weeks prior to the major creative development that followed the cathedral's first consecration in 1924. The foundation stone of what was to be a vast building was laid in 1904, the Lady Chapel was dedicated in 1910, and now the completion of the choir and the eastern transept – comprising just one-third of the great project – gave a clear indication of its scale as well as its scope for dramatic use. The bishop, A. A. David, was still officially the dean but in preparation for the consecration appointed one of his diocesan clergy, Frederick Dwelly, to the office of 'Ceremoniarius'. This was an inspired choice, since Dwelly, who was both autocratic and eccentric, had a superb sense of theatre and, given a free hand, created forms of ceremonial that were always colourful, sometimes spectacular, and never other than dignified.

Raven arrived in time to read the Deed of Consecration at a service attended by King George V and Queen Mary as well as 40 bishops, and an array of civic dignitaries. More importantly, he and Dwelly established the most cordial of relations, leading to a close lifelong friendship. Dwelly was in no sense an intellectual, but they shared a liberal approach to the Christian faith and an understanding of the importance of worship that owed little to liturgical correctness. Raven's own special contribution was the leading of a simple service at 8.30 on Sunday evenings, when the emphasis was on the sermon. He did most of the preaching himself, though distinguished thinkers from other parts of the country were sometimes invited, and congregations, drawn from all parts of Liverpool and including many young people, became very large. His other special responsibility was not directly related to the life of the cathedral, though it took place in the building, and involved the post-ordination training of the clergy. Among these was a young priest named Michael Ramsey, serving as a curate at Liverpool Parish Church, and a future Archbishop of Canterbury.

He, being under the influence of Barth's Biblical Theology, was able enough to challenge Raven's natural theology – adding spice to the seminars. Most of the younger clergy of Liverpool diocese were however far less bright and required more patience than their tutor always had available. He was sometimes, and perhaps with justice, described as an intellectual snob.

In the opinion of Raven's biographer, F. W. Dillistone, these were the happiest years of his life, but even in the Church of England there was no possibility of a man of Raven's ability being left at Liverpool indefinitely. In 1930 he was invited to become rector of Holy Trinity, Boston, Massachusetts – one of America's great pulpits, made famous by the preaching of Bishop Phillips Brooks in the late nineteenth century – but he firmly declined. A year later Liverpool Cathedral was given a formal constitution and there was talk of Raven replacing the bishop in the deanery. But the office went rightly, and with Raven's fullest support, to Dwelly. Raven became chancellor, but by now his days on Merseyside were numbered.

Appointment to the Regius Professorship of Divinity at Cambridge in 1932 carried with it a residentiary canonry of Ely Cathedral. This was unusual inasmuch as the stall was normally occupied by the Professor of Hebrew, but a layman had recently been appointed to this chair, so it was decreed that the ordained Regius Professor should have it. This might have been agreeable enough had not the cathedral's life at that time been more or less moribund and apparently impervious to change. Dean Kirkpatrick had been there for almost 50 years, first as a canon and for the last 30 as dean. Raven was required to be in residence for two months of the year and to attend chapter meetings, though in practice he attended the cathedral services and other activities whenever at home. His home was in the Prior's House, dating from the twelfth to the thirteenth centuries and one of the historic houses of Cambridgeshire. This appealed to the romantic side of his nature and was a delightful abode for a family of four children. But it was very cold and when engulfed by the winter mists of Fenland seemed gaunt and inhospitable.

There was also the problem of commuting to Cambridge – 13 miles away. Like a number of other intellectual clergymen he never learned to drive a car and had therefore to rely on his wife or one of his daughters to get him to and from his Cambridge study in Christ's College, where he was a fellow – sometimes as often as three times a day. The inconvenience of this was partly alleviated by his preference for working at home, in the spacious drawing room, surrounded by his family. Had the cathedral itself offered any kind of stimulation, or been responsive to his own ideas and gifts, he might perhaps have been happier and less frustrated. In the end he was driven to exclaim, 'Ely Cathedral is a great white elephant which feeds on the souls of men.' Other cathedral canons have sometimes felt the same, without being able to express their frustration quite so vividly. Relief came for Raven in 1938 when the Regius Chair was separated from the canonry. He was mightily thankful.

Other frustrations, though of a different sort, awaited him. In 1936 the Master of Christ's had died, leaving Raven and C. H. Waddington, later to become a world-famous geneticist, as the chief contenders for the succession. The fellows turned out to be equally divided in their support for the two colleagues, so the mastership went instead to Sir Charles Darwin, a former college lecturer in mathematics. But after only two years he resigned to become Director of the National Physical Laboratory and Raven was elected in his place. The jockeyings for position during this immediate pre-war period were to provide rich material for C. P. Snow's novel *The Masters* (1956), he also being a fellow of the college at the time.

Christ's was the right college for Raven, since in its constitution it prided itself on its 'large-minded comprehensiveness where men of all creeds and parties enjoy harmonious college intercourse'. The element of harmony was not always prominent and, initially, Raven had the handicap of knowing that only two years earlier he had been rejected by the fellowship. But the Master's Lodge became a place of warm hospitality and he saw the college through the critical years of the 1939–45 war and the surge of new life that followed. Not the least of his achievements was his influence on a young chaplain, Ian T. Ramsey, who went on to become a notable Professor of Religious Philosophy at Oxford and a remarkable Bishop of Durham. As vice-chancellor from 1947 to 1949 Raven played a leading part in the admission of women to full membership of the university and in 1948 conferred, in the absence of the Chancellor, an honorary degree on the Queen – the first woman to be so honoured by Cambridge.

Charles Earle Raven was born in Paddington in 1885. His father was a barrister and his paternal grandmother was a sister of Samuel Reynolds Hole, the rose-growing Dean of Rochester in Victorian times. Charles's half-holidays from school were usually spent in the National History Museum in Kensington, where he was fascinated by the specimens of bird and plant life. He was taken to church by his mother and quite soon noted the contrast between what he found in

the life of the church and the wide vision of the gospel it existed to pro-
claim. At Uppingham School, where he went on a scholarship, he was
happy enough for the first two years, but then came to hate the place
and felt lonely and afraid. He was particularly unhappy about the content of religious studies, but whenever he could find space he studied
the local bird life and in the end had a substantial school record as a
house captain, a player of cricket, fives and hockey, and the winner of
a few prizes.

In 1904 he went up to Gonville and Caius College, Cambridge,
already a centre of scientific study, and began a close association with
Cambridge that lasted 60 years. Even during his ten years in Liverpool he was often there delivering lectures or preaching sermons. His
achievements as an undergraduate were notable: he took Firsts in
Classics and Theology, was joint editor of *Granta*, the leading Cambridge literary review, to which he introduced reviews, often written
by himself, of scientific books, and became engaged to the niece of the
master of his college. At the end of his first year, moreover, he had a
family holiday experience in the Lake District that proved to be a turning point in his life. Having climbed to the summit of Great Gable, he
felt that:

> to be alone in such a place on such a day is to be drawn up from
> delight to rapture, and from rapture to adoration. When you have
> marked the lie of the land and spied out its secrets, when you have
> absorbed bit by bit every aspect of that glorious panorama, slowly
> the width of it and the far-off glimpses of plain and ocean give wings
> to your soul; the little hills rejoice on every side; the stark strength of
> the mountains usher you into the presence chamber of the eternal.
> Free, joyous, abiding, their quality infects you with its own influ-
> ence. You, this tiny, tragic, transient creature, are at one with the
> universe, seized of its age-long glories, harmonised to its rhythm,
> enfolded in its peace. This is worship: here is holy ground.

It was this sense of the unity of the whole of the created order, and
the place of human beings within its grand, evolutionary scheme, that
informed and directed his future studies and teaching.

First, however, there was the destructive effect of fallen human
nature to be experienced. On leaving Cambridge in 1908, Raven
became Assistant Secretary for Education on the staff of Liverpool
City Council. This took him into the heart of the city's worst slums,
where he was appalled by the conditions in which young people had to
live. He became involved in the Colosseum – a recently refounded Vic-

torian mission which combined recreational, artistic, social work and religious activities under one roof and on a considerable scale. A visit to a friend who was working as a curate in a slum parish in Stoke-on-Trent revealed a form of sacrificial life akin to that of Jesus Christ and caused Raven to wonder if he might himself be ordained one day.

Pressure towards this came in 1909 with an invitation to become Dean of Emmanuel College, Cambridge, conditional upon his first taking holy orders. This he did in Ely Cathedral at Advent that year and immediately found himself embroiled in a Cambridge controversy arising from the publication of a paper by the Master of Emmanuel, William Chawner, denying the truth of the Christian faith. As the official upholder of this faith in the college, and with conflicting opinions being voiced throughout the university, Raven was trapped in an unenviable position, made worse when, because of the master's known views, the flow of ordinands reading Theology virtually ceased. Nonetheless he enjoyed very good relations with the undergraduates and was strongly sustained by his wife, Bee, and the situation was resolved by the death of the master.

Before long, however, the life of the college was seriously interrupted by the outbreak of war in 1914. As its members left for the army it became apparent that there would soon be no work for a dean, so he became a form master at Tonbridge School, at the same time deputizing for the vicar of the parish church, who was serving as an army chaplain. He also published his first book, *What Think Ye of Christ?* (1916), in which he emphasized the humanity of Jesus and asserted that it was in his human perfection that Jesus became the true representative of God to man. The book marked Raven out as a theologian to watch. A year later he felt unable to resist the call to serve his country and in next to no time was at the front line in France, ministering to soldiers of the Berkshire Regiment in the thick of battle. This experience, during which he was injured by a shell, gassed, and in constant danger from snipers, he described at the end of a week of bitter fighting as 'a descent into the valley of death', though he said, when the war was over, that it was an experience he was glad to have had and amongst the most inspiring of his life.

On demobilization in 1919 Raven returned to Cambridge to complete a history of the origins of Christian Socialism during the years 1848 to 1854 and to continue a large-scale study of Apollinarianism – a fourth-century heresy which denied the full humanity of Christ. This won him a Cambridge DD and became a landmark in the study of its subject. Raven believed that Apollinarius, a Greek theologian, had not been properly understood and that his ruthless condemnation by Rome was, from the Christian point of view, far more dangerous than his alleged heresy.

Meanwhile Raven had moved in 1920 to the college living of Bletchingley in Surrey, and, in acknowledgement of his gifts as a preacher, became a chaplain to the King. The next four years of parish ministry were only moderately successful, not because of any lack of pastoral skill, but because his mind, and increasingly his presence, were elsewhere. He took on the editorship of *The Challenge* – a weekly church paper that was independent of party allegiance and, in the hands of William Temple, had presented a wide variety of Christian concerns in language accessible to laypeople. It was already ailing when Raven took over and, although for 15 months he made an heroic effort to revive its fortunes, his health began to suffer under the strain of combining editorial work with parish and other responsibilities. His doctor insisted that he give it up.

A university sermon at Cambridge in 1921, printed in *The Challenge* under the heading 'The New Reformation', gave a clear indication of how he saw the future of the Church. It must, he said, stop busying itself about side-shows and instead concentrate its efforts on the duty of evangelism, taking full account of the new scientific learning. In a later essay on the same subject he accused the theological faculties in the universities of being 'still in the iron grip of a rigid and tyrannical convention' and went on:

> When they ought to be pressing on to meet the needs of the time they are refusing to leave the beggarly elements of Hebrew and Greek. Theology to its professors seems to mean little more than a minute acquaintance with the linguistic and textual problems of the Scriptures and with the niceties of fourth century controversies, as if a detailed study of the authorship of Isaiah or of the manuscript evidence for a few verses in the Gospels helped a man to see God or to preach Christ.

That he was himself ready to turn from fourth-century controversies to the more pressing issues of the twentieth-century church led to his acceptance of an invitation from William Temple to become the joint secretary of a major conference on Christian social concerns to be held in Birmingham in 1924. The preparations for this extended over four years and proved to be a massive undertaking. Attended by 1,500 people, the Christian Conference on Politics, Economics and

Citizenship (COPEC) came to be seen as one of the most significant ecumenical enterprises of the twentieth century and one of the most substantial contributions of the churches to the consideration of contemporary problems. It was all very important but the churchwardens of Bletchingley paid him the compliment of wishing to see more of him in the parish, and the fact that he had an able curate to hold the fort whenever he was away did not meet their point. After a cordial meeting with the church council, Raven decided that he should seek fresh pastures and, the Bishop of Liverpool having come to the rescue with the offer of a canonry, he resigned, leaving behind a fine rock garden and a special collection of gentians. Liverpool, lacking a garden, was to be devoted to birds, and so was Cambridge.

Some courage was needed for the head of a Cambridge college to be an outspoken pacifist during a time of total war, when the survival of the nation was under threat. It was in 1924 that Raven declared the abolition of war to be the chief issue of the time. His own traumatic war experiences undoubtedly coloured his views, but his rejection of war owed more to his conviction that Christians must formulate absolute standards and follow them absolutely. In 1930 he committed himself to pacifism by joining the Fellowship of Reconciliation, then recruiting strongly, and served as its chairman from 1932 to 1945. His Sir Halley Stewart Lectures, published as *Is War Obsolete?* (1935), argued from natural theology that the evolutionary principle left the individual no choice: full-scale war had become so fearsome that renunciation was the only possible response for a sane person. In 1934 he joined Dick Sheppard in sponsoring the Peace Pledge Union and declared the doctrine of the just war to be out of date. As war clouds grew ever darker he went with George Lansbury, the veteran Labour leader, and five other pacifist leaders to No. 10 Downing Street to plead for the espousal of non-violence and the calling of a new peace conference. In May 1939 he was a co-signatory of a letter to *The Times* which described war as 'fundamentally unchristian' and urged Parliament not to introduce conscription if war came. All of this proved to be of no avail, but throughout the war years Raven stood out as the most prominent Anglican churchman to embrace the pacifist cause.

Another minority cause to which Raven devoted himself was feminism. As early as 1922 he wrote an article for *The Challenge* in which he urged the Church to adopt a new attitude towards women, and in a book, *Women and Holy Orders* (1928), he declared:

For some years the conviction has grown in me that the admission of women to Holy Orders on an equality with men is inherent in the teaching of Jesus and necessitated by a true understanding of the nature of the Church; and my experience of their spiritual fitness and of the needs of the time confirm this conclusion.

He became joint president of an interdenominational society for the equal ministry of men and women in the Church, but as with several other issues he was at least half a century ahead of his time.

During his Cambridge years Raven gave a good deal of time to work in public schools, where his influence became considerable. If invited to preach at a Sunday service during university vacations he would ask the headmaster if he might spend a day or two in the school beforehand. He would then use this time to give one or more talks on some scientific subject and establish his credentials as a serious thinker before going into the pulpit on Sunday. This proved to be very attractive to the schools, and many of those who encountered him in this way decided to read Theology when they went up to Oxford or Cambridge. Christ's College was never short of applicants.

His gifts as a communicator were no less valued by the BBC – at least until the war came – and he was a brilliant broadcaster, both on radio and, later, on television. His gift was that of making profound subjects understandable without loss of depth. By 1939 he was well known to radio listeners, but then fell victim to a government-imposed blanket ban on any kind of broadcast by notable pacifists. F. R. Barry, at that time a canon of Westminster, wrote to the Director-General of the BBC enquiring if it was the case that Canon Raven would not even be able to talk about birds. The answer was 'Yes'. When the war ended, however, Raven soon returned to the microphone, especially that of the Third Programme, with some memorable series on scientific subjects. His only difficulty lay in producing and conforming to a script.

As a preacher and lecturer Raven was almost without a peer. Shortly after his ordination, when on holiday with his parents, he preached in the parish church at Rye. In the congregation was a young man named Alec Vidler, who lived in Rye and described the sermons as 'electrifying'. Later, in the chapel of Christ's College, Raven walked up and down the aisle between the inward-facing pews and captivated the congregation by the stimulating content of his sermons, by their rhythmic language, and by what one of them called his 'compelling look'. He was also a welcome preacher at Holy Trinity Church, Cambridge during the time Max Warren was its vicar, and sometimes gave sermons at Emmanuel Congregational Church. There was something of the actor about him and, although he always spoke without notes and apparently extempore, he would often devote a lot of time to rehearsing his lines. His lectures, too, were compelling and attracted large numbers of undergraduates, though their content was not usually related very closely to examination requirements. On the whole he was much loved, though some were put off by his apparent high regard for his own undoubted ability.

Curiously as it might seem for someone whose career bore all the hallmarks of success, he often felt disappointed that he had not been raised to the bench of bishops. In 1940 there was talk of his becoming Bishop of St Edmundsbury and Ipswich, and later Liverpool was mentioned, but no letter from 10 Downing Street ever came. He was convinced that his pacifism, his views on the ordination of women, and his liberal theological position always stood in the way, which may well have been the case. Certainly it was unrealistic to suppose that Winston Churchill would have appointed so militant a pacifist to an English diocese at a time when the nation was fighting for its survival. In many ways Raven felt isolated and lonely – the common lot of the prophet – but had he been born 50 years later he might well have felt that the lot of a Regius Professor of Divinity and the master of a Cambridge college was infinitely preferable to that of a diocesan bishop.

In the end he was left free to exercise influence through his studies and his books. *Jesus and the Gospel of Love* (1931) was a powerful defence of theological liberalism, while *Science, Religion and the Future* (1943), based on some public lectures, proved to be a magisterial treatment of a subject that no other theologian was capable of tackling. His two volumes of Gifford Lectures, *Natural Religion and Christian Theology* (1953), were, incredibly, delivered extempore at St Andrew's University and represented his mature thought on what was then a deeply unfashionable subject. During the war years he began pioneering work on the history of science with *John Ray: Naturalist* (1942), which won international acclaim, and *English Naturalism: From Neckham to Ray* (1947) drew attention to the fact that the beginnings of modern zoology and botany are to be found in the work of late medieval artists, rather than in the books of philosophers.

Raven was married three times. His first wife, Bee, to whom he had become engaged while still an undergraduate and by whom he had four children, collapsed and died while on holiday in Anglesey in 1944. He was devastated. Ten years later he married in Boston, Masachusetts,

Ethel Moore – an old friend, a widow and a millionairess. She was 80, he was 69, and she died while they were on their honeymoon in Lyme Regis, leaving him well off for the rest of his life. Within two years he had remarried at St Martin-in-the-Fields in London (where he had become a regular preacher), this time to a Belgian, Hélène Jeanty. Her husband had been shot in a German concentration camp, and she met Raven when he interviewed her on a television programme about the arts and religion. She was an intellectual who shared many of his interests and their home in Cambridge became a place of welcome for a seemingly endless stream of friends and visitors, many of them from continental Europe, who brought him much stimulation during his final years. He died in 1964, a few weeks after preaching in the University Church at Oxford a sermon on 'Christ and the Laboratory'. This ended with the assertion that 'the growing points of modern science are towards the unity of the cosmos', and he linked this with the conviction of the truth of the words in Ephesians attributed to St Paul that 'we all come home into the unity which is supplied by our faith, and our full knowledge of the Son of God, into mature manhood, unto the measure of the stature of the fullness of the Christ'.

15

The Extraordinary Headmaster
John Shirley, Canterbury

John Shirley, who was a canon of Canterbury Cathedral from 1935 to 1967 and for almost 27 years of that time Headmaster of King's School, Canterbury, was a most extraordinary man. He rescued two public schools from the edge of extinction and made them among the most successful in the country simply (though it was not simple) by the force of his own personality, his insights into how the best could be drawn, or forced, out of boys, and his skill as an educational entrepreneur. During the twentieth century he was without a peer and became one of the few headmasters of that century to be accorded an entry in *The Dictionary of National Biography* – a well-merited distinction that he would himself have considered appropriate and would have much enjoyed.

But it is not certain that he should be regarded as a *great* headmaster and within the public school world he was regarded by many as a rogue. There is, nonetheless, a great deal to be said in his favour. The two schools he resurrected – Worksop College was the first – were, as he himself confessed, his life and devotion. He served them ceaselessly, day and night, with few holidays and sometimes considerable sacrifice of salary. Although he came from a background of near-poverty and had his local priest to thank for gaining a grammar school place, he was possessed by the vision of what a great public school might become. It was to this that he dedicated his life. He was also able to inspire others by this vision and win from many their loyalty and affection. Unlike many men of vision, he was endowed with important practical gifts. He had a flair for publicity and his schools often found their way into national newspapers with items to their credit. He was a superb fundraiser and astute at enlisting the support of the famous for his schools. He knew how to spend money economically and at the end of his time at King's, he pointed out that even though the number of pupils had increased fourfold and the buildings and activities of the school had grown almost beyond belief, the number employed on the administrative staff was no larger than when he arrived. New buildings were another of his specialisms and, although he was sometimes criticized for not embracing modern architecture for his projects, it is now possible to be thankful that none of the designs of his period were inflicted on the precincts of Canterbury Cathedral.

The boys were all known to him by name and he was always available to them, usually without appointment. The door of his house was open from after lunch until early evening and anyone who wished to see him had simply to turn up. He tended to address the boys as 'm'dear', or sometimes 'old chap', and if he wished to emphasize a point his words were accompanied by a prod in the stomach. Being human, he had favourites and if a boy indicated a calling to holy orders he could be sure of special attention. His closest relationships, however, were with school captains, monitors and other senior boys who wore court dress and purple gowns on special occasions. These he treated almost as if they were colleagues, confiding in them his hopes and plans for the school and, more questionably, his views, usually adverse, on members of the teaching staff. But his greatest gift was the ability to take a boy of modest background and ability and create in him the confidence to aim for the highest and work hard to win an Oxbridge scholarship – bringing honour to the boy and most importantly to Shirley's school.

A volume titled *Fred Remembered*, published in 1997 as a companion to a biography, *An Extraordinary Headmaster* (1969), written by David L. Edwards, one of his star pupils, contains the brief recollections of his daughter and 26 others who at various times were in his schools as teachers or pupils. Within them there is ample testimony to his achievements and often to his kindness. One recalled how he went to see the headmaster, only to be ushered to a bedroom where he was in bed ill. During the course of the interview Shirley noticed that the boy's shoes were down at heel and unpolished – serious crimes – but instead of administering a rebuke he asked him, 'What size shoes do you take?' 'Size seven, Sir,' said the boy. 'So do I', came the reply; 'open that door of that cupboard'. Within it were two rows of gleamingly polished, handmade shoes, from which the boy was invited to select a pair – these becoming the best shoes he was ever to possess. Shirley's life generated a number of anecdotes and, as David Edwards remarked, they were all true. The fact that a book of recollections should be published some thirty years after his death suggests a man of unusual influence.

But these recollections reveal another, and much less attractive, side of his personality. Members of his teaching staff, to whom he could be rude and ruthless, had special difficulties. A former matron and wife of a housemaster wrote:

The atmosphere between Shirley and his staff was often tense. He had one goal – to rescue King's (which he did) – and it would be fair to say that he trampled on those who got in the way of this.

Another former colleague wrote:

Shirley could legitimately take credit for his great achievements at King's, but my view was (and still is) that the price he made the community pay for it was profoundly degrading. Mark 8.36 says it all: '. . . For what shall it profit a man if he gain the whole world and lose his own soul?'

These are harsh words, equalled by another former master, who described him as 'an unpredictable despot'. A more gentle, but hardly attractive, opinion was that:

one had to remember that one could work for him and sometimes (for he was often absent or just plain bored) instead of him, but not in any sense with him.

It is important to record, however, that these judgements were made in the context of a certain admiration for him, and even of gratitude for some aspects of schoolmastering they had learned from him.

Many of the boys who were educated under Shirley's rule at Worksop, and more especially at Canterbury, went through life with a sense of enormous gratitude to him, not least those who earned distinction at either Oxford or Cambridge and had very successful careers afterwards. But even among these there were reservations about his methods, and particularly his severe discipline. A Worksop boy and future headmaster remembered him as 'a strange and frightening personality' who kept his pupils 'always under the threat of the cane'. A future president of the Paediatric Section of the Royal College of Medicine wrote:

He liked inflicting pain – not in an evil way but because he realised that a nice stinging is often the simplest and quickest way to bring out the best in a boy – and fun for him too.

A future distinguished diplomat and sometime private secretary to Margaret Thatcher during her years as prime minister confirmed this evidence:

> Shirley was one of those flashy headmasters who believed in the utility of a good thrashing . . . if not in the beaters' first division, he was fairly high up in the second.

A boy summoned by the headmaster, either on the noticeboard or by a postcard, would then go in fear and trembling, not knowing whether he was due for congratulations, a beating, or kind, helpful advice about his future. The noticeboard was used to record the names of miscreants and the number of strokes of the cane administered – the highest, it seems, being 37. A boy who failed to answer a question, or was hesitant in answering, in a class conducted by Shirley was let off with a single stroke. Sports teams that committed the unpardonable offence of losing to another school were summoned for a dressing down by a headmaster who had gone into a tantrum on the touchline when players had not responded adequately to his waving stick and shouted instructions.

Such a complex, and it might seem heavily damaged, personality (not uncommon in a genius) could only be, in the words of another of his housemasters, 'either hated and deeply feared or else swallowed whole and more or less worshipped'. He was fortunate indeed to have a wife who was gentle and tolerant, albeit often neglected and sometimes publicly humiliated by him. She provided the stable, loving home essential to a man of volatile temperament, who when disappointed was subject to bouts of depression and ill-health. She bore him a daughter and four sons and he thought the fact that she was the niece of a recently created peer important enough to include in his *Who's Who* entry. Shirley himself was of rubicund complexion, with a hint of the agricultural about him. But he was never other than immaculately dressed in Savile Row suits and wore a large, broad-brimmed hat. Polishing shoes, to guardsman standard, was for him a form of relaxation, but he rarely took a cigarette out of his mouth, thus allowing the ash to fall on to his waistcoat. Claret and whisky were his favourite drinks and at times he was known to indulge in them too heavily.

It was hardly to be expected that such a man – single-minded to the point of fanaticism – would regard his cathedral canonry as anything more than a sideline, albeit a very useful one, until he retired from the school in 1962. That he was a convinced Christian and a committed Anglican churchman was never open to doubt and during his early years at Worksop College he continued to embrace the Anglo-Catholicism in which he had been nurtured. But study of Hooker led him to abandon this and he became a classic middle-of-the-road Anglican who valued the Establishment, partly because it provided some protection for the Church but chiefly because it offered opportunities for the Church's infiltration of society. In many ways his faith was more akin to that of a layman than to that of an ecclesiastical dignitary. Apart from his interest as an historian of the Reformation he had no concern for theological niceties and disputes, and he made much of the fact that the motto on the shield of King's School is simply 'Jesus Christ'. In a sermon at the school's Commemoration Service in 1961 he said:

> Why should you not be content with a comfortable life, undisturbed by the sadnesses and shames of others? Because 'Jesus Christ is the same yesterday, today and for ever' – the friend of man without respect of person, the friend of sinner and social outcast, of the neurotic and the unwanted, your friend and mine, who washed the feet of working-class men; because in the thirty years he lived here he showed you the nature and character of God; because his spirit is within you to enable you to live for others as well as yourself and so live in the forever now; because as Judge he will by this estimate the worthwhileness of your life. And you must spend your life in his service or in slavery to yourself; and if you think to find joy and freedom in serving yourself, you will be in error since it is only the service of God which brings perfect freedom.

Difficult though it was sometimes to believe, there was in Shirley a real concern for the underdog, reflecting perhaps his own early years, and there were periods of his life when he was considered to be left-wing. This may have had something to do with his great admiration for Archbishop William Temple, but not much with his membership of Brookes's Club in London. On the other hand, he fought in chapter meetings on behalf of tenants who were threatened with sudden rent increases, or employees facing what he considered to be unfair dismissal. He had a strong sense of justice.

In church affairs he could be scathing in his criticism of the inefficiency of the ecclesiastical machinery, believing there to be no reason why the Church of England should not be run at the same level of competence as a well-organized public school such as his own. This belief was accompanied by the further conviction that the laity, rather than the clergy, should have the chief say in how the Church at every level should be organized, and indeed what kind of church the Church of England should be. To this end he had reprinted at his own expense a learned report of 1902 on *The Position of the Laity in the Church* and he was credited with some responsibility for the increased share of the laity in church government that came in the 1960s. It may be assumed, however, that its outcome in synodical bureaucracy was not what he had in mind and he was fond of pointing out that as church committees multiplied, so congregations dwindled. For him, new emphasis on evangelism was essential to the Church of England's survival, reunion with the Free Churches highly desirable.

On liturgical matters his approach was, as always, essentially pragmatic and never doctrinaire. He quickly discerned that Canterbury Cathedral's Sunday services were unsuitable for adolescent boys and reduced the school's attendance at them to once a month. Instead, they had their own Sunday morning service in the choir, and an evening service in the crypt, which was more intimate. Shirley produced his own version of the Prayer Book, which excluded the Psalms, but took in a wide variety of extracts from saintly spiritual writers. There was also a special lectionary of Bible readings and a school hymnal designed to encourage congregational singing. The cathedral became, in effect, the school chapel – all under the headmaster's control and thus irreverently known as 'Shirley's Temple'.

That he was not one of the more congenial, collaborative members of the chapter goes without saying, but he took the affairs of the cathedral very seriously, revelling in its history and tradition, and fought to make its administration more efficient. Shortly before his retirement from the school he became treasurer and in 1961 librarian – posts he held until his death in 1967. Meanwhile he used his position on the chapter to secure precincts property for the school to aid its expansion, and always on terms most favourable to the school. Cosmo Gordon Lang, who was archbishop during Shirley's early years, named him 'Octopus'. But when the dean and chapter decided that the time had come to create a boarding house for choristers in order to be less dependent on local boys, it was to Shirley that they naturally turned for advice and the drive necessary for its realization. It was unfortunate, even if predictable, that he did not get on with any of the choir school's headmasters, though they provided a constant stream of pupils for King's. Immediately after the war, when the dean and chapter were short of money, he assumed responsibility for a worldwide appeal, detached a member of his teaching staff to conduct it, and raised £270,000. Having secured this large sum (several million pounds in today's money) he urged the utmost care and economy in its expenditure – a constant theme of his contributions to chapter meetings. An illustrated Pitkin Guide to the cathedral, written by him, was a best-seller and a useful source of income for many years.

His chapter colleagues generally recognized how difficult it was for him to combine his two roles and were ready to deputize for him at the cathedral's daily services, though they were sometimes suspicious when he had to take to bed on the eve of a period in residence. Whatever difficulties they might have had, however, were usually overcome by their unity in opposing the 'Red Dean' – Hewlett Johnson – whose naïve support for the Stalinist Soviet Union was more than a source of embarrassment inasmuch as his worldwide reputation was likely to lead the less well-informed in distant lands to suppose that others responsible for Canterbury Cathedral might share his views. In March 1940 the canons sent to *The Times* a strongly worded letter deploring his writings and utterances on the subject and disassociating themselves from them. For Shirley there was the further, and for him the frightening, possibility that parents might be reluctant to send, or even keep, their sons at King's lest they be contaminated by Communism. He acted swiftly: the deanery, to which a few boys had sometimes been invited to meet Russian visitors, was placed out of bounds and the school's governing body was persuaded to attempt to depose the dean from the chairmanship of its meetings. Johnson was not prepared to accept this and, after a considerable fuss, it was agreed that the archbishop, as Visitor, would take the chair. There was another problem inasmuch as Johnson and Shirley were prima donnas and there was insufficient room for them on the same stage without frequent collision. Ironically, Johnson's long absences abroad served to increase Shirley's power in the chapter considerably.

Frederick John Shirley was born in 1890 in the Jericho district of Oxford – then one of the city's poorest areas, consisting of Victorian working-class terraces. His father was a carpenter and the poverty of the family required one of his brothers to leave school when only 12 and his sister at 13. Another brother ran away to sea when 11. All attended the local St Barnabas Church – one of the leading Anglo-Catholic churches in Oxford – and young John, who was a server and a member of the choir, was greatly influenced by the vicar, Father Cyril Hallett, who enabled him to go from the church school to Oxford High School for Boys on a scholarship. T. E. Lawrence was a fellow pupil. The vicar also provided money for his entry into St Edmund Hall, Oxford, which at that time catered mainly for poor ordinands, but for financial reasons Shirley had to live at home and could never afford to take part in college life.

On coming down he taught for a time in a preparatory school in Surbiton, then at another independent school on the outskirts of Bedford. In December 1915, however, he was commissioned in the Royal Marines Light Infantry, but soon had to resign on medical grounds, having succumbed to rheumatic fever. Following his recovery he re-enlisted, this time as an RNVR paymaster, and spent some time as an intelligence officer at Invergordon, in the north of Scotland, followed by spells at the Admiralty and Dover. While in London he seized the opportunity to study part-time for a law degree and to qualify as a barrister.

Following demobilization in 1919 he became a Sixth Form master at Framlingham College in Suffolk, taking a full part in the life of the school, excelling as a sports coach and CO of the Officers' Training Corps, eventually becoming a housemaster. Even at this stage, however, his martinet character was becoming obvious and one of his pupils later recalled:

> We always thought of Shirley as something of a sadist. He taught us History and English and was what I would call a crammer: he crammed it into you but you were always in fear of him. He always brought his cane into class with him; he would ask you a question – it was a matter of luck which question you had, some you knew, some you didn't – and if you failed to answer you were in danger of getting the stick. I used to hate his lessons.

But when he left the boys presented him with four silver candlesticks and the headmaster described him as 'almost an ideal schoolmaster'.

From boyhood Shirley had felt drawn to holy orders and, after taking a special examination in theology for ex-servicemen, he was ordained in 1920 to a part-time curacy in Framlingham parish church. His particular responsibility was for a daughter church in the hamlet of Saxted, where he raised money for the restoration of the medieval building and filled it by his preaching and visiting. Three years later he was appointed rector of the High Church parish of Sternfield, eight miles from Framlingham, which again he combined with teaching and where, again, he was very popular in the village.

In 1924, however, he replied to an advertisement for a headmaster of St Cuthbert's College, Worksop in north Nottinghamshire and was appointed. This minor public school of the Woodard Foundation was in dire straits. Although the fine building had a wonderful setting in the 'Dukeries' it was in a poor state of repair, the accommodation for the boys was inadequate, the food was poor, the teaching lamentable and most boys left at 16, often with few or no academic qualifications. The finances were precarious and the inspectors told the newly appointed headmaster that they had never visited a more unsatisfactory school. Shirley quickly took matters in hand and soon there was no part of school life beyond his scrutiny and, in most instances, his direct control. Teaching standards were raised – masters who did not get results were axed – and boys showing unusual promise were carefully groomed for Oxbridge scholarships. Any finance required by poorer boys was found from a variety of sources.

The building was modernized, more classrooms and laboratories were erected, the library and the sanatorium were brought up to date, new tennis and squash courts were created, and land purchased from an adjacent farm brought the school site to a total of 250 acres. Over the course of ten years more than £100,000 (a very great deal of money in those days) was spent on these projects and raised by Shirley from loans and gifts, from a browbeaten governing body, and by exercising the utmost economy in the running of the school. At one point the teaching staff were required to take a temporary cut in their salaries. The name of the school was changed to Worksop College.

When the prime minister, Ramsay MacDonald, came to open a new wing in 1934 he said that it was 'fast becoming famous among the public schools of England'. The inspectors now reported that its progress had been 'phenomenal' and the Woodard Foundation recognized Worksop as its leading school. The number of pupils had increased from 213 in 1924 to 330 in 1931 and to 387 in 1934. During this time 13 open scholarships had been won to Oxford and Cambridge, along with 15 exhibitions. Moreover, Shirley, while always frantically busy, had not neglected his own studies and in 1931 completed a University of London Ph.D. on 'The Political Theory of Richard Hooker'. He was later to be awarded an Oxford DD for some further work on Hooker and wrote *Elizabeth's First Archbishop* (1948), a defence of the validity of Matthew Parker's episcopal orders, but he was not really a scholar or even an intellectual.

By 1935 King's School, Canterbury, was also in dire straits. The number of boys in the senior school had fallen to 182, the financing of a new junior school had left the governing body in debt, morale was low and there appeared to be only a bleak choice between closure and incorporation into the state system. But Shirley's achievements at Worksop were by now widely acknowledged and it was decided to invite him to take over the headmastership in the hope that he would repeat his performance. The school vacancy chanced to coincide with the move of Dr Claude Jenkins, a member of the cathedral chapter, to the Regius Professorship of Ecclesiastical History at Oxford, and it was decided to combine the headmastership with the vacant residentiary canonry. How this decision came to be made is not altogether clear. There is some evidence that the dean and chapter, who were effectively the governing body, regarded the joint appointment as a way of saving a headmaster's salary and of freeing his house for other school purposes. Others believe that Shirley demanded the canonry as a condition of his acceptance, since he was not prepared to work under the thumb of a body in which he had no influence. In the event he exploited his position on the chapter mercilessly to further the school's interests and when he retired a resolution was passed by the chapter indicating that never again should these two offices be combined.

Having surveyed the scene, Shirley, while still at Worksop, addressed a very long letter to the dean, Hewlett Johnson, indicating what he required from the governing body of the cathedral. This amounted to a detailed policy statement and included an uncompromising demand for a free hand:

> At the moment it would seem that I can do nothing which is not approved at a Governors' Meeting, which may be held several weeks after the need for action arises. I am not a young, rash, hot-headed fool. I used to be all these, but I have a lot more sense now that I have grown up. But nobody can expect me to do what seems to be the toughest job in the school world in England if I am to be the mouthpiece of the Governing Body.

He went on to point out that by accepting the post he had burnt his boats at Worksop and warned that if he found himself without the support of the governing body he would have no alternative but to resign and, remaining a member of the chapter, simply offer his counsels. There could be no quarrelling with this, but the public school world soon quarrelled with his first move and he was expelled from the Headmasters' Conference. His offence was to persuade, or at least allow, the parents of 30 Worksop boys to let their sons accompany him to Canterbury, where they formed a new house under a former

Worksop master – one of three who joined him there. In his defence he pointed out that he had been personally responsible for getting Worksop back on its feet, that he had been its recruiting agent, that many of the 30 boys had not yet arrived at the school, and that he had entered into an arrangement with Worksop's governing body whereby he would recruit a further 30 boys to replace those whose allegiance had shifted to Canterbury. But the other headmasters, some of whom felt distinctly threatened by his methods and great success, were unconvinced and he was barred from their conference for several years. Not that this troubled him, and of greater satisfaction to him than the company of the headmasters was the immediate impact on King's made by the arrival of 30 additional boys with their teachers and the creation of a new house. From the outset things were on the move.

And so they continued for the next 26 years, interrupted only when the school had to be evacuated, for safety reasons, to Cornwall during the 1939–45 war. Even then his ingenuity and enterprise kept up academic standards and the best possible use was made of the hotels in which the school was accommodated, with a large garage serving as its chapel and assembly hall. During the absence the music school and his own house were destroyed by German bombs. By the time he came to retire in 1962, when he was 72, he was able to report that the number of boys in the school had reached 830 and that the profit for the previous year was £40,347, the highest in the school's history. He also told the governing body that whereas scholarships to Oxford and Cambridge during the 20 years prior to his arrival had totalled 26, during his reign they had totalled 260. Moreover, a leading authority had told him that no school in the country was comparable for its music. The Rugby XV and the Cricket XI had gone through their last seasons undefeated, and the first VIII of the Boat Club had only just missed winning at Henley. As for the teaching staff, he believed they were, on the whole, definitely good, with (a characteristic Shirley reservation) only three or four changes desirable. During his time something approaching £400,000 had been spent on new buildings and other facilities.

Following his retirement, by which time he had mellowed somewhat, he had five good years devoted to the cathedral, liberated from the presence of Hewlett Johnson, who had resigned, aged 88, and more than ready to welcome Ian White-Thomson, who had worked closely with five archbishops and was able to initiate changes that had hitherto been impossible. Unable to resist the opportunity to deal in bricks and mortar, Shirley secured a grant from the Wolfson Foundation to enlarge the cathedral's fine library, but he found much more time to spend with his wife and his books and had the great satisfaction of seeing his school continue to flourish under new leadership. He died of leukaemia in 1967 and it was left to his only daughter, Janet, to sum him up most accurately:

> Devout, doubting, an ardent left-winger, a thorough snob, loving, self-centred, compassionate, hurtful, my father was, like anyone else, a mass of contradictions.

16

The Belgian Monk
Emmanuel Amand de Mendieta,
Winchester

Emmanuel Amand de Mendieta, who was at Winchester from 1962 to 1976, was one of the most unusual occupants of an English cathedral stall since the Reformation. The first 49 years of his life were spent in Belgium, 23 of them as a Roman Catholic Benedictine monk – and no ordinary monk, for he was one of his order's leading scholars and a world authority on St Basil of Caesarea, a fourth-century Father of the Eastern church. In 1956, however, he decided that the Anglican Church was his true spiritual home and, moreover, a sphere in which he could continue to exercise his vocation as a priest-scholar while no longer under monastic vows. He was received into the Church of England and, after a short spell at St Augustine's College, Canterbury, and three years at Gonville and Caius College, Cambridge, became a canon of Winchester.

There is a long and honourable tradition of distinguished scholars becoming residentiary canons, to the benefit of their studies, their cathedrals, and the wider church. But there are bound to be problems when a learned canon's grasp of the English language is so imperfect that his sermons are virtually incomprehensible, and when his particular field of study, in which he is totally absorbed, is so specialized and technical that there may be no more than a small number of other scholars in the entire world who understand what he is about. If the language difficulty includes an inability to distinguish between numbers, such as ten, one hundred and one thousand, and is accompanied by an unworldly ignorance of the realms of administration and finance, it is to be expected that such a scholar's contribution to chapter meetings and the like will be slight and sometimes a cause of confusion.

This was Winchester's experience of de Mendieta during the 1960s and 1970s. Yet the eminent scholar, always deeply engrossed in his books, was much valued and admired by the cathedral community. No one could ever accuse him of idleness, and the portly – eventually almost spherical – figure, known to have an extreme fondness for Dubonnet and milk chocolate, won the affection of many by his geniality, kindness and good humour. The solemn tolling of the passing bell announcing his death while still in office caused much sadness, as well as sympathy for his young widow and their schoolboy son. (Another child had died within a few hours of birth.) There was also a recognition that at Winchester the old world of Barchester was now ended, though for the rest of the century people would recall the late canon's struggles when reading lessons: for example, 'Jozeph's bruzzers vent on zheir own vay. Jozeph, 'owevair, reemained in goal'; and on the first Easter Day 'ze disciples came to ze empty tum'. The announcement of hymns was sometimes bewildering: "'ymn numberre two souzand one eleven' (i.e. 211) or 'ze 'ymn is one souzand elephant' (i.e. 111).

Anecdotes abound. The dean was never able to convince him that his academic achievements did not entitle him to more pay than the other canons. The head sidesman, when needing to discipline another sidesman for some failure of duty, would sentence him to four 'Emmanuels', i.e. being on duty four times when de Mendieta was preaching. The boys of the Pilgrims' School, attending Mattins, were advised by their headmaster to spend time studying the cathedral's architecture, this being a more profitable exercise than listening to de Mendieta preach.

Emmanuel Amand de Mendieta was born in 1907 in the chateau of Bouvignes-sur-Meuse, not far from the fashionable Belgian town of Dinant and about 12 miles from the French border. His father, a lawyer, had at one time been burgomaster of Bouvignes and narrowly escaped execution by the German invaders in 1914. His mother, a baroness, was highly intelligent, a monarchist, and a devotee of Marie-Antoinette. French was the family's mother tongue and the household was steeped in Catholicism and French culture. The children were expected to attend weekday Mass frequently – often being dragged out of bed to get there – and confession was required every week and several decades of the rosary every day.

When he was ten, young Emmanuel was sent to a school in Dinant run by Roman Catholic secular clergy. Discipline was severe. The day boys were forbidden to speak to the boarders and the young boys who wore shorts were required to wear long black stockings to cover their knees. Emmanuel was poor at mathematics but developed what was to become a lifelong love of Greek literature. At about the age of 14 he was greatly attracted by the life at the major Benedictine abbey of Maredsous, about 12 miles from his home and a stronghold of Roman Catholicism in Belgium.

The abbey was famous for the beauty of its worship and especially its use of Gregorian chant. Whenever he cycled there, particularly at great festivals, he was always warmly welcomed by the abbot, Columba Marmion – an Irishman who had become a naturalized Belgian and a widely acknowledged master of the spiritual life. Emmanuel was permitted to attend all the divine offices, starting with Mattins at 4.20 a.m., and felt increasingly drawn to the religious life, primarily, it seems, in order to be able to share in its liturgy. Through his visits he also discovered the Bible, it being strictly forbidden at school to read it in French, and the Gospels were a revelation to him.

In 1924 his request to be allowed to test his vocation to the religious life was met by the sensible requirement that he should first spend a probationary year 'in the world'. This involved daily attendance at the Catholic Faculty of Namur to study philosophy and literature, together with frequent visits to Maredsous. His parents were happy with this development, though his mother would have preferred him to become a Jesuit. On completion of the probationary year, he spent three months as a postulant, then one year as a novice, but by the time of his admission Abbot Marmion had been succeeded by Dom Célestin Gelevaux – a tall, ascetic monk who was a good administrator, yet rigid and authoritarian, and with little interest in intellectual matters. His welcome to the new novice was icy – 'Do not think you are indispensable. I do not need you. The door is wide open; you may go back home.' This was a bad start to a relationship that was to remain difficult for the next 25 years. After he left the order de Mendieta said that if he had known at the time all the difficulties he would later encounter in his personal dealings with Gelevaux he would not have put himself under his direction and obedience. He would have chosen a different monastery and might not have decided to become a Benedictine monk.

The regime was tough and involved weekly self-inflicted flagellation, twice a week in Lent, together with the wearing of goat- or camel-hair shirts, and instruments of penance such as spiked bracelets and chains. Nonetheless, under the guidance of a wise and sensitive master of the novices, de Mendieta had four happy years, three of which were spent mainly in the study of Scholastic theology under some able teachers, followed by a spell at the Abbey of Mont-César, a daughter house of Maredsous at Louvain. At Epiphany 1930 he took solemn life-vows on what was, he said, 'one of the happiest and most crowded days of my life'. But soon afterwards he had a very painful conversation with his abbot, who accused him of having an individualistic and critical spirit, not compatible with the religious life. Furthermore, he had revolutionary ideas and was an undesirable element in the monastery. He was therefore to be placed under the strict supervision of two other monks. In retrospect, de Mendieta saw this as the beginning of his dissatisfaction with the Benedictine Order and the Roman Catholic Church.

Meanwhile, he continued his studies at Mont-César, delighting in the worship – the chapel being the cradle of the Liturgical Movement in Belgium – and appreciating the fact that the theology taught at Louvain University was not rigidly doctrinaire or over-systematic. This was already causing anxiety in the Vatican where it was believed the teachers were promoting 'historicism', which had, it was said, affinities with Modernism. De Mendieta was in fact being drawn increasingly to the study of Patristic theology, and in particular to the writings of Basil of Caesarea – one of the great theologians of the early church, whose allegiance was to the see of Constantinople rather than to Rome, and who denied the Bishop of Rome's claim to supremacy. Following his ordination to the priesthood by the Bishop of Namur in 1932, de Mendieta established contact with the Institut russe Saint-Georges, which had moved there from Constantinople and was attended by Russian Orthodox students, mainly from aristocratic émigré families. This stimulated what would become a long-standing concern for the reunion of the Orthodox and Roman churches and also connected with his interest in St Basil. He kept up his studies of classical philology, which was against the wishes of the Abbot of Maredsous, but had the support of an advisory council of senior monks. They saw the possibility of his one day joining a small team of editors of *La Revue Benedictine* – an important annual journal of international Benedictine learning.

In 1936 he returned to Maredsous, where his conflict with the abbot showed no sign of resolution, and began to write for the *Revue*. For the next 16 years he contributed 20 to 30 book reviews to each issue. These dealt with a wide variety of subjects, but mainly ancient history, classical philology and Patristics, and involved him in the reading of hundreds of newly published books. During the early years of his return he also prepared a thesis for a Louvain doctorate, having already taken a licentiate with a study of the ascetic writings of St Basil.

For the doctorate he first considered producing a critical edition of the complete works of the theologian, but soon concluded that this was far too demanding an assignment for one scholar. He settled instead for a critical edition of St Basil's nine homilies on the biblical narrative of creation. The particular interest of these homilies is that St Basil was attempting to rethink and restate theology in terms of the scientific data and philosophical principles taught in the university of Athens in the fourth century, and to relate this to the first chapter of Genesis. De Mendieta set himself to track down, describe, collate and classify all the known MSS of Basil's homilies from the ninth to the sixteenth centuries – a task that was to engage him for almost 20 years. But for the purpose of his doctorate, which he was awarded in 1939, he undertook just a part of the project. This involved no more than a month or so away from the abbey every year for research in the Bibliothèque Nationale in Paris.

Soon, however, the combination of research, writing and rewriting, together with the demands of monastic life, began to put him under considerable mental and physical strain. At 17 stone he was much overweight, and a liver disorder became chronic. This brought no sympathy from the abbot and relations between the two monks virtually broke down. The abbot accused him of 'individualism' and 'pernicious humanism' but the war, which broke out in September 1939, separated them for a time.

Although Belgium declared her neutrality, the Germans invaded the country on 10 May 1940 and three days later the abbot and the older monks were evacuated on the last train to France. De Mendieta and two young monks followed, but on bicycles. At first they could move only slowly on roads crowded with retreating soldiers and refugees, but eventually they got clear and completed a 500-mile zigzag journey to the Benedictine abbey at Solesmes. De Mendieta stayed for three weeks and during this time compiled a Patristic bibliography for the library, but then the Germany army reached Solesmes and all but the elderly and infirm monks were obliged to leave. On his bike again, he rode south for ten days until he reached an abbey on the Tarn, where he spent about a month before being summoned back to Maredsous.

He was in no hurry to return and spent an idyllic August on the Côte d'Azur and in Provence, staying in various monasteries, before turning north and being arrested by the Germans at Chalon-sur-Saône, on the demarcation line between Occupied and Vichy France. Notwithstanding the fact that his papers were in order and he had not served in the Belgian army, he was held for seven days in a squalid camp near Dijon.

He was then handed over to the French Red Cross, who put him on a train for Dinant, from where, after being greeted by his parents, he returned to the abbey at Maredsous. There he was given a chilly reception by the abbot, who had returned earlier and was very suspicious of de Mendieta's long absence, during which he had cycled more than 1,200 miles. The rest of the war was spent in this destructive relationship and on a meagre diet consisting largely of potatoes, turnips and a little bread. This had the useful effect of reducing his excessive weight and, besides resuming his work for the *La Revue Benedictine*, which soon closed down because of censorship problems, he completed a general index of its volumes from 1905 to 1942 and edited a collection of six philosophical and theological texts rebutting the claims of astrological fatalism during the first five centuries of the Christian era. Both volumes were published after the war.

The immediate post-war years proved to be increasingly painful for de Mendieta. The prior, Dom Jules Harmel, had been an influence for good in the community and a restraining hand on the despotic rule of the abbot, but in 1944 he heroically gave himself up to the Gestapo in place of the abbot and, during the early part of 1945, was executed. The abbot became increasingly senile, yet unwilling to retire, though he was more than happy to give his 'difficult' scholar-monk leave of absence to pursue his research in the libraries of France, Italy, Greece and England.

Having written a 390-page volume on the ascetic and monastic doctrines of St Basil, and secured a useful bursary from the Belgian Ministry of Education and Fine Arts, de Mendieta resumed his project of tracking down the known manuscripts of the saint's homilies on Genesis 1 in order to produce a definitive critical edition of the original text. During the course of his travels two experiences proved to be particularly significant. The first resulted from a stay of three months in Rome during 1948, working in the Vatican Library, and at the same time having his eyes opened to what he called 'the faults and corruptions in the Roman system'. He was particularly shocked by the procedures for putting a book on the Index which followed exactly those of the Inquisition. The second, rather more positive, experience arose from a visit to Athens in 1949, where he received from the Patriarch of Constantinople an introductory letter to the monks of Mount Athos. This resulted in a substantial book about the religious life on the Holy Mountain and, although this led to problems with some Greek monks and the refusal of an imprimatur by the abbot of his own community, it eventually saw the light of day after he had left Maredsous and was under the canonical jurisdiction of the Roman Catholic Archbishop of Washington.

Another visit to Italy, in 1950, coincided with Pope Pius XII's definition of the dogma of the bodily assumption of the Virgin Mary, and in his autobiography de Mendieta wrote:

> I think that, by that day, I had quite ceased to believe in the personal infallibility of the Roman Pontiff, who had just offered the church and the world such a striking proof of his own fallibility, and of a complete lack of respect or charity towards the Orthodox Church, the vast Anglican Communion and all the other Christian churches, who could not but lodge a protest against a dogmatic definition so rash, inopportune and contrary to the ecumenical spirit.

Most significant of all, however, was his attendance at the first International Conference on Patristic Studies, held in Oxford in June 1951, to which he contributed a short paper on his work on St Basil. This was his first encounter with the Church of England – experienced through worship at Christ Church Cathedral and visits to the university church and college chapels. It was all very beguiling. So was the openness of the conference and the delights of working in the Bodleian Library for a fortnight afterwards.

Soon after his return to Maredsous he told the abbot that he could no longer cope with the monastic regime, which was now affecting his health, and he was immediately given leave to spend six months in Paris, working at the Bibliothèque Nationale on its Basilean manuscripts and earning his keep as a convent chaplain. This arrangement extended well beyond six months and in 1954 he applied to the Vatican, ostensibly on health grounds, for exclaustration, which would permit him to live outside his monastery for another two years. By this time he had in fact decided to leave the Benedictine Order and it only remained for him to decide whether to break altogether with the Roman Catholic Church. He hoped for a time that he might secure a position as a priest in one of the French Instituts Catholiques, which would have enabled him to continue his studies, but when nothing materialized he decided to follow his conscience and cease to be a Roman Catholic.

This decision, de Mendieta was always at pains to emphasize, preceded his encounter in the summer of 1953 with a young Parisian woman, Ginette, to whom he later became engaged, and subsequently married. He returned to Maredsous for a few days to discuss his situation with a new and more understanding abbot, before taking up a visiting scholarship at Dumbarton Oaks in the USA. This was followed by another scholarship at Harvard, after which he applied, without success, for several academic posts in America. He returned to France in 1956 to rejoin his fiancée and to despatch a letter to the Archbishop of Washington announcing his decisions. The months preceding this action had been agonizing for him and once the decision was conveyed by letter to his family in Belgium his relationship with them was severed, though one of his five sisters kept in touch with him and, after about two years, his father resumed an affectionate correspondence.

De Mendieta now decided it was time to become an Anglican, so he contacted the chaplain of the British Embassy in Paris, who handed him on to a London friend, Patrick Gilliatt, then vicar of Holy Trinity, Brompton. This was long before the church became a centre of Evangelical charismatic renewal, and the curate, John de Satge, who chanced to be of French origin and a fluent French speaker, prepared the new convert for reception into the Church of England. A week after this ceremony, in June 1956, de Mendieta and his bride were married in South Kensington's registrar's office, the legal union being followed by a blessing and a nuptial Eucharist in Holy Trinity Church. He then spent nine months on the staff of the church as a lay assistant, learning the ropes of the Anglican liturgy and parish life, as well as the problems posed by the English language.

A decision was now needed about the sphere of his ministry as an Anglican priest. Several bishops were approached, but for a variety of reasons felt unable to help. So the Bishop of Kensington arranged for him to spend four months in 1957 at St Augustine's College, Canterbury, which had recently been turned into a kind of staff college for the Anglican Communion and was attracting priests from all parts of the world. De Mendieta felt, probably correctly, that the bishops were suspicious of his motives for moving from Rome to Canterbury, not least because of the proximity of his marriage to his reception. In the event, his time at St Augustine's was well spent and a decision about his future ministry was further postponed by immediate appointment to a bye-fellowship at Gonville and Caius College, Cambridge. Tenable for two years, later extended to three, this involved no teaching or administrative responsibilities and was designed to leave its occupant entirely free to pursue his own studies.

De Mendieta got on well with the master, Joseph Needham, the dean, Hugh Montefiore, and William Frend, a distinguished church historian, and produced some substantial work. This included a 50-page article, contrasting the differing styles of Basilean and Pachomian monasticism, for *La Revue de L'histoire des Religions*, a critical edition of a Latin translation of St Basil's Genesis homilies, and another book on Mount Athos, which was not published until he had moved to Winchester. Not long after his arrival in Cambridge, Archbishop Geoffrey Fisher, who regarded him as a great 'catch' for the Anglican Communion, authorized him to resume his priestly ministry, which he did by helping at the Sunday services at St George's, Chesterton. He was also appointed a lecturer in the Faculty of Divinity, though his problem with spoken, as well as written, English restricted his usefulness.

During his Cambridge years he wrote in French *Rome and Canterbury* (translated into English by the Professor of Biblical Greek at Trinity College, Dublin, and published in 1962). This was partly autobiographical and partly a vigorous assault on some aspects of Roman Catholicism, which had caused him to reject its claims, particularly papal infallibility, Marian devotions and the lack of individual liberty. His decision to become an Anglican had shocked many Roman Catholics, some of whom were not slow to allege that the move owed more to a desire to marry than it did to a change of conviction. The book was designed to answer this charge and it was perhaps natural that, in common with other converts, he tended to regard the Church of England more favourably and the Roman Catholic Church less favourably than many of those whose company he had joined were accustomed to do.

Another book, *Anglican Vision* (1971), looked forward to 'a dynamic restoration of the One, Holy, Catholic and Apostolic Church based on the Anglican model of faith and order', and, somewhat unrealistically, believed this to be feasible within the foreseeable future. Little notice was taken of this book – the failure of which he took to be an indication of the failure of the Church to listen to its prophets.

But his home in Winchester Close continued to be a small-scale ecumenical centre in which the visitor was more than likely to meet an Orthodox Christian, or a Roman Catholic or some other sort of Christian from almost any part of the world. Alec Vidler, who got to know him well at Cambridge, said that 'his courage, integrity and moral and spiritual sensibility outshone even the splendour of his erudition'.

17

The Missionary Statesman
Max Warren, Westminster

Max Warren, who was a canon of Westminster from 1963 to 1973 and before that an honorary canon of Truro for 18 years, was one of the twentieth century's greatest missionary statesmen and in other circumstances would have made a notable Archbishop of Canterbury. It is arguable, however, that during his 21 years as General Secretary of the Church Missionary Society (CMS) his contribution to the life of the world Church was far greater than anything he might have achieved at Canterbury.

His appointment to this key post at the age of 38 came in 1942, when wartime travel restrictions required him to remain in London. But the next three years were not wasted. The relative inactivity enabled him to apply a first-class mind, prophetic insights derived from deep biblical knowledge, and a burning missionary zeal to the radical changes that would inevitably face all the Churches in the post-war world. When the war ended, therefore, he was able to produce a strategy that enabled the CMS and, through his influence on Archbishop Geoffrey Fisher, the Anglican Communion as a whole, to meet the demands of new forms of nationalism. Thus it became possible to encourage and support the emergence of indigenous, autonomous Churches some time before Prime Minister Harold Macmillan discerned that 'a wind of change' was blowing throughout Africa. These Churches were to play a significant part in the conversion of the British Empire to a Commonwealth of independent nations.

By the time Warren moved to Westminster Abbey his chief work was ended, but the freedom afforded by his canonry, and its location, enabled him to spend ten years as the missionary movement's elder statesman. In this role he continued to make a major contribution. He was consulted by archbishops, bishops and other church leaders, and often by governments in their dealings with the Biafran conflict in Nigeria and what turned out to be a lengthy civil war in the Sudan.

He was one of the best-informed and most experienced experts on international affairs in the country, and bishops planning to speak in the House of Lords on these and related matters turned to him for briefings.

In this he kept up to date, not only through his omnivorous reading, but also by means of the generous hospitality he offered in his house in the Little Cloister to overseas bishops and other churchmen and churchwomen when they were in London. Twice a week and sometimes at weekends, he and his wife Mary provided their visitors with dinner, bed and breakfast and during the summer of 1968 meals were served to 294 bishops and others attending the Lambeth Conference. No longer able as before to go into all the world – he suffered a severe thrombosis in 1967 – friends from all parts of the world came to him. And besides those who came to stay, there was a constant stream of other visitors who sought advice or brought information – or simply came to renew friendships, for he firmly believed that friendship was the primary means of sharing the Christian faith. During his time at the CMS he worked strenuously to ensure that his relations with the many hundreds of overseas missionaries were conducted in terms of friendship and even at Westminster he often wrote in his own hand as many as 30 letters a day.

Westminster Abbey was an ideal base for all this and Warren loved the view from his house of the Palace of Westminster and the Abbey's involvement in national and Commonwealth life. But it was not quite paradise for him – there were some frustrations. He had never been used to a regular round of formal worship and had reached the conclusion during the few days he spent at Romsey Abbey, immediately before his ordination in Winchester Cathedral, that daily services were unlikely to become a necessary part of his spiritual life. Unfortunately, his installation at Westminster took place on the fifteenth evening of the month, when the choir sang all 73 verses of the appointed Psalm 78. He never forgot this and came to feel that often the services were hardly different from a sacred concert. Thus he wrote in his diary one Sunday after experiencing Leighton's *Missa Brevis*:

The sheer cacophony of sound without a single word being distinguished was a ghastly ordeal I, and many others, had to endure when attending the Sung Eucharist this morning. The enormous sense of relief at the said portions of the service could almost be felt. After the uproar the still small voice. What quaint musical conceit induces organists to produce this ghastly cacophony?

This comment obviously reflected Warren's personal tastes and preferences, but more important for him was the likely effect of such an act of worship on the large congregation assembled in the Abbey. Ever the missionary and one who believed that well-ordered worship could for some people have a converting power, he longed for something less elaborate and more direct that might conceivably touch the hearts of those, of all sorts and conditions of humanity, who had come from all quarters of the globe on a once-in-a-lifetime visit to Westminster Abbey. Besides the problem of the music, the Bible readings prescribed by the official lectionary often seemed to him to be totally unsuitable for public reading in a missionary context and the Evangelical in him found the elaborate ceremonial unhelpful. For a time he urged a reconsideration of the pattern and style of the Abbey's worship but he eventually came to recognize, as many other canons before and since him have done, that capitular institutions are impregnably fortified against such assaults on their traditions.

Another source of disappointment to him was the lack of close collaboration and fellowship which he had experienced during his long years at the CMS. There he and the departmental secretaries had met every Thursday, and sometimes during weekends away, not only to discuss the nuts and bolts of the Society's administration but also the biblical and theological basis of their decision-making in the realm of missionary strategy. He found none of this at Westminster Abbey. Apart from the dean, Eric Abbott, the other members of the chapter, who were all distinguished churchmen – Edward Carpenter, Ronald Jasper and David L. Edwards – had not been appointed to their canonries primarily in order to run the Abbey. Rather were they, like Warren himself, sent there in order that their gifts and experience might be made available to the wider Church.

Thus chapter meetings were concerned only with necessary administrative matters, often of a very tedious sort, and, apart from sharing in worship and brief encounters in the Cloisters, no one – and this almost certainly included Warren himself – had time enough left for the deepening of fellowship and the devising of strategies. It would be a matter of only a few years before the demands of the Abbey's own developing ministry – in common with those of the major cathedrals – made it virtually impossible to appoint men, and later women, of Warren's distinction.

Max Warren was born in Dún Laoghaire, not far from Dublin, in 1904. His father, an Irish clergyman, was a CMS missionary in India, at the time on furlough, and when Max was three months old the family returned to India. He had two older brothers, one of whom was killed in the 1914–18 war; the other died soon after of tuberculosis contracted while in the army. His sister died of bubonic plague in Benares, and his father died in India in 1920 at the age of 53.

During his early years Max was educated largely by his mother, who instilled in him a love of books and reading, but in 1913 he was sent to a preparatory school at Cockfosters and from there, just as the war was ending, went to Marlborough College. There he played rugby, hockey and cricket, and did well enough academically to win a scholarship to Jesus College, Cambridge. The religious influence of Marlborough College on him was minimal and his confirmation was only a formality, but the death of his father, who was his hero, had a considerable effect and by the time he reached Cambridge he had more or less decided to follow in his missionary footsteps.

The family home now being in Upper Norwood in South London, he had also come under the influence of the local Evangelical Christ Church, Gipsy Hill. Every summer from 1920 to 1927 he was involved in the Children's Special Service Mission, which held services on the beaches of Eastbourne and West Kirby on the Wirral, and eventually succeeded his brother as its leader. Being thrown in at the deep end and required to preach in the open air when still very young was, he always said, the best possible preparation for the work of an overseas missionary.

At Cambridge he took Firsts in History and Theology and won the coveted Lightfoot Scholarship in Ecclesiastical History. He was also much involved in the Evangelical Cambridge Inter-Collegiate Christian Union, as well as the Student Christian Movement – an unusual combination which was soon to be forbidden by CICCU because of the SCM's 'unsound' liberalism. Warren became, in fact, an outstanding figure in the university and was almost certainly one of the last of its gifted undergraduates to respond to a particular missionary challenge. It was during his first term that the CMS Secretary for Africa spoke at a tea party and appealed for a team of men to take the gospel to the Hausa tribes in northern Nigeria. Warren offered his services, recruited two of his friends, was joined by two more senior men and then by another and before long found himself the acknowledged leader of what became known as the Hausa Band – it being understood that each member would go to Africa on completion of his degree.

For some time Warren was not clear as to whether he was also being called to holy orders but, having taken his degree, went to Ridley Hall, Cambridge, for the ordination course so that he might be prepared should the call come to him in Africa. Towards the end of his time in Cambridge he became engaged to Mary Collett, who also had a missionary vocation, and it was understood that she would join him, after their marriage about 18 months hence. In November 1927 therefore he sailed for Nigeria as a layman and on his arrival at the mission station in Zaria spent some months learning the Hausa language, teaching and helping in the dispensary. But in October of 1928 he was struck down by a very virulent form of tuberculosis and, having been immediately sent back to England, spent the next three years in bed, first in a sanatorium in the New Forest, then in a nursing home at Alton. Various parts of his body were affected and his right eye had to be removed. The physical exhaustion also led to an emotional breakdown and a darkness of the soul from which he was eventually liberated through the guidance of a fellow patient, George Lyward, in the nursing home. Lyward had also suffered a breakdown and received some important insights in the process of recovery. Later, Warren regarded these three years, during which he had undertaken a vast amount of reading, as 'one of the most worthwhile experiences of my life'.

On 7 May 1932 Max and Mary, who had assiduously visited him during his illness, were married in Tunbridge Wells and a fortnight later he was ordained by Bishop Theodore Woods in Winchester Cathedral. It was now accepted that his problematic health would not permit him ever to work as an overseas missionary, so he became instead a curate at St John's, Boscombe – the leading Evangelical parish in Winchester Diocese – combining this with the new post of Diocesan Youth Organiser. During the next few years he learned the ropes of parish ministry and did a great deal of work among young people, including youth weekends, an annual camp and a major youth campaign in Bournemouth. Bryan Green, at that time chaplain to the Oxford Pastorate, and henceforth a lifelong friend, brought 120 undergraduates from Oxford and Cambridge to reinforce the local effort.

These were heady days and when Bishop Cyril Garbett, who had succeeded Theodore Woods, asked him to become vicar of a parish in Southampton he declined on the grounds that he did not feel called to traditional parish ministry. Before long, however, he had accepted the call to become vicar of Holy Trinity, Cambridge – a church made famous by the 50-year-long ministry of Charles Simeon (the leader of the late eighteenth-century Evangelical revival) and still the chief Evangelical presence in both the university and the town. This was a huge responsibility for a 32-year-old priest, who had been ordained for only four years and was also to be head of the Cambridge Pastorate, which, from an Evangelical standpoint, augmented the work of the college chaplains. But Warren soon made a considerable impact through his leadership of worship and the power of his sermons. There was nothing extravagant about his style. He believed the Book of Common Prayer to be still useable and provided carefully planned sermons with appropriate lessons, hymns and intercessions. In his sermons he used a distinctive and attractive voice to expand biblical themes to which he had applied a considerable intellect and an ever-deepening faith.

The threat of war and its outbreak in 1939 caused him to relate the Bible more closely to contemporary problems and experiences and this brought him great influence, for the services were always crowded, long queues sought admission and the parish magazine was transformed into a widely read monthly bulletin. Town as well as gown was fully involved in the church's life and from 1937 onwards hospitality was offered to a congregation of German refugees. Some joint German–English services were also held, but these came to an end in 1940 when most of the refugees were interned. As a preacher and lecturer, Warren was in the highest class and never went into the pulpit without the most thorough preparation. This makes it all the more surprising that during his years at Westminster he believed his sermons never really connected with the Abbey's congregations. This was strongly disputed by many who heard him and it may be that for most of his ministry, particularly during his time at the CMS, he had spoken mainly to clearly defined groups of people, whereas the large and ever-changing congregations of Westminster Abbey were quite impossible to identify or relate to.

While at Cambridge Warren became a member of the CMS Executive Committee and in 1942 was largely instrumental in the founding of the Evangelical Fellowship for Christian Literature – a project which he supported and guided for the whole of its 30-year existence. In the same year the General Secretary of the CMS, Wilson Cash, became Bishop of Worcester, and Warren was a member of the committee responsible for finding his successor. When his own name appeared on the first list of likely candidates he asked for it to be struck off. But the first choice declined and Warren, unable to attend the next meeting of the committee owing to illness, was, in his absence, unanimously nominated.

Thus began his 21 years of outstanding service to the world Church, but within a month he was seriously ill and had to spend two months away from London. Again, he came to regard this as a blessing, since it enabled him to reflect on his leadership role and on the future of the CMS when post-war changes would require fewer missionaries – at least of the traditional sort – from Britain. Following his recovery, he travelled the length and breadth of the country, getting to know the Church of England and the Society's supporters, and he also became a regular reader of *The Economist*. This continued until the end of his life and, combined with his worldwide contacts, put him among the best-informed men in the country.

One of the most significant ways in which his knowledge was expressed and shared was through the *CMS Newsletter*. He inherited this from his predecessor, who had started the monthly publication as a means of keeping in touch with the Society's missionaries and supporters, and had got as far as issue number 31. Warren made it the organ of his own prophetic ministry and was responsible for the next 232 issues published over the course of 21 years. It was, and remains, a modest affair, consisting of no more than 1,700 words. His method was to select a theme, sometimes to be covered over several months, then get an able research assistant to gather and collate the appropriate material, together with a selection of relevant books for him to read. Often, after composing a first draft, he would send this to three or four experts on the subject, inviting their comments and criticisms. Only then would he write the final version.

The result, over the years, was a substantial contribution to Christian thinking on world affairs and a very wide circulation that extended far beyond the original readership to include the Foreign and Commonwealth Office, overseas embassies and virtually everyone with a serious concern for the international as well as the church scene. The arrival of the monthly *Newsletter* was eagerly awaited by its subscribers, who knew that its contents would be fresh, stimulating and without a single platitude. A constant theme was that in a rapidly changing world the Church itself must change radically and present the gospel in what he called 'the vernacular of particular localities'. The maintaining of the *Newsletter*'s high standard for so long was a very remarkable achievement, and its continuation at the same level by his successor, John V. Taylor, not less so.

Taylor, who later became Bishop of Winchester, was the Africa Secretary in a highly gifted team that met Warren every Thursday in what constituted his cabinet. While keeping himself sufficiently well informed so as to direct overall strategy, Warren was content for the regional secretaries and other specialists to manage their own departments. Once the war was over he travelled extensively – something he greatly enjoyed – and over his 21 years as General Secretary undertook 21 journeys, each of which was meticulously detailed in nearly 40 travel diaries, usually written daily, and each averaging at least 200 pages. He maintained that all candidates for high office in the Church of England should have spent some time living abroad.

Inevitably, he was himself often considered for such office. In May 1946 the prime minister, Clement Attlee, offered him the bishopric of Carlisle and the Archbishops of Canterbury and York pressed him to accept, believing there to be a need for young Evangelicals on the episcopal bench. But Warren pointed out that he had been at the CMS for scarcely four years and declined on the grounds that he did not feel called to be a bishop. Later Archbishop Fisher would from time to time sound him out when bishoprics fell vacant, but he always said no, as he did to suggestions that he become a co-adjutor bishop in the puritanical Archdiocese of Sydney in Australia, with the near-certainty of succeeding to the primacy when next it became vacant. His own unwillingness to become a bishop did not, however, stand in the way of his being the chief adviser to Archbishop Fisher over appointments to overseas bishoprics, many of which were at that time still in the hands of the Archbishop of Canterbury.

Warren was in fact always strongly opposed to centralizing tendencies in the Church, particularly when these attempted to embrace overseas missionary work. Soon after becoming General Secretary of the CMS a powerfully argued Church of England report proposed that all the missionary societies should be amalgamated to form a single missionary department of the Church Assembly. He totally rejected this, as he did a proposal to bring the work of the International Missionary Council – an informal association of the world's non-Roman Catholic missionary societies – under the umbrella of the World Council of Churches. He insisted that missionary work required the kind of passion that could only be evangelical and sustained in flexible associations of people who had responded to the call to be evangelists and needed the personal freedom to take initiatives. Centralized bureaucracy would destroy this, and in a pamphlet, *Iona and Rome* (1947), he said, 'Human nature being what it is, it is commonly more attracted to be organised by "Rome" than to be disturbed by "Iona"'.

There could be no doubting Warren's own personal identification with the free-ranging approach of the missionaries from Iona who evangelized the north of England in the seventh century. He spoke often of 'the untidiness of the Holy Spirit' and strongly supported the formation of the United Church of South India, while at the same time deploring what he called 'the failure of missionary nerve' that came over the western churches in the early 1950s and was never to be overcome. Although nurtured in the Church of England's Evangelical tradition and always ready to own its designation, Warren's outlook and style were markedly different from that of the more charismatic Evangelicals who came to the fore in the closing decades of the twentieth century. He believed the Bible to be the primary source of religious truth and inspiration, and the cross the effective sign and symbol of human salvation. Moreover, he shared the Evangelical sense of assurance, of being at home with God in every sphere of life, and above all the need for obedience to what they called the Great Commission – 'Go ye into all the world, and preach the gospel to every creature'.

He wrote upwards of 25 books on these and related subjects, and his understanding of the theory and practice of mission was most powerfully expressed in *The Christian Mission* (1951), *The Christian Imperative* (1955) and *Partnership* (1956). These were all fairly small works and the heavy demands of the CMS made it impossible for him to produce the larger-scale volume on mission for which many had hoped. All of this located him firmly in the Evangelical tradition, yet there was a marked distinction arising from the rigour of his scholarship and the breadth of his vision. His distinctiveness also had a good deal to do with his personality, for he was in no sense a larger-than-life figure who might have delivered a barnstorming message to thousands assembled in a stadium. On the contrary, his style tended to be avuncular. There was a modesty and an older-style courtesy about him. He had an unforgettable smile and a twinkle in his remaining eye that immediately set new acquaintances at their ease. Friendships were made for life and his family was specially important to him. Yet although, after his physical and emotional breakdown when a young man, he never lost hope, there was a melancholic side to his nature that sometimes emerged. This, in company with a romantic tendency, may have owed something to his Irish origins, and all contributed to his undoubted greatness.

When he retired from the general secretaryship of the CMS his mind turned from preoccupation with the theology and methodology of spreading the gospel to a consideration of the content of the gospel itself. Not long before leaving office he received from Bishop John Robinson, with whom he had had a long friendship, a manuscript of his *Honest to God*, the liberal character of which was to cause a sensation. Warren recognized that he was raising important questions and urged him to publish it. Warren's own special concern was now with the relationship between Christianity and the other great religious faiths, an area in which he confessed to having been a 'slow starter'. He was considerably helped by a long correspondence with his son-in-law, Roger Hooker, who was a missionary in India, and Warren still argued strongly along orthodox lines for the saving character of Christ's work, while at the same time recognizing that God is no less active among people of other faiths. In a later letter on the subject to Professor John Hick he said he had come to feel that the word 'uniqueness' was no longer appropriate since it required too much definition. He added, 'Salvation is a word far too great, and an experience far too glorious, to be defined and limited by a dogma. Strictly speaking only God knows what it encompasses.'

The ill-health he suffered from 1967 onwards, and which severely restricted his activities, caused him intense frustration but he went on for another six years at Westminster, and accomplished a great deal, including the writing of his autobiography, *Crowded Canvas*, which appeared in 1974. His final four years were spent in a cottage at East Dean, Sussex, where he continued to read and write and add 300 to 400 words every day to his diary. He died in 1977 and his remains were interred in Westminster, where there is a memorial tablet to him out in the cloisters bearing the text 'Into all the world'.

18

The Patristic Scholar
Geoffrey Lampe, Ely

The Ely Professorship of Divinity at Cambridge was created in 1889, its teaching functions having previously been subsumed under the Regius Professorship of Greek. The funding of the new chair was provided by its annexation to a residentiary canonry of Ely Cathedral, some 16 miles from Cambridge, where the duties were light and the Black Hostelry (a reminder of Ely's Benedictine past) provided an appropriate residence.

Geoffrey Lampe was the eighth occupant of the chair, from 1960 to 1971, and the first to take the canonry with the degree of seriousness necessary to the evolving life of a cathedral. By the end of his time there he was as well known and popular in Ely as in Cambridge and there was great sadness when his move to the Regius Professorship of Divinity necessitated his resignation from the canonry. Beyond Cambridge and Ely he was a scholar of international reputation. Patristics – the name given to the study of the theology of the Church's teachers during its earliest, formative years – was his subject. Its literature, requiring expertise in the classical languages and philosophies of the ancient world, is extensive and complex and to most modern minds not immediately interesting. But Lampe had the ability and the passionate desire, not only to make it interesting to the non-specialist student, but also to demonstrate its relevance to the pursuit of theological study in any era.

Lampe discovered through his work on the early Christian theologians three significant elements in their method. The first was that the overwhelming majority of them regarded as their priority the fundamental Christian beliefs – the being of God, the nature of the incarnation, the activity of the Holy Spirit, the character of faith, grace, righteousness, justification, atonement and so on. These were their concerns. Secondly, they always, and inevitably it might be thought, expressed their convictions about these central beliefs in the thought-forms of their own day. How otherwise could they expect them to be understood and to have saving power? Thirdly, this led to a considerable variety of insight, interpretation and expression, the first signs of which were visible in the New Testament itself, following a tradition clearly delineated in the Old Testament. Creeds and other confessional statements were formulated from time to time by the early Church for its own catechetical purposes and membership needs, but these are never to be confused with the Christian faith itself, which requires continual exploration on a voyage of discovery. The effect of all this was, paradoxically as it might at first seem, to make Lampe, the Patristic scholar, one of the most radical British theologians of his time. An Easter Day sermon televised from Birmingham Parish Church in 1965 brought him a thousand letters of protest from viewers.

Physically, as well as intellectually, he was a big man. Tall, well-built and from his middle years endowed with a bare, domed head, he could not easily be overlooked in a crowd. Yet there was nothing 'superior' about him. He radiated warmth and kindness, was a wonderfully witty raconteur and, although meticulous in his scholarship, always saw this as something to inform or inspire service of the Kingdom of God, rather than to gather dust in libraries. At different times he was accused of heresy, and sometimes of being a Deist – usually by those who had never read any of his books.

Geoffrey William Hugo Lampe was born in 1912. His father, who came from Alsace, was a distinguished conductor of the Bournemouth Symphony Orchestra, but left England before the 1914–18 war, never to be seen again. Geoffrey was therefore brought up by his mother, to whom he was devoted and who lived long enough to see him installed as Ely Professor at Cambridge. He was educated at Blundell's School, from where he went as a scholar to Exeter College, Oxford. Being interested in neither politics nor sport, he concentrated mainly on his academic work, relieved by long walks with a friend. He was rewarded by a First in Greats and a congratulatory First in Theology. His choice of Theology was dictated by a vocation to holy orders and, his religious outlook being of the liberal sort, he decided to complete his training for ordination at the Queen's College, Birmingham, rather than at one of the Oxford or Cambridge partisan theological colleges. In 1937 he became a curate at Okehampton in Devon but, although he pitched into the life of the parish and the town with enthusiasm and energy, it was already clear that his future lay in education and after a year he left to become an assistant master at King's School, Canterbury. This, as it turned out, was not a good time to move to Kent, which, by the summer of 1940, was in the front line of war.

When the decision was made to evacuate the school to Cornwall, Lampe enlisted as an army chaplain, ministering to various units in England before his attachment to 34 Tank Brigade, which was preparing for its involvement in the invasion of Normandy at the end of June 1944. By this time a firm bridgehead had been established and a fortnight later the brigade was in action with its Churchill tanks. The role of a chaplain in this form of warfare was limited, but Lampe soon found one in the evacuation of the regiment's casualties. This he undertook with such courage under fire that he became the first chaplain in the Battle of Normandy to be decorated with the Military Cross. The citation read:

> The Revd. G. W. H. Lampe, R.A.Ch.D. has been in action with 147 Regiment R.A.C. continuously and is still in action with the Regiment. Throughout he has been in and amongst the forward troops under shell and mortar fire. His presence there and his complete disregard of personal safety has done much to maintain the high standard of morale in this Regiment.
>
> On a great many occasions he has assisted in recovering the bodies of fatal casualties from destroyed and burnt out tanks and has conducted burials under shell and mortar fire. These actions have further heightened the morale of the troops. No praise is high enough for the conduct of this Chaplain in and among the forward troops, and without doubt his presence and personal example have been of the greatest value and of a very high order.
>
> His gallantry and devotion to duty have been an inspiration to all.

He was also a very popular figure with all ranks, one of whom recalled, 'I met him outside a dressing station coming from the wounded. His eyes had sunk back into his head and he was sooty black under the eyes. He had seen awful things and I think he was as badly shocked as the wounded.' Later, when the brigade had crossed France to Holland, fighting its way to Germany, another soldier recalled how the chaplain had memorably held a Communion service under difficult conditions. He added, 'He was a wonderful brigade padre.' Towards the end of the war Church Houses were set up in German country houses to provide soldiers with courses of reflective preparation for their return to civilian life and the churches were permitted to use these for the selection of ordination candidates. Lampe was given responsibility for one near Hanover and was ideally equipped for lecturing, selection and the creation of a warm, hospitable atmosphere.

In 1943 he had been elected *in absentia* to a fellowship of St John's College, Oxford; this to be combined with the offices of chaplain and tutor, and on his demobilization in 1945 he immediately took up the post. As in the army, so in the college, his large-hearted, generous personality made a considerable impact, and his distinguished war record won the respect of the ex-servicemen undergraduates – who formed the overwhelming majority. He made himself available to everyone in the college, though he always maintained a somewhat formal relationship with his pupils. These were given a weekly personal tutorial; on Saturday morning there was a class on set texts and on Monday evening a discussion was open to all. Among his pupils was Kenneth Woollcombe, who succeeded him at St John's and later became Bishop of Oxford; he recalled,

To read theology was not to be admitted to a kind of holy club but rather to be admitted to membership of a family which extended in different ways and included all kinds of people, not all of whom were churchmen or Christians. The fact that we were often welcomed to the house in Museum Road (and sometimes invited to baby-sit!) gave us a strong sense of loyalty to Geoffrey as our paterfamilias.

It was while Lampe was at St John's that he took over the editorship of *The Patristic Greek Lexicon*, work on which had been started as long ago as 1906 by the then Regius Professor of Divinity, H. B. Swete, and put under the formal editorship of the Principal of Pusey House, Darwell Stone, in 1915. It was designed to be a companion volume to Liddell and Scott's long-established *New Testament Greek Lexicon* and to include all the key words in the writings of the most important theologians of the earliest centuries of the Church. This was a formidable task, given the number and complexity of these writings, and the work progressed in fits and starts until 1946, when the latest editor, F. L. Cross, recruited a much larger team of scholars, including Geoffrey Lampe, to bring the great volume to completion. In 1948, having become distracted by the editorship of *The Oxford Dictionary of the Christian Church*, Cross handed over the editorship of the *Lexicon* to Lampe, who enlarged the team even further, found money to pay them, wrote many of the major articles himself, and had the older material updated and improved. Although the research team were wont to describe themselves as 'The Slaves of the Lampe', he ensured that it was a stimulating and enjoyable experience and the whole enterprise was brought to a triumphant conclusion with publication in instalments during the period 1961 to 1968. By this time its editor was Ely Professor of Divinity at Cambridge, and an acknowledged authority on the early Fathers of the Church, as they are often called. The work greatly influenced his own thought and writings.

Before moving to Cambridge he had occupied the Edward Cadbury Chair of Theology at Birmingham University from 1953 to 1959. There he inherited a small department consisting only of another full-time colleague and ten part-time lecturers who had other responsibilities in various parts of the Midlands. By the time he left a second full-time lecturer had been appointed, negotiations with a charitable trust to fund a second chair were well advanced, and the annual intake of students had risen to just under 50. Besides his own departmental responsibilities he was also Dean of the Arts Faculty and eventually Vice-Principal of the University itself. His approach to administration, which he did not like, was relaxed and the meetings he chaired were always short, none of which much mattered in the days when the universities were smaller and less accountable to others than they were destined to become. His charm and ease of manner was useful in the resolution of conflict. Chairmanship of the university's Board of Extra-Mural Studies was another much valued contribution, and he was always ready to respond himself to requests for lectures and sermons. One such request came from William Temple College, Rugby, where someone was needed to teach Church History. He not only took this on, but also extended this teaching to other subjects, visiting the college on a weekly basis for 14 years – well into his time in Cambridge. He was made an honorary canon of Birmingham Cathedral in 1957 and two years later Edinburgh University awarded him a DD.

This coincided more or less with his appointment to Cambridge, where he was also allocated a Professorial Fellowship at Gonville and Caius College. The dean of Caius at the time was one of his former pupils, Hugh Montefiore, who was to become Bishop of Birmingham, and with whom he got on particularly well. Lampe made the college his main place of study, becoming notorious for his frequent requests for more bookshelves, and although he managed to avoid much committee work he was secretary of the Patronage Committee, responsible for appointments to the college's parishes, and eventually joined the College Council. He rarely spoke at its meetings, unless his opinion was openly sought, whereupon he made a number of succinct points that were generally recognized as wise and therefore carried the day. This was not the case, however, when the issue of admitting women undergraduates came on to the agenda in the late 1960s. Lampe, who strongly favoured their admission, found himself in a narrowly defeated minority over this and in a sharply divided fellowship, but he and two other professorial fellows sought to solve the problem by proposing that Caius should take the initiative in creating more educational opportunities for women, possibly by the founding of a new, mixed college. Fortune smiled on his proposal at the end of 1971 when an anonymous benefactor, who ten years later was revealed to be Mr David Robinson, provided, via the university, the necessary substantial endowment. Thus Robinson College was born, with a Caius representative always on its board of trustees.

Soon after taking up the Ely chair Lampe joined the Cambridge Extra-Mural Board, becoming its chairman in 1968 and continuing until his retirement 11 years later. And, as at Birmingham, he contributed a great deal to the board's work, travelling to the towns and villages of East Anglia to give lectures, courses or seminars. Co-operation between the board and Local Education Authorities and the Workers' Educational Association became increasingly important, and demand for residential courses led to the taking over of Madingley Hall for this purpose.

Surprisingly, perhaps, for one who was no great lover of committees, Lampe got himself elected, as a university representative, to the Church of England's General Synod. Admittedly, this was during its earlier years, when the agenda was of greater significance than it later was, and although he found administration tedious he was a formidable debater. He was also interested in the practical application in the life of the Church of the theological subjects with which he was more normally concerned – none more so than the proposal to ordain women to the priesthood, which was debated in 1972, 1973 and 1975. Long before then he had accepted the chairmanship of the Anglican Group for the Ordination of Women, when it was only a very small body and regarded by many as eccentric, so there was no uncertainty as to his position. His contributions to these debates were, as always, magisterial and, with the aid of his considerable knowledge of the Bible and theology, he had no difficulty in demolishing one by one the arguments of the opponents of women priests. This was to no avail in his lifetime, though the Synod accepted in 1975 that there were no theological objections to their ordination. It would take another 17 years to convert this into action.

Debates about baptism, confirmation and the Eucharist were also of special interest to him, because of his own theological work on their relations to each other, as were matters relating to church unity. His understanding of the place of the ordained ministry within the ministerial life of the whole Church enabled him to plead for greater understanding and acceptance of the Free Churches. These same beliefs drove him to make a sharp and sustained criticism in 1977 of an 'Agreed Statement' published by the Anglican–Roman Catholic International Commission. This was in the heady days when some significant movement towards uniting the two churches seemed not altogether impossible and Anglicans were inclined to be less critical of certain aspects of Roman Catholicism than their predecessors had been. Lampe wondered, however, what the Anglican representatives on the commission were doing when it was claimed that councils of the Church were protected from error and that the Pope, as well as councils, had the authority to define dogmas. While it might well be possible for Anglicans to accept some form of papal primacy – seniority, rather than authority – a 'stupendous evolution, requiring the dismantling of the curia and no more encyclicals like *Humanae vitae*', would be required in Rome. He doubted the likelihood of this. Yet he always longed for closer union between Anglicans and Roman Catholics and believed that the theological justification for intercommunion already existed.

He felt this, equally, about relations between the Anglican Church and the Lutheran churches of Scandinavia. A bi-annual Anglo–Scandinavian Theology Conference, attended by 16 to 20 theologians and churchmen, was begun in 1929 and Lampe, having started to attend in 1961, became its chairman four years later and continued until 1979. Its combination of size and seriousness suited him well, as did the opportunity of making friendships and dispensing hospitality whenever it met in Cambridge. He generally chose the subjects and recruited distinguished theologians to present papers, including a few by himself. The Lutheran delegates greatly admired him and shortly before he retired from the chairmanship, the King of Sweden awarded him the Northern Star, the University of Lund having marked the beginning of his term with the award of an honorary DD. During Lampe's lifetime it seemed that little progress towards ecclesiastical unity was being made, but during the mid-1990s the four participating Anglican churches and six of the eight Nordic and Baltic churches agreed to a mutual acceptance of ordained ministries and the practice of intercommunion on a theological basis of which he would, had he lived to see the day, undoubtedly approved.

His predecessor in the Ely chair had been a somewhat remote figure in the precincts of the cathedral, being content to perform the statutory requirements of the canonry and then hurry straight back to Cambridge. There was nothing in the cathedral's statutes to forbid this, but Lampe, churchman as well as scholar, was determined to contribute more and also to enjoy his membership of the Ely community. A bar was installed in the undercroft of his official house, which soon became a centre of generous hospitality. He and his wife, Elizabeth, tackled the garden and became well known in Ely through their joint shopping expeditions and their readiness to talk to anyone they chanced to meet.

Within the cathedral he was not altogether happy with the forms of worship, which were strictly in accordance with the 1662 Prayer Book and took no account of the new, experimental forms of service then emerging from the General Synod. But he played his full part, celebrating Holy Communion on Thursday mornings, and even wearing the Eucharistic vestments, to which he was not accustomed. His preaching was powerful and always intellectually demanding. Appropriately, he became Chapter Librarian and was responsible for the transfer of the greater part of the books to Cambridge, partly to ensure their proper care but chiefly to encourage their greater use. His educational skills were employed as a lecturer at the theological college in Ely, until its closure in 1964, and he was always ready to address clergy and deanery meetings in the diocese. He was, in fact, prepared to turn his hand to anything – assisting vergers with the removal of chairs and the works department with simple house repairs. It was a memorable 11 years in the cathedral's history.

Lampe established his reputation as an important theologian with the publication in 1951 of *The Seal of the Spirit*. This is an examination of the relation between baptism and confirmation in the New Testament and its development during the Church's earliest centuries. The question at issue is whether at baptism an individual is, through the operation of the Holy Spirit, fully incorporated into the life of the Church, or whether this is something that requires completion through a further outpouring of the Holy Spirit at confirmation. There has never been a Christian consensus over the answer to this question, but during his time at St John's College, Oxford, Lampe noted, through his Patristic studies, the importance of the subject and also the apparent conflict between the belief and practice of the early church and that of the Church of England. The running had been made recently by the Catholic wing – A. J. Mason, Dom Gregory Dix, Kenneth Kirk and to some extent A. M. Ramsey – who threw most of the emphasis on confirmation, thereby relegating baptism to something akin to a preliminary ceremony in which the Holy Spirit had hardly a look in. This theological opinion seemed also to have pastoral usefulness in a church where a high proportion of the population brought their infants for baptism, but without much prospect of these being nurtured in the Christian faith.

Lampe used the full weight of his formidable learning to demonstrate that this understanding of baptism and confirmation had no foundation in the New Testament, nor any clear support by the early Fathers. It was only later, when the Church began the practice of baptizing infants and leaving until later the signing with the cross or the laying on of hands in blessing by a bishop, that the doctrine of confirmation was developed to justify the change. But, argued Lampe, this did not invalidate the original belief in the completeness of baptism on its own. The presence in his book of untranslated Latin and Greek suggests that it was intended chiefly for his fellow professorial theologians, not all of whom accepted his argument, but by and large it carried the day and made the Anglo-Catholic position untenable.

Although Lampe made no proposals for change in the Church's current practice, the publication of *The Seal of the Spirit* and the discussion that followed had three significant effects on the life of the Church of England. The first of these was that theologically literate bishops and parish clergy changed their teaching on the subject and stressed the fundamental importance of baptism as the primary sacrament of the gospel. The second became evident in the liturgical revision which began in the 1960s, when the new services for baptism and confirmation showed clear signs of the change of emphasis. Later, in his Bampton Lectures, *God as Spirit* (1977), Lampe insisted that it was misleading and altogether wrong to administer confirmation immediately after the baptism of an adult, and even went so far as to suggest that confirmation could be received several times in the lifetime of an individual Christian as a reaffirmation of the Holy Spirit given in baptism. But neither of these views found much support in the Church.

More immediately significant than his influence on matters related to Christian initiation, however, was the Church of England's changed attitude to intercommunion. Previously the sharing of Holy Communion with members of the Free Churches had been actively discouraged, partly because it was believed that sacramental communion required a stronger expression of ecclesial community than currently existed, and partly because those in the Free Churches had not been episcopally confirmed and their churches lacked the authenticity provided by bishops ordained in an historic succession. But what if baptism alone was recognized as the only means of sacramental incorporation into the Church's life? And if baptism created a deep unity among Christians that was not dependent upon further spiritual embellishment, how could the sharing of the Lord's Supper at the Lord's Table be denied? Faced with these questions, a Commission on Intercommunion came to the conclusion that it could not be denied, and the General Synod agreed. A major improvement in inter-church relations soon followed, much to Lampe's pleasure.

The publication in 1976 of the report *Christian Believing* should have been a milestone in the expression and development of Anglican theology. Produced by the Doctrine Commission, it was the work of 17 leading theologians, of every tradition and of a calibre that could never again be matched. The report itself occupied only 41 pages and was concerned with the Christian faith and its expression in the Bible and the creeds. The main conclusion, to which all subscribed, was that the ineffable mystery of God made divergence of belief not only inevitable but actually desirable, provided it encouraged dialogue within the community of faith. In order to illustrate this point, eight individual essays on related subjects by members of the commission were appended to the report. Some of these proved to be highly controversial – so much so that the report was never even presented to the General Synod. This was a lost opportunity of considerable magnitude and reflected badly on the leadership of Archbishop Donald Coggan.

Lampe's influence on the report is not difficult to discern. Besides providing a useful appendix on the origins of the creeds, he contributed one of the personal essays. This, on the nature of divine revelation, challenged the commonly held view that in the Bible, the creeds and other conciliar definitions, as well as in the writings of some of the early Fathers, there are to be found revealed doctrines, a divinely authenticated theology. 'This is not the case,' he declared. 'Theological propositions and systems of belief are not revealed. Theology is a process of reflection that arises from revelatory experience; it is not itself the locus of revelation.'

The year of the report's publication also saw Lampe delivering his Bampton Lectures. These consisted for the most part of a learned examination of the various ways in which the early Fathers of the

Church had written about the Holy Spirit and, in particular, how they grappled with the theological and metaphysical problem of regarding the Holy Spirit as a third divine 'person'. He came to the conclusion that this is an insoluble problem, since it can be solved only by adopting some form of tritheism, which is unacceptable. It is therefore better to regard the Holy Spirit not as a third 'person' but as God himself in a personal relationship with his creation and inspiring and informing the spirit of man. He returned to the theme of the lectures in 1978 in a sermon preached in the chapel of Trinity College, Cambridge. This began, 'What future is there for the traditional, classical doctrine of the Trinity? I am bound to reply even within these walls of Trinity College, "Not much".' He immediately added, however, that he was talking about the doctrine of the Trinity, not about the faith experience of God as Trinity. He went on to point out, once again, that doctrines are human inventions, designed to articulate faith experience in the thought-forms of a particular culture. They are therefore variable, even disposable, in future ages, and, to illustrate his point, he declared, 'I believe that the Trinitarian model is in the end less satisfactory for the articulation of our basic Christian experience than the unifying concept of God as Spirit.'

Since 1976 Lampe had been battling against what turned out to be extensive cancer. Drastic surgery and radiotherapy took their toll, but he continued his busy life and few, apart from his family and close friends, were aware of his problems. On the day following his retirement in 1979 he celebrated with a 72-mile walk, with his son and daughter, along the South Downs Way, and in July of the following year he and his wife had a holiday tour of Russia, the Balkans, Greece and Italy. But by the time they returned he was desperately ill, and he died soon afterwards. Four months earlier he had chosen as the subject of his Mere's Commemoration Sermon 'Preparation for Death', and, without any reference to his own circumstances, ended:

To prepare against the fear of death, we need to make the most of life: to enjoy ourselves and to be thankful for it; to do our best to make it possible for other people to enjoy it more; to move through the enjoyment of life into enjoyment of God the source and giver of life, and to begin to experience that renewal of ourselves through his love which gives us the promise of fuller life to come.

19

The Sceptical Believer
Alec Vidler, Windsor

An innocent television viewer in the early 1960s who tuned in to a religious programme in the expectation of a broadcast interview with the traditional sort of Anglican scholar – the first in a Sunday evening series – was astonished to find himself listening to what appeared to be a sceptical *savant* of the French Third Republic. This was Canon Alec Vidler, lately of St George's Chapel, Windsor, and now Dean of King's College, Cambridge, wearing a trim 'spade'-beard and clad in a black shirt with a white tie. An engaging personality was matched by what was obviously an acute mind and deep wisdom.

Vidler, who was at Windsor from 1948 until 1956 and before that spent ten years as Warden of St Deiniol's Library, Hawarden, was a prominent and much-loved Cambridge figure in the 1960s. For almost 30 years he was also highly influential in the Church of England, mainly through his writing, though he had an unusual ability, without even trying, to gather around him other gifted scholars who achieved together what they might not have attempted on their own. He was academically a church historian with a specialist knowledge of the early-twentieth-century Modernist movement in the Roman Catholic Church, but he once described himself as a theological mid- wife – one who interpreted and communicated to others the thought of interesting theologians. He did this mainly through his editorship for a quarter of a century of the monthly magazine *Theology*. Read mainly by thoughtful clergy, this was eagerly awaited in rectories and vicarages, since it was never dull and some of its contents, not least the editorials, were always stimulating. That an editor could, with the aid of a few advisers, sustain a magazine of such quality for so long was an astonishing achievement.

Part of the explanation of his success was the character as well as the quality of his mind. Among other revealing descriptions of himself were 'a sceptic in faith's clothing' and 'an agnostic believer', while Malcolm

Muggeridge, a lifelong friend since their undergraduate days, said that he was 'a man who believed with all his heart and doubted with all his mind'. Yet, liberal thinker though he undoubtedly was, there was nothing remotely superficial about Vidler's mind. New ideas must be subjected to rigorous analysis and, after *Soundings* – an explosive volume of essays edited by him in 1962 – he never identified himself with such 1960s outbursts as *Honest to God*, secular Christianity, and the new morality. And this, not because their concepts were too radical, but rather because they were not radical enough – that is to say, they did not dig deeply enough into the roots of the categories under examination. Neither did he have any real interest in church reform. Again, this was not because he had no concern for the Church – he was a devout priest and a deeply committed member of the Oratory of the Good Shepherd, which, he being celibate, provided him with a substitute family – but simply because he believed ecclesiastical affairs to be very dull and of little importance when compared with the fundamental challenges to faith now posited by the cultural changes in the modern world.

Alexander Roper Vidler was born in the Sussex Cinque Port of Rye a few days before the end of the nineteenth century and was pleased to have lived during the reign of Queen Victoria. There was always to be an element of the Victorian about him. The Vidler family were central figures in the Rye community. They lived in the town's oldest house, which they had acquired in 1801 and named Friars of the Sack, believing it to date from 1263 when it was a friary. Young Alec's father, grandfather and great-grandfather were all mayors of Rye and it seemed inevitable that he would one day hold this office. He did – twice.

At his Eastbourne prep school he was often in trouble and was lucky to escape expulsion for being the ringleader of a spitting match. Nonetheless he made a good start at Sutton Valence public school and eventually became head boy, though financial problems led to his withdrawal for more than a year during the 1914–18 war. He worked in the family shipping business, which had come on hard times, but friends of his devout mother came to the rescue by funding his return to school. He believed himself to have been one of the last pupils in any school who never had a single lesson in the natural sciences.

He went straight from school into the army, where he completed his officer training in the Royal Field Artillery just as the war ended. At Selwyn College, Cambridge, he read Theology – mainly in vacations, preferring to devote term-time to a variety of extra-curricular activities, details of which have never been revealed. It is known, however, that his leadership of a campaign against compulsory chapel attendance was unsuccessful. As a boy at Rye he had been a chorister and a server in the parish church and by the time he reached Cambridge he was moving steadily towards Anglo-Catholicism and holy orders. He frequented the Cambridge house of the Oratory of the Good Shepherd, which he joined in 1923, but before this went to Wells Theological College to complete his preparation for ordination. There he soon became disenchanted with the life of the cathedral close, in which the college was located – 'it exuded the odour of establishment – moderation, caution and the virtues associated with public schools' – so he left early and returned to the Oratory house.

Vidler was ordained in 1922 and became a curate of the Anglo-Catholic Mission of the Holy Spirit, serving one of the worst slum areas on Tyneside. Many of the children had neither shoes nor stockings and were dressed in rags, and the grinding poverty drove him into membership of the Labour Party. He addressed election meetings and was on the platform in Newcastle when Ramsay MacDonald spoke at the 1924 general election which made him Britain's first Labour prime minister. Later that year he moved to a curacy at St Aidan's, Small Heath, Birmingham and soon found himself embroiled in what was to become a national *cause célèbre*. The modernist E. W. Barnes had recently been appointed Bishop of Birmingham and decreed that whenever the Sacrament was reserved (something he did not like) it must be kept in a closed or curtained-off chapel to which the public had no access, thus ruling out its use for devotional purposes. Vidler arrived in the parish shortly before a change of vicar and the new one, having refused to accept this ruling, was refused institution by Barnes. A lengthy legal case ensued and in the end the Archbishop of Canterbury, Cosmo Gordon Lang, was directed by the court to institute the priest, which he did in the chapel of Lambeth Palace. During the two years while all this was going on, and attracting massive publicity, Vidler was holding the parish fort single-handed, and when in 1932 he came to leave after seven years of devoted ministry Barnes sent him a letter, which he had framed and displayed on the walls of his study until the end of his life:

Dear Mr. Vidler,

I thank you for your letter of August 21 informing me that you propose to leave the Diocese early in October. Will you allow me to

urge that in any Diocese to which you may go you should carefully
keep the pledge which you make in taking the Oath of Canonical
Obedience.

Yours sincerely,
E. W. BIRMINGHAM

He was actually moving to the Oratory house at Cambridge, where
he remained for eight years, undertaking pastoral work among the
undergraduates, preaching and conducting missions in various parts of
the country, and writing. During his final year in Birmingham he had
completed his first book, *Sex, Marriage and Religion* (1932), in which
he argued for the permissibility of contraception within marriage,
equal status for women, and the possibility of married couples being
called to the religious life. The liberal influence of his Cambridge
tutors was now beginning to show and his next project was a study
of a development in the Roman Catholic Church which had created
a stir at the beginning of the century and had been condemned by
Pope Pius X in 1907. This led to a substantial book, *The Modernist
Movement in the Roman Catholic Church*, which was published in
1934 and remains the standard work on its subject. Now established
as a significant modern church historian, Vidler had in the course of
his studies come under the influence of the controversial thought of
George Tyrrell, a British exponent of Modernism and a theologian
of considerable depth and originality. This, combined with the earlier
and lasting influence of F. D. Maurice, settled the foundations for
Vidler's own subsequent thinking.

In 1938 he was appointed Warden of St Deiniol's Library at
Hawarden. A gift to the nation from W. E. Gladstone, this had a
magnificent collection of books and, although wartime problems soon
hampered the use of the residential facilities, Vidler turned it into a
lively centre of Christian thought and influence. Conferences of theologians were held and groups came at weekends to discuss current
theological, political and social questions. Some scholars stayed for
several weeks to pursue their studies and a number of middle-aged
men came for directed reading in preparation for their ordination. A
daily round of services was started in the chapel. This still left Vidler
with ample time for other activities, in particular the editorship of
Theology, appointment to which had coincided deliberately with his
move to the library. When he took it over its circulation stood at 1,700
and this grew quickly to about 5,000, which he considered, probably

correctly, to be the ceiling for a publication of its kind. In 1946 A. E. J. Rawlinson, the scholarly Bishop of Derby, made him an honorary canon of his cathedral.

In the same year Vidler was asked to consider a proposal that he and Lesslie Newbigin, who had been a noted theologian in the Church of South India, should become joint secretaries of the British Council of Churches, with the aim of cultivating a more imaginative approach to ecumenism, but neither of them felt inclined to move to an office job in London and Vidler stayed at St Deiniol's for two more years until an offer came to be a canon of St George's Chapel, Windsor. Again there was a simultaneous and by no means coincidental invitation to take over the leadership of the Christian Frontier Council. This had been started in 1942 by J. H. Oldham, one of the foremost laymen of that time and a colleague of William Temple, Reinhold Niebuhr and other pioneers of the twentieth-century ecumenical movement. It sought to carry forward some of the thinking of an international conference on Church, Community and State held in Oxford in 1937, in particular the responsibility of the layman, rather than the cleric, for the application of Christian moral principles to secular social and economic problems. Oldham convened a small group of people, who held positions of responsibility in public life and who were ready to attend regular meetings, to consider 'frontier' subjects, and lunchtime meetings were also held for wider participation. A journal, *Frontier,* achieved a substantial circulation and a number of important books were published.

Vidler was well equipped by outlook and skill to succeed Oldham and, once installed at Windsor, he travelled to London twice a week either for meetings of the council or for related work – inviting speakers, arranging conferences and publications, and co-editing *Frontier.* Being a clergyman, however, he was never able to capture the lay mind in quite the manner of Oldham, though members of the council valued his acute theological judgement and under his leadership the work continued to flourish. His Firth Lectures at Nottingham University in 1955 were published under the title *Christian Belief and this World* and placed him squarely in the Oldham, Temple and Niebuhr tradition.

Although Vidler would have been happy to remain at St Deiniol's Library for the remainder of his life, he greatly enjoyed his Windsor years, recognizing from their outset that he had been fortunate to secure a position where, as he put it, 'the statutory duties are minimal and probably leave more time for outside appointments than any other office in the church'. Nonetheless he took those duties seriously and valued the daily choral services as well as the pageantry of the annual service of the Order of the Garter and the funerals of King George VI and Queen Mary. He got on well with the Windsor Castle community, which numbered about 200, and especially with the military knights, whose company he found a refreshing change from that of his clerical colleagues. While in no sense an Establishment man he always argued strongly for the retention of the Church of England's established status, believing it not only to be a safeguard against sectarian introspection but also to demand of the Church a concern for the wider community.

Relations with the dean and his fellow canons were warm and co-operative, except in the case of Canon Duncan Armitage, who had oversight of the buildings and finance. Vidler described him as 'a man of piety and charm with a strong pastoral sense, but an ecclesiastical fanatic, tiresomely obstreperous and unco-operative and liable to sulk if he did not get his way: he thus made himself and other people unhappy.' It seems that Armitage's two immediate predecessors in the office of Steward had been of the same mould and got across their colleagues in one way or another. J. N. Dalton, the father of Hugh Dalton, a Labour Chancellor of the Exchequer, had evidently tyrannized over his colleagues while Anthony Deane had made a misery of the life of a new dean, Eric Hamilton. Things improved when, following the sudden death of Armitage, Vidler succeeded to the stewardship and found the duties 'full of interest, particularly the regular meetings with the architect'.

It was to Armitage, however, that Vidler owed a suggestion that turned out to be useful to the Church and personally satisfying. At St Deiniol's Library he had been content to occupy no more than a good-sized study and a bedroom, but at Windsor he inherited an official house with about 20 rooms. The problem of furnishing these was solved by loans of surplus items from friends, but the rooms still needed to be heated and cleaned, and preferably used. Armitage, who was involved in the church's Central Council for the Ministry, therefore asked Vidler if he would consider using some of the spare rooms for accommodating a number of middle-aged ordination candidates, and also oversee their training in whatever ways he considered appropriate. He was immediately attracted to this idea and during the remainder of his time at Windsor about 50 men passed through his hands.

There were usually six or seven ordinands in residence. Vidler did not give lectures, but directed their reading, conducted seminars and brought in specialists on pastoral matters. The students worshipped in St George's Chapel and on Sundays took services in country churches. The scheme was deemed a great success and also helped to solve the problem of financing a large house. At the outset there was an inevitable discussion as to what the students were to be called and Armitage, who in spite of some other shortcomings was evidently not devoid of humour, suggested 'Vidler's Vipers'. In the end they were called 'Doves' – a title used by C. J. Vaughan, a notable nineteenth-century Master of the Temple, who had trained ordination candidates by a similar method. Vidler continued to edit *Theology* – a responsibility he had brought with him to Windsor – and in 1955 led a delegation of Anglican theologians in a series of meetings with Roman Catholic theologians in England and Italy. This was some years before the reforms of the Second Vatican Council and, although the Pope and the Archbishop of Canterbury approved of the exercise, the meetings had to be held in secret. The Windsor years were also devoted to the writing of several books and numerous university lectures, so Vidler was more than fully occupied.

The invitation to become Dean of King's College, Cambridge arrived right out of the blue in 1956 and was accompanied by a degree of pressure, since the college had recently lost by early death both its provost and its dean. As at St Deiniol's, Vidler was free to remain at Windsor for the rest of his days, and no one would have blamed him for doing so, but he recognized that so comfortable a stall, occupied indefinitely, might not be good for his spiritual health. He was also feeling the need to be a bit more stretched and concluded that if he ever left Windsor it should be for an academic appointment, rather than another ecclesiastical post.

The atmosphere of the college was very much to his taste, combining, as he wrote later in his *Scenes from Clerical Life* (1977), 'intellectual integrity and acumen, honesty and tolerance'. His own style suited the college no less well and he found the other fellows much more friendly than he had been led to believe they would be to a churchman. He was in any case secure enough in himself not to require approval. The transition from the choral services at Windsor to those of King's could hardly have been easier, though he substituted a sung Eucharist for Evensong on Ascension Day, All Souls' Day and other important festivals. At Sunday Mattins passages from great religious literature, read by fellows, were substituted for sermons. Towards the end of his time he was deeply involved in the decision to place Rubens' great painting

The Adoration of the Magi at the east end of the chapel, though it was not actually installed until shortly after his retirement.

He was Director of Studies in Theology in the college and an exemplary tutor whose pupils invariably got good degrees. Loveable though he undoubtedly was, he was not someone who could be taken for granted, since he had firm ideas about what was proper and could be fierce with offenders. He and the lay dean held a joint At Home for undergraduates every week at which fellows and others were invited to open a discussion on something they were knowledgeable about, and there was another weekly group of a 'frontier' sort when senior and junior members of the college discussed ethical and religious questions. Vidler was also a university lecturer in Church History and when in due course he became Chairman of the Faculty Board of Divinity he abandoned the tradition of starting its meetings with prayer, on the grounds that in a pluralistic university it should not be assumed that everyone could conscientiously join in prayer. For several years he was a syndic of Cambridge University Press and being a prolific author (he wrote over 20 books) he petitioned for a DLitt. rather than a DD, to indicate that he did not regard himself as a true theologian.

In another characteristically idiosyncratic move he dug out statutes dating from the reign of Queen Elizabeth I which had never been repealed and which empowered the university to license a number of its members to preach throughout England without the permission of the local diocesan bishop. These statutes had not been used since the eighteenth century, when a licence was granted to Thomas Bray the founder of the Society for the Propagation of the Gospel. Having been involved in contretemps with some bishops over his views, Vidler decided to petition for a university licence, partly to protect his freedom and partly to ensure that the statute should not be lost by default, but also, as he confessed, to annoy the Archbishop of Canterbury, Geoffrey Fisher, who had declared himself opposed to the revival of the university's power. A formal vote of the university was required and sufficient of the dean's colleagues and friends turned out to give the necessary approval.

When Vidler arrived at King's, Biblical Theology was still in vogue and in some parts of the country, not least in college chapels, there was something of a revival of church attendance. Archbishop Fisher, on his retirement in 1961, declared the Church of England to be 'in good heart'. But some of the younger Cambridge theologians became anxious about the complacency of churchmen and the apparent unwillingness of their senior colleagues to face the challenging questions raised by some European and American scholars. Howard Root, Dean of Emmanuel College, suggested to Vidler that he should convene a group to consider what might be done about this. Vidler readily agreed and about 12 members of the Divinity Faculty began to meet in his rooms. They exchanged papers, spent a long weekend away together and in 1962 produced a volume, *Soundings: Essays Concerning Christian Understanding*, which made a considerable impact and caused great alarm in conservative circles. The essays were on subjects such as 'The Uneasy Truce between Science and Religion' (John Habgood), 'The Meaning and Authority of the New Testament' (J. N. Sanders) and 'Theology and Self-Awareness' (H. A. Williams), and in his introduction Vidler, who had suggested the title, explained:

The authors of this volume of essays cannot persuade themselves that the time is ripe for major works of theological reconstruction. It is a time for ploughing, not reaping; or to use the metaphor chosen for our title, it is a time for making soundings, not charts or maps. If this be so, we do not have to apologise for our inability to do what we hope will be possible in a future generation. We can best serve the cause of truth and of the Church by candidly confessing where our perplexities lie, and not by making claims which, so far as we can see, theologians are not at present in a position to justify.

Thus was inaugurated, though quite unconsciously by its authors, the lively and important debate that was to dominate academic and church circles throughout the rest of the 1960s. Forty years on the number of high-calibre Church of England theologians then working in Cambridge is a matter for wonderment. In the year following the publication of *Soundings* Vidler contributed to a course of four Cambridge lectures on 'Fundamental Objections to Christianity'. These attracted weekly audiences of about 1,500 and were edited by him into a volume titled *Objections to Christian Belief* (1963), which, for several weeks, was listed among the top ten best-selling books. He explained in his introduction, 'We hold that it is more important to try to plumb the depths of the objections, without complacently assuming that answers are readily available.'

Besides all this and, until 1963, the continuing editorship of *Theology*, he wrote several more books, including *Twentieth Century Defenders of the Faith* (1965) and *The Church in an Age of Revolution* (1968), both of which remain valuable works of reference. There was also an introduction to a new edition of F. D. Maurice's *The King-*

dom of Christ (1958) and the same for George Tyrrell's *Christianity at the Cross-roads* (1963) – acts of homage to his mentors.

On his retirement to his beloved Rye in 1967 Vidler remained active. His beard had now assumed patriarchal proportions and, with a Jack Russell terrier and a cat for company, he baked his own bread, continued to keep bees, offered hospitality to his friends, kept open house once a month for his neighbours and anyone else in the vicinity who cared to call, and played golf. He was for a time much involved in local government and was the last Mayor of Rye before the town was absorbed into a larger borough council. He travelled far and wide, preaching and lecturing, and from time to time submitted inimitable letters to *The Times*. The last and longest of these appeared on 6 May 1976 and was headed 'An Awkward Shortage':

I shall be grateful if you will allow me to draw public attention to the hardship that is increasingly experienced by septuagenarian men when they go away from home, and *a fortiori* by octogenarians and nonagenarians. I refer to the disappearance of the chamber pot as an article of bedroom furniture, or rather of guestroom furniture. Of course some bedrooms have a bathroom directly attached to them and in that case I make no complaint. But, like many of my contemporaries, I am often invited to spend a night in a room that has no such convenience. We do not like to disturb our hosts by wandering about dark passages in quest of light switches and uncertain doors and at last by the noise of flushing.

We plead for the restoration of the traditional chamber pot to its rightful place either under the bed or in a bedside cabinet. It is true that most of them now seem to have made their way into antique shops and thence to the United States. But various sizes in plastic are obtainable and, for my part, I am ready to settle for one of these as a substitute for an elegant piece of china.

I would add that I entirely agree with the late Dick Sheppard that the recipients of such relief should always be responsible in the morning for emptying and cleansing the receptacle which they have used and not leave the operation as a chore for their hostess or any minion of hers.

He died in July 1987 as he had always hoped, 'a penitent Catholic and an impenitent liberal'.

20

The Protester
John Collins, St Paul's

'Hang Canon Collins' was an unusual slogan to find painted on a house in a cathedral close, but this, together with several others of a threatening sort, appeared in Amen Court at St Paul's in the 1950s. John Collins, who provoked them, was the most notable cathedral canon of the second half of the twentieth century and the Church's most prominent social reformer of that time. In spite of the Herculean efforts of Archbishop William Temple before and during the 1939–45 war, there remained little concern for the social implications of the Christian faith, and under the leadership of Temple's successor, Geoffrey Fisher, the Church of England's energy was devoted primarily to internal matters related to the preservation of its own life. It is a measure of Collins's achievements that by the end of his life this was less evidently the case, though the quality and influence of today's Christian social witness would have greatly depressed him, since it hardly bears comparison with the major projects that flourished under his leadership.

Collins combined a good mind with broad vision, courage, dynamic energy and unusual organizational skill. He was essentially a man of action who could not be content until he had got something done. Obstacles, including people who disagreed with him or counselled caution, were no more than challenges to be overcome. Yet, as a churchman, he was conservative about some matters, not least in his defence of the traditional rites and ceremonies of St Paul's, though in the pulpit he often used vivid language to denounce what he perceived to be the great evils of his day.

Born and brought up in a politically Conservative home, he joined the Labour Party in the 1930s when he was teaching at Westcott House, Cambridge. This was due largely to the influence of one of his pupils, Mervyn Stockwood, the future Bishop of Southwark, and his socialism, like that of Stockwood, was of the champagne sort. It did not hinder the sending of his four sons to Eton, and although his right-wing enemies sometimes dubbed him a Communist, such accusations would not stick and he won a libel action against a careless retired general who went too far in this direction. Nonetheless, his major campaigns against the international stockpiling of nuclear weapons and apartheid in South Africa, together with his lesser battles against capital punishment and homelessness in Britain, attracted much support from the middle-class Left and encapsulated the ideals and hopes of many who were growing up in the 1950s and 1960s. Collins became for them an icon, if not of revolution, then of a better, more humane world.

A canonry of St Paul's was an ideal base from which to exercise such a ministry. It gave him easy access to people of influence and was only a stone's throw from Fleet Street, where St Paul's was one of the few churches known to journalists. At the practical level it provided generous space for what became a sizeable office and, most important of all, time to devote to great causes. Collins belonged to the last generation of canons who were not expected to be concerned primarily with the running of their cathedrals, and he had no difficulty in combining the discharge of his capitular responsibilities with the role of international reformer. He also had the good fortune to be among the last to owe their appointment to a prime minister who preferred his own judgement to the always-cautious advice offered him by the hierarchy of the Church.

He was no less fortunate in his choice of a wife after several previous engagements. Diana Elliott was a very able woman – more able in many ways than her husband – and, besides her total commitment to his way of life and his causes, was able to cope creatively with his mercurial temperament. Their relationship was accurately described by the title of her acclaimed *Partners in Protest* (1992), consisting of both biography and autobiography. Her contribution to his achievements was largely unseen but vital and it was entirely appropriate that, shortly before her death, this should have been nationally recognized by appointment as a dame. In this, as in other respects, there was a marked affinity between the shared ministry of John and Diana Collins and that of Samuel and Henrietta Barnett, exercised more than half a century earlier.

John Collins was born in 1905 at Hawkhurst in Kent, where his father was a master-builder. At the age of six, young John declared his intention of becoming a priest. He went to Cranbrook School, where he was captain of the school as well as of the Shooting VIII at Bisley and a keen member of the Army Cadet Corps. He was also confirmed and attracted by Anglo-Catholicism. At Sidney Sussex College, Cambridge, he started to read Mathematics, but soon recognized this to have been a mistake and switched to Theology. A Second and a First in the Tripos, together with the coveted Carus Greek Testament Prize, indicated a possible academic career, but he was not over-studious and had played hard at tennis, rugby and rowing. Active membership of the Conservative Association led to his enrolment as a Special Constable during the 1926 General Strike.

The childhood attraction to holy orders had never left him and after a year of further preparation at Westcott House, Cambridge, he was ordained by Archbishop Cosmo Gordon Lang in 1928 for a curacy at Whitchurch. This Kentish parish, mainly middle-class and conventional, aroused his impatience and after a mere 12 months he was relieved to be invited back to Sidney Sussex College as chaplain. This offered the opportunity to study German theology, but he found it too heavy and turned his attention to the French Roman Catholic Modernists, whose liberal theology and ensuing conflict with the Vatican was beginning to arouse interest in England. As a college chaplain he offered friendship to the undergraduates, displaying a particular sensitivity to the misfits. It was in defending one of these against unfair treatment by the senior tutor that he clashed with the college authorities and felt obliged to leave after only two years.

Collins then applied for a vacant minor canonry at St Paul's Cathedral and, in spite of the fact that his good baritone voice was untrained, managed to get appointed. The dean, W. R. Inge, who disliked choral services, had told the music department not to choose a 'singing bird' but someone who also had academic gifts. Inge, himself a Modernist, appreciated Collins's interest in the subject and established a better relationship with him than he had previously had with most of the cathedral's clergy. During the 1930s (Collins was there from 1931 to 1934) St Paul's remained strictly formal – it was not until 1940 that the clergy forsook their frock coats and top hats on Sundays – but he soon came to value the great building and its national role, learned to sing the services well and, after a course of speech training, became one of the few preachers able to make himself heard in the vast spaces of a cathedral that lacked a sound-reinforcement system. His warm, friendly manner also made him a popular figure with the large lay staff.

The emoluments of the minor canonry, which included accommodation in Amen Court, were far too small to keep body and soul together, so he managed to get an assistant lectureship in theology at King's College, London and also became a Deputy Priest-in-Ordinary to King George V, which involved him in conducting services at the Chapel Royal. This still left him with time to improve his French and resume his studies of Roman Catholic Modernists. A close friendship with Alfred Loisy, the excommunicated priest-scholar who was the most prominent figure in this movement, followed. Collins made many visits to the village in northern France where Loisy was living in retirement and the influence of the French priest on him was considerable. 'I had not considered before', Collins wrote later, 'that Christianity stands or falls at the existential level . . . questions of faith can be assessed only by reference to their effects in human experience. Where faith is concerned, the proof of the pudding is in the eating.' The emphasis on Christian action which characterized his ministry after the 1939–45 war sprang from this conviction.

His next move, however, was to Westcott House, Cambridge, in response to a request from its legendary principal, B. K. Cunningham, that he should become his vice-principal. But the decision to accept was not entirely straightforward. Tall, dark, handsome and unmarried, Collins had many female admirers. During his years at Whitchurch he was unofficially engaged to a girl from the parish, but when he moved to Sidney Sussex College they gradually drifted apart and the relationship ended. Then, soon after his arrival at St Paul's, his engagement to a girl he had met in Cambridge was announced in *The Times*. This was broken off by mutual consent and followed by a brief fling with an attractive student at the Royal College of Music. But then things became complicated. In order to help Collins overcome a domestic problem in Amen Court, Maurice Relton, a formidable professor of dogmatic theology at King's College, under whom he served, invited him to spend a fortnight in his own home. In these comfortable surroundings Collins found an unmarried daughter, whom he took out for meals on several occasions, and whose late-night company over a glass of wine he much enjoyed. The consequence of this was that on the morning of his departure Mrs Relton expressed her joy at their engagement, and added that the professor had sent an announcement to *The Times*.

Collins was astonished but, for some reason, felt unable to spoil the family's happiness by disavowing any commitment to marriage, and it was not until some time later, and after consulting a psychiatrist over what seemed to be an emotional breakdown, that he felt bold enough to stand firm and to despatch a notice to *The Times* – 'the marriage will not now take place'. Relton was furious and threatened to 'break' him, while some newspapers, having dug out details of his two previous engagements, published articles with headlines such as 'Priest-in-Ordinary to the King breaks engagement' which detailed what they described as reprehensible behaviour.

It was now deemed necessary for Collins to resign from his post at King's College and, although Dean Inge did not press him to leave St Paul's, being content with the remark, 'You've been a fool, but we're all fools at some time or other in our lives', he decided that it was prudent to get away from London. Inge co-operated by strongly recommending him for the post of Fellow and Dean of Peterhouse College, Cambridge, but this did not materialize and he went instead to Westcott House, where he taught from 1934 to 1937. His role on the small staff was that of theologian, in which he was perfectly competent, though some were shocked by his liberal views, expressed moderately in his first book, *The New Testament Problem* (1936). The influence of Loisy was apparent, as was that of Alec Vidler, who had written the standard work on the Modernist movement in the Roman Catholic Church and become a lifelong friend.

He also kept in touch with Mervyn Stockwood, who had won him over to socialism, and when his erstwhile pupil became a curate in Bristol, Stockwood introduced his former tutor to Sir Stafford Cripps, the local MP, and Victor Gollancz, both of whom would become key figures in the founding of Christian Action. 'If ever a master owed more to his pupil than the pupil to his master, I was that man,' confessed Collins. 'It is certainly more to him, than to anybody else, that I owe my first attempts to relate the Gospel to social and political matters.' To many of his other pupils, whom he took out to pubs and picnics, he seemed a somewhat worldly priest and B. K. Cunningham, while greatly valuing his contribution to the college, noted that he did not appear to have much time for prayer and other forms of devotion.

After three years at Westcott House, Collins felt that it was too small and too ecclesiastical an establishment to satisfy him, and he applied successfully for the post of Fellow, Chaplain and Dean of Oriel College, Oxford. There he was soon appreciated, but his strong political opinions – he had by this time joined the Labour Party – and informal style did not commend him to all the fellows. And before long he was head over heels in love with an undergraduate and Lacrosse Blue at Lady Margaret Hall. But Diana Elliott came from a very different social background – her maternal grandfather, who owned the Fison's chemical fertilizer business, lived at Stutton Hall in Suffolk – and the family was totally opposed to her proposal to marry a poor parson, even though he might be an Oxford don. With the outbreak of war in September 1939, however, their opposition collapsed and a few weeks later John and Diana were married.

An idyllic few months together was broken in the following July when, after Dunkirk, he felt it right to enlist as a chaplain in the RAF. His first posting was to a reception centre for recruits at Cardington in Bedfordshire, but he was soon moved to Yatesbury, where he spent most of the rest of the war. This camp, at a bleak place on the Wilt-shire Downs, did not provide one of the RAF's most glamorous assign-ments, being a training centre for aircrew and ground radio and radar operators, but it was very large, with five to six thousand personnel, and eventually Collins became the senior of four Anglican chaplains. There was ample scope for his reforming zeal and soon after his arrival he described the camp as corrupt and inefficient. This inevitably brought him into conflict with the authorities and four times during his three years at Yatesbury he was threatened with a court-martial. Compulsory church parades, at which officers were allocated seats at the front rows of the church, displeased him and, after insisting that there should be no privileged places at acts of worship, he moved on to get compulsory attendance abolished. Instead, large voluntary congre-gations assembled for what became, after a time, a pioneering Parish Communion followed by breakfast.

The size of the camp and the scale of his ministry within it – he usually wore a black cassock rather than an officer's uniform – made him feel the need of a cell in which the Christian life could be more intensely experienced and expressed. Thus there came into being the Fellowship of the Transfiguration. About 20 strong, and drawn from all ranks, its members accepted a rule of life which included daily prayer and Bible reading, regular attendance at the Eucharist on Sundays and special weekdays, self-examination, almsgiving, work for the Church and commitment to trying to make the social, economic and political implications of the Gospel effective in local, national and international affairs'.

In order to encourage thought about these matters Collins began to invite distinguished speakers to address camp meetings on current issues. Archbishop William Temple was the first to accept and he was to be followed by Sir Richard Acland (on 'The Christian and Politics'), the 'Red Dean' of Canterbury, Hewlett Johnson (on 'The Christian and Communism') and Barbara Ward, a Roman Catholic economist.

But when news of this reached the Commander-in-Chief of Technical Training Command he panicked and, fearing that socialism might be advocated, tried to get Collins to withdraw the invitations. He refused and the matter went as far as the prime minister, Winston Churchill, who minuted, 'The chaplain at Yatesbury must be either a Communist or a dupe'. But after a meeting of senior RAF officers it was decided that the meetings could go ahead. Later, when an invitation was extended to the Soviet ambassador in London, there was more fuss, but eventually he came and, in common with most of the other speakers, addressed an audience of over a thousand.

In July 1944 Collins was posted to Bomber Command Headquarters at High Wycombe, where, with the bomber offensive against Germany still being waged, it might have been supposed that he would soon be in trouble for questioning this policy. But in fact he had a high opinion of the Commander-in-Chief, Arthur 'Bomber' Harris, who chanced to be a first cousin of Diana's father. A television programme on Harris broadcast in the 1990s, which showed him and Collins in open conflict over the issue, was totally misleading and excused by the BBC as 'faction'. There was, however, a big problem when Sir Stafford Cripps, at that time Minister of Aircraft Production, gave a lecture in which he asserted that in some circumstances it might be necessary, even for a serviceman under orders, to say 'I must obey God, rather than man.' For the rest, Collins was content to see compulsory church parades abolished and to form the Fellowship of Transfiguration, of which there were now about 120 cells on various RAF stations. Reunions of these continued to be held for many years after the war ended.

The dropping of nuclear bombs on two Japanese cities, which brought the war to an end, troubled him greatly, though as a member of the RAF he could not voice his disquiet publicly. Living in an officers' mess where everyone else was rejoicing in the decisive ending of the war made him almost physically sick. He therefore wrote to Archbishop Fisher asking why there had been no official protest from the Church against America's first use of the indiscriminate weapon. All pretence to be fighting to preserve a decent way of life had, he claimed, been thrown overboard. Collins was not the only protester and Fisher eventually made a public statement in which he weighed the pros and cons for the use of the new weapon and concluded, 'The way of deliverance is the Charter of the United Nations'. But this did not satisfy Collins, who became a nuclear pacifist, and eventually an unqualified pacifist – a further step he took with reluctance.

A few months before his correspondence with Fisher he had been summoned to Downing Street to discuss with the Secretary for Appointments what form of ministry he might exercise when the war was over. It was explained to him that the Crown had its disposal a canonry of Worcester Cathedral and the large parish of Nuneaton. Did he have a preference? After careful consideration he opted for Nuneaton, but for some unstated reason was offered neither. Meanwhile Sir Stafford Cripps advised him not to get fixed up too soon. In January 1946, therefore, Collins returned to Oriel College and took over the office of Domestic Bursar, which gave him the opportunity to improve the pay and working conditions of the college staff. His first sermon in the chapel called for the embracing of an all-out Christianity which, after the pattern of the early Church, would be committed to 'turning the world upside down'. Members of the congregation were invited to his rooms for coffee afterwards and out of this grew a small fellowship on Yatesbury lines.

By this time, Victor Gollancz, now a close friend, had written an influential book, *Our Threatened Values* (1946), which the fellowship studied and then decided to hold a public meeting about it in Oxford Town Hall. This took place on 5 December 1946 under the slogan 'A call to Christian action in public affairs'. The Bishop of Chichester, George Bell, was in the chair and the speakers were Sir Richard Acland, Victor Gollancz, Barbara Ward and Roger Wilson, the former secretary of the Friends' Relief Organisation in Europe. In spite of appalling weather, the Town Hall was filled to capacity, as was the university church, used for an overflow meeting, and it was estimated that some 3,000 people had turned out for the event. Two resolutions were passed by acclamation:

1. There must be a large increase in the number of committed Christians actually engaged in public life, and Church life must become an example of the application of Christian principles to everyday life.
2. In view of the special dangers which arise at this time in connection with our recently defeated enemies we urge the leaders of the Churches to press the Government for a more Christian policy towards Germany.

Afterwards a small organization, named Christian Action and based in Oriel, came into being and Collins got various notables, including the Masters of Balliol and Oriel, Quintin Hogg (the future Lord

Hailsham), Lord Halifax and Sir Stafford Cripps, to become patrons or to serve on the committee. It was decided to back Gollancz's 'Save Europe Now' campaign and to emphasize the importance of reconciliation between Britain and Germany, including pressure for increased food supplies, repatriation of prisoners of war, and the saving of factories from unnecessary destruction. Collins was then asked by Lord Pakenham (the future Earl of Longford), Cripps and Lord Halifax to organize a meeting in London's Albert Hall to rally support for Churchill's idea of a Western European Union. This attracted enormous support and tickets had to be refused to over 4,000 applicants. As with the Oxford meeting, a potent post-war idealism was at work and some prominent Conservatives were involved, though not for long.

Once again, though, the question of Collins's personal future came to the fore and Archbishop Fisher tried to persuade Collins to become General Secretary of the British Council of Churches. He wisely declined, and shortly afterwards, when a canonry of St Paul's fell vacant, the prime minister, Clement Attlee, gladly accepted the suggestion of Cripps that it should be offered to Collins to enable him to develop Christian Action from a London base. Fisher opposed this move on the grounds that Collins would not be an easy member of the chapter and would spend most of his time on his own outside concerns. William Wand, the Bishop of London, was also against it and the dean, Walter Matthews – the most agreeable and gentle of men – was annoyed that for the first time he had not been consulted about an appointment to his chapter. And Diana did not want to go, but she never regretted the decision to face the formidable challenge.

Collins was installed on All Saints' Day 1948 and made an immediate impact by bringing to St Paul's the first post-war performance in England of the Berlin Philharmonic Orchestra. He had already been involved in the organization of an English tour designed to help restore relations between the former enemies, and those who were fortunate enough to get into the crowded cathedral found it a deeply moving experience. Less so, for Collins, was his first chapter meeting, when most of the time was taken up by a dispute between the Senior Canon and the Archdeacon of London, also a canon, about precedence in processions and at formal events. This took 18 months to settle. His frustration at this and other trivial matters led to an unfortunate incident at the annual chapter dinner, held not long after his arrival, when as the junior canon he was required to respond to the speeches of the distinguished guests. These had praised the cathedral's ministry, but

Collins began, 'As a dog returns to its vomit so have I returned to St Paul's.' He went on to speak of the darker side of the cathedral's life and quoted his friend Dick Sheppard, who had spent his closing years at St Paul's and lamented, 'Those cold, cold stones, they crush to death all that is human in the place.'

The speech caused massive offence, and the dean received many complaints, but controversial utterances were something they had to become used to. In his first sermon Collins asserted that the cathedral should not be content to remain a nineteenth-century museum, but should bring in artists and craftsmen to create contemporary works of art. Likewise, the choir should experiment with modern music. Reports of this appeared in the press, whereupon the organist threatened to resign. The chapter, for its part, sent a letter to the preacher suggesting that he ought to resign but he took this to the next chapter meeting and tore it up in the face of its signatories. Like some other churchmen who were radical on ethical and social questions, Collins was, in fact, markedly conservative on anything relating to liturgy and worship. Neither did his controversial sermons attract large congregations, but, with Fleet Street on the doorstep and copies of the sermons readily available, they often received worldwide publicity. The *Church Times*, on the other hand, refused to report anything about St Paul's whenever Collins was in residence. Much later, when reflecting on his own time at St Paul's, Dean Matthews wrote of Collins:

> He had such a reputation for stirring up trouble because he preached so fiercely about love. He would be a magnificent leader of a violent revolution, but he would never appeal to emotions of revenge or hate.

Within the cathedral community as a whole he came to be greatly liked even by those who strongly disagreed with his views and actions. The pulpit was often placed at the disposal of other notable preachers, some of whom attracted huge congregations. Paul Robeson chose to sing, rather than to preach, while Martin Luther King, who arrived an hour late owing to a delayed aircraft, electrified a packed congregation for over an hour. His widow, Coretta King, later occupied the pulpit for the launching of a Martin Luther King Memorial Fund masterminded by Collins. Earlier, an invitation to Sir Stafford Cripps caused a considerable public outcry and led to the blackballing of Collins's application to join the Athenaeum Club. His own negative vote in the Greater Chapter of St Paul's failed to prevent the election of Robert

Stopford to the bishopric of London. The objection was partly to the antiquated election procedure but chiefly to Stopford himself, who was on record as saying that it would be better for Britain to be entirely destroyed than for the country to have to live under Communist tyranny.

Meanwhile, Christian Action was absorbing an ever-increasing amount of his time. An office was set up in the basement of 2 Amen Court, where he lived, a full-time secretary was employed and volunteers came in to help with mailings and the like. Diana took on a good deal of responsibility, including the editorship of a journal. Sir Stafford Cripps and other supporters hoped that Christian Action would become a national movement with cells throughout the length and breadth of the country, but this never materialized. Instead it became a powerful support organization for Collins's personal, prophetic mission, and so it remained until the end of his life. A council was formed and several hundreds of members recruited.

Collins's work developed in three ways, the first of which might broadly be described as home affairs. Concern for reconciliation and care of some of the war's casualties continued, with particular emphasis on the future of the many millions who had been displaced from their own countries. This involved the constant drawing of attention to their plight and the organization of relief. During the 1950s an Anti-Capital Punishment Campaign, launched by Victor Gollancz and with Collins, Arthur Koestler and Sydney Silverman MP on the committee, was run from the Christian Action office, but it was not until 1969 that the death penalty was finally abolished. The previous year saw the launching of a 'Homeless in Britain' campaign, designed to draw attention to a national problem but one that was particularly acute in Birmingham, Clydeside and London, where there were as many as 7,500 homeless on the London County Council's books. Support was offered to other voluntary organizations tackling the problem and over the next four years 19 Christian Action Housing Associations were established. Homes for unmarried and deserted mothers were opened, together with a shelter for vagrant women at Lambeth and several houses for the rehabilitation of alcoholics and other addicts. A feature of Christian Action's work was its provision of financial and administrative support, including office accommodation for other small projects dealing with special problems. These included RAP (Radical Alternative to Prison) and CHAR (Campaign for the Homeless and Rootless) – two causes that also found a voice in the St Paul's pulpit.

In 1950 there was little concern in Britain about the rapid development of racist rule in South Africa. Gratitude for the support of South Africa during the war and the leadership of Jan Christian Smuts, including his major role in the drafting of the constitution of the United Nations, tended to obscure the evil of apartheid. But not for John Collins, who had been profoundly influenced by his reading of Alan Paton's *Cry the Beloved Country*, and was enlisted by Victor Gollancz to support Michael Scott – an unusual tramp-like Anglican priest who had been expelled from South Africa for encouraging Indians in Durban to adopt Ghandian methods of non-violent resistance. A public meeting in Central Hall, Westminster, addressed by Scott attracted a huge crowd and he also spoke from the pulpit of St Paul's. It was then arranged that he should develop a race relations section of Christian Action but, being an inveterate individualist, he decided that he needed his own organization and started what became the influential Africa Bureau. A Race Relations Fund was established to help black students and immigrant workers in London, and Trevor Huddleston, then working in Sophiatown, Johannesburg, asked Collins to raise money for the families of men who were being imprisoned for their non-violent resistance to apartheid. This was followed by an extended visit to South Africa, in which lasting friendships with Huddleston, Ambrose Reeves, Nelson Mandela, Chief Luthuli, Oliver Tambo and other African leaders were established and his determination to support them reinforced. Further work on his part was delayed, however, for 12 months, since he had contracted tuberculosis during his travels and needed a long period for treatment and convalescence.

In 1956 Christian Action launched a Treason Trial Defence Fund and raised £170,000 for the defence of 156 black and white South Africans whose opposition to government policy had led to their trial on charges of high treason. The trial lasted four years and all were acquitted. By this time the fund's terms of reference had been extended to cover support for Rhodesian rebels and eventually it became the International Defence and Aid Fund, through which the Swedish and several other governments channelled their money for the legal and humanitarian assistance of apartheid's victims. The fund became too large to shelter under the Christian Action umbrella, so a separate organization was established, with its own office, but with Collins still at the helm, supported by a high-powered international committee. Before long he was banned from entry into South Africa and it became illegal for money from the Fund to be received by South Africans, though the flow continued by clandestine means. In 1976, some 20 years after his exile from the country he loved, Trevor Huddleston wrote:

I am certain, and am proud to go on saying it, that *informed* opposition to apartheid in Britain owes as much to John Collins and Christian Action as *informed* opposition to the slave trade owed to Wilberforce. And when history comes to be written, the name of John Collins will have an equally honoured place.

Two years later the United Nations, which also channelled money through the fund, honoured him with a Gold Medal for his work against apartheid. The King of Sweden made him a Commander of the Northern Star.

But South Africa was not Collins's only major concern. Deeply shocked by the use of nuclear weapons to end the war in 1945, and never ceasing to preach against their subsequent proliferation by the leading world powers, he convened a meeting at 2 Amen Court in January 1958 to consider the possibility of mounting organized opposition to their stockpiling as well as to their possible use. Among the 50 people present were Bertrand Russell, J. B. Priestley, Kingsley Martin, Michael Foot and Peggy Duff – all firmly located on the Left, and none of them Christian. It was decided to launch a Campaign for Nuclear Disarmament (CND) with Russell as president, Collins as chairman and Duff as secretary. The timing proved to be exactly right. The Campaign struck a chord among a significant section of the British public and soon became a mass movement, albeit somewhat chaotic, united in a moral crusade against something they believed to be intrinsically evil. Groups sprang up in most parts of the country.

The chief rallying-point of the campaign was an annual march at Easter from Trafalgar Square to the nuclear research centre at Aldermaston in Berkshire. This was later reversed to enable the event to end with a mass meeting in Trafalgar Square. The numbers taking part were never fewer than 7,000 and sometimes reached 20,000 and for many years no Easter seemed complete without media pictures of a motley procession headed by Collins, in his cassock, and various left-wing intellectuals, trade union leaders and Labour MPs. A white-on-black banner identified them. For most of those who marched it was an enjoyable experience, combining serious purpose with fun, but, since a high proportion of them firmly believed that a nuclear war might start at any time, it was hardly surprising that some began to show signs of impatience when none of their efforts made a scrap of difference to government policy. Eventually this led to a sharp policy disagreement between Collins and Bertrand Russell, who formed a 'Committee of 100' to engage in direct action, including such gestures as lying down in Whitehall until forcibly removed by the police. Infighting, some of it bitter, followed among the leaders of the Campaign and in April 1964 Collins, believing correctly that he could no longer hold the movement together, resigned from the chairmanship. CND then went into a fairly steep decline, though it enjoyed a mini-revival in the late 1970s and early 1980s. It is not easy to discern what CND actually achieved, though it undoubtedly spread among the public a wider perception of the danger and horror of nuclear weapons and Collins believed that this, combined with similar campaigns in other countries, helped to create the atmosphere in which the signing of a Test Ban Treaty in 1963 became possible. It also provided him with his one experience of being arrested, locked in a police cell and charged with a public order offence after a demonstration in Trafalgar Square. The Bow Street magistrate subsequently dismissed the case.

Meanwhile, some at St Paul's – usually those who found his outlook and actions unacceptable – complained that his national and international responsibilities were getting in the way of his expected contribution to St Paul's. This was hurtful and he strenuously denied it. He held at different times all the great offices of the chapter, and during his years as precentor organized and supervised the building of a new choir school. Viewed in the light of what was normal among cathedral canons at the time, he did more than his fair share of capitular work, and was in fact deeply attached to St Paul's. This made it all the more painful when, on the retirement of the 86-year-old Walter Matthews in 1967, he was passed over for the deanery. During the vacancy there was, as is often the case, strong pressure from the cathedral community (though not from the other canons) for Collins to be appointed dean. The only other strong candidate was Canon Edward Carpenter of Westminster Abbey, and the two men, who were close friends, agreed that they would be quite happy if the other were to be appointed. In the event it went, to widespread astonishment, to the junior canon of the cathedral – Martin Sullivan – who turned out to be something of a disaster.

Inasmuch as there is usually a bias against the appointment of a dean from within his own chapter, it is hard to fathom why the Crown, in the person of Prime Minister Harold Wilson, chose Sullivan in preference to Collins. The Bishop of London, still Stopford, was almost certainly against Collins and, unlike Sullivan, Collins was not a popular after-dinner speaker in the City, from which financial support was always likely to be needed. Collins had created many enemies in the Establishment and, although Wilson greatly appreciated his outstanding social and political witness, he lacked the concern for appointments that sometimes impelled Attlee to override church advice. J. B. Priestley, a close friend of Collins, expressed his dismay memorably – 'It is rather like a man who, with a certain course to run, leaves a racehorse in its stables and uses circus ponies.'

As senior canon, Collins was responsible for the running of the cathedral during the interregnum, then for the installation of his junior colleague as dean. It was not to be expected that relations between the two men would be easy but Collins did his best to conceal his feelings and, remaining at St Paul's for another 13 years until his reluctant retirement in 1981, continued to discharge his responsibilities diligently, though distancing himself from the new dean's more ludicrous enterprises. There was still more than enough to keep him occupied elsewhere and he remained the Church's leading social reformer, in spite of suffering a coronary in 1974. At the time of his retirement he relinquished his leadership of Christian Action, retaining that of the Defence and Aid Fund, but in the event lived for only another 12 months and died on 31 December 1982. Trevor Huddleston, by now Archbishop of the Indian Ocean, preached at a service of thanksgiving in St Paul's, and a special memorial meeting was held at the United Nations in New York. A slate memorial stone in the crypt of St Paul's records that 'He worked for reconciliation between races and nations, and helped those who were deprived, persecuted, imprisoned or exiled', and includes the words of Jesus, 'In as much as ye have done it unto the least of these my brethren, ye have done it unto me.'

21

The Original Theologian
W. H. Vanstone, Chester

W. H. (Bill – but only to his friends) Vanstone was perhaps the only truly original Anglican theologian of the twentieth century to remain uncompromised in the Christian camp. He was, paradoxically, a deeply conservative churchman who would use only the Book of Common Prayer and withstood most of the church reforms effected during his lifetime. His profound thought is expressed primarily in two slender books which were the result of the application of an outstandingly able academic mind to 21 years of devoted pastoral work on a new housing estate in Lancashire. He had intended this parochial ministry to be his life's work and was driven to accept a canonry of Chester Cathedral in 1978 only when ill-health would permit him to remain in his parish no longer.

William Hubert Vanstone was born in 1923, one of four children of a clergyman who devoted 26 years to ministry in a Bradford parish that was partly very poor and partly fairly well off. These included the years of the 1930s depression when the Church was deeply involved in social work among the unemployed and as a boy young William was much affected by the experience of apprehending some other boys who were stealing apples from the vicarage orchard. Noting their slender arms, he resolved to devote his own career to one of 'service to people'. But the 1939–45 war intervened and he went straight from school into the Royal Air Force and trained as a pilot. He was lucky to escape when the Mosquito aircraft in which he was flying as an instructor in Canada crashed. On demobilization in 1945 he went to Balliol College, Oxford, where he took a Double First in Classics and, having decided that his future did not lie in politics, offered himself for holy orders. This took him to Cambridge to study under Professor C. F. D. Moule, a distinguished New Testament scholar, who described him as 'the most gifted pupil I ever taught'. He was awarded a 'starred First' and at the same time completed his ordination training at Westcott House.

There he established what became close and lifelong friendships with Robert Runcie, the future Archbishop of Canterbury, and Victor Whitsey, the future Bishop of Chester, who was to play an important part in the second, final phase of his ministry. Unlike many of their fellow ordinands, neither he nor Whitsey came from a public school background and their experience of the robust life of northern communities drew them together in opposing the 'camp' homosexual atmosphere of the college. Before proceeding to ordination, however, Vanstone went to New York for further study at the Union Theological Seminary under Reinhold Niebuhr and Paul Tillich – two of the twentieth century's most influential theologians. Tillich's insights into the religious significance of psychology and symbolism and Niebuhr's discernment of the church's partial responsibility for the disorders of society were to colour his own future thinking. Vanstone told his fellow students in Cambridge that he had learned from Tillich the truth that 'it is essential to accept that one is accepted by God'.

Returning to England in 1950 he was ordained and spent the next five years as a curate of St Thomas's, Halliwell in Bolton. Within two years he had received seven offers of fellowships at Oxford and Cambridge, but declined them all, stating, 'My vocation is simply to serve God and my fellow human beings.' For him this meant a celibate life. The working-class parish was not unlike his father's. It was well run and Vanstone described his vicar, Harold Kirkman, as 'a pattern of pastoral ministry'. But it was different from pre-war Bradford in that social relief work was no longer needed and the community was not lacking in hope. He threw himself into every aspect of parish life, particularly the youth club, and came to the conclusion that the Church's task now was to foster community life and to enrich the life experience of individuals. This would be achieved through well-ordered worship, strong teaching and sensitive pastoral work.

In 1955 he was appointed curate-in-charge of Kirkholt – a new corporation housing estate in Rochdale where it was necessary to start the Church's work from scratch and where he remained for the next 21 years, becoming its vicar in 1964. A simple building, to be used for both worship and other church activities, was being erected but there was nowhere for him to live and it was arranged that for the first six months he would remain at Halliwell, about 20 miles away, and visit Kirkholt every ten days or so to supervise the completion of the building and prepare for its dedication. The initial encounters with his

future parishioners were not encouraging. Those he chanced to meet
in the streets seemed hardly aware of the plans for a new church and
indicated no need of its ministry. At a meeting with civic officials he
was assured that community life was developing well, various organizations were flourishing, and there were no social problems such as
loneliness among the elderly or misbehaviour among the young. This
was intended by way of encouragement but it left him feeling that
perhaps the estate had no need of a church and was, as he put it,
'getting on very well and very happily without one'. This seemed to
support Dietrich Bonhoeffer's belief that man would soon 'come of
age' and no longer need religion.

These early days at Kirkholt were to have a decisive impact on both
his ministry and his future thinking, raising the fundamental question,
what is the Church really for? Other young priests taking on similar assignments about this time were finding their answers through
the insights of the Biblical Theology and the Liturgical movements
but these did not satisfy Vanstone, who believed it necessary to dig
deeper. He had a very considerable knowledge of theology, but confessed that only one or two aspects of it applied to his pastoral work,
so he decided to concentrate on these. Meanwhile he was approaching despair about his role in this pioneering situation until, as he later
related it, one lovely May evening when returning from a visit to a
parishioner he suddenly crossed the road and:

> as I did so, I experienced, in one moment, a sudden and complete
> revolution of attitude. It was as if my world turned upside down: or
> as if, having been perplexed by looking at a picture upside down,
> I suddenly saw it the right way up, and understood it. What I saw
> was still the same – a good world, full of innocent contentment and
> human fulfilment; but I suddenly realised that its goodness made the
> presence of the Church not less important but much more so, not
> empty of significance but more than ever full.

He had been shown that the importance of the Church lies in something other than its service to, or satisfaction of, the needs of man. The
content of this 'something other' was to be hammered out over the
coming years in a dedicated ministry informed by a prayerful dialectic
between what he discerned in theology and what he experienced in the
daily life of a parish of 6,500 people.

It turned out that a few of these people had been looking forward
to the coming of a priest to help start a church and that beneath the
surface of community life there was a fair amount of personal need.

Intensive pastoral work was initiated and sustained over the next two decades. He kept open house and, as this became known, many enquirers, students, tramps, drug addicts and drop-outs found their way to his door. All were welcomed and, although he did not give them money, he was generous with food and time. David Wyatt, who was working in another part of Rochdale in the early 1960s and subsequently became the Bishop of Manchester's chaplain, described in an obituary how Vanstone 'put love at the centre of his ministry, constantly demonstrating what it means to be human, embodying what he taught'. He had a particular concern for the underdog, and there was a large Sunday School as well as a network of organizations – youth clubs, Scouts and Guides and the like. The summer camps for boys were long remembered.

The dual-purpose building he inherited did not please him. He believed strongly that churches have an important symbolic significance, sacramental almost, both as places where God's presence is more deeply experienced and as expressions of a response to God's love on the part of those who build them and care for them. Such buildings must therefore be set aside only for worship and prayer, and he soon began fund-raising which led in 1964 to the consecration of a beautiful parish church, with an oval altar to symbolize brotherhood, equality and communion; a large metal crown of thorns suspended above it as a reminder of the true cost of the divine love; and a stark, simple, life-size wooden cross to remind both preacher and congregation of the central truth of the Christian gospel. In his address at Vanstone's funeral, Archbishop Robert Runcie spoke of his sermons, which – like his writings – 'give the impression of being effortless, beautiful in style and concise in content. In fact they were the result of giving himself again and again to writing, refining and polishing.' Sadly, as it may be thought, few of these sermons are extant, and this because of his high doctrine of preaching. He saw the sermon as an offering of thought to God, which if fashioned well will become the offering also of those who hear. In the same way therefore that an anthem has done its work when it has been sung:

so the sermon has done its work when it has been preached and offered. The preacher, having prepared it with the greatest care, will now destroy the script or erase it from his memory; for the occasion of this particular offering will not recur, and if the same should be preached again there would then be no cost involved in it, and therefore no offering.

Inasmuch as the contents of his books were initially worked out in his sermons, parish magazine articles and other occasional writings, it might be wondered just what the congregation at Kirkholt made of his profound thoughts. The answer seems to be a great deal, since he was a master of the illuminating illustration, invariably drawn from his own pastoral experience in the parish. Many of these found their way eventually into his books, to the great benefit of their readers. It was also the case that Vanstone's insights were not expressed in dry intellectual categories but always had a devotional element which ensured that gems of wisdom were available even to those who had difficulty with the logical thrust of his exposition.

Those who were close to him could hardly have been surprised when in 1974 he suffered a severe heart attack. He had driven himself relentlessly for far too long and been disinclined to heed his bishop and others who urged him to slow down. For some time his deteriorating health had been noticeable. Heavy smoking had not helped. But sacrificial offering as a response to and recognition of God's limitless love was an integral part of his life and ministry. After a ten-week convalescence he returned to duty and resumed the leading of services as well as his usual pastoral work. During the next 18 months, however, he was always struggling and, on the edge of complete physical and emotional exhaustion, he was told by his doctors that he must give up. The parish church services register records for 1 February 1976:

> On this day, being somewhat afflicted with disease of the heart, I laid down my ministry at Kirkholt with great gratitude to Almighty God for his unending mercies.

At this point Bishop Victor Whitsey came to his aid by providing him with accommodation and appointing him as his theological adviser – an undemanding post but one that presumably facilitated the payment of a salary. Vanstone used the time now available to him to complete his first book, *Love's Endeavour, Love's Expense* (1977), which won the Collins Biennial Religious Book Award and went through several reprints. H. A. Williams, a notable Dean of Chapel at Trinity College, Cambridge, and by now a Mirfield monk, wrote in the foreword: 'It is, I believe, a masterpiece and will become a classic. And certainly it leads us out into the fresh air.' He was right on all counts.

This task completed, Vanstone felt impelled to return to parish life and pressed Bishop Whitsey to appoint him vicar of Hattersley – another large housing estate which had a macabre association with the so-called 'Moors Murders', a notorious series of crimes which had involved the torture, murder and clandestine burial of children on the nearby moors. No other priest was willing to take it on and, after Vanstone had repeatedly offered himself, Whitsey, against his own better judgement, relented and instituted him to the parish. But to no avail: after only 12 months Vanstone had to acknowledge that he lacked the strength to continue and that the days of his parish ministry were ended.

Once more Whitsey facilitated a period of recovery and this enabled Vanstone to write most of *The Stature of Waiting*, which was published to considerable acclaim in 1982 and also went through several reprints. In common with *Love's Endeavour, Love's Expense*, it had been a long time in preparation – in his mind, in sermons and in articles – and reflected his own experience, particularly since his disabling heart attack. In 1978 he was deemed well enough to become a residentiary canon of Chester and remained there, happily, until his retirement in 1990. He was said to have declined, at different times, two bishoprics and, Robert Runcie and Victor Whitsey apart, he had a low estimate of bishops, once describing them as 'either stupid or vain, and in some cases, both'.

Like most Church of England clergymen, Vanstone was an individualist and his extraordinary ability inevitably set him apart from most of his colleagues. Until he joined the chapter at Chester he had no experience of working in a team and, given the English cathedral tradition, it was not to be expected that his contribution to capitular life would be one of glad collaboration. Nor did it turn out to be. But he found common cause with his fellow canons in opposing the reforming tendencies of the dean. Ingram Cleasby, who had once been Archbishop Garbett's chaplain and had acquired strong experience of northern parish life as Vicar and Archdeacon of Chesterfield, had himself only recently arrived at Chester, where he inherited a cathedral which had long turned its back on the inspired, innovative decanate of Frank Bennett in the 1920s and 1930s.

Elsewhere the influence of the rebuilt Coventry Cathedral was spreading quickly and bringing significant renewal. Cleasby, well aware of this development, believed it to be his responsibility to move Chester in the same direction. Unfortunately, no one else associated with the cathedral had the slightest desire to move and Cleasby's proposal that some of the experimental Communion services, now in common use, should be introduced to complement the Book of Common Prayer was firmly rejected. A later request that the revived Chester Mystery Plays might be performed in the cathedral was, in spite of Cleasby's support, no less firmly declined. Vanstone's part in all this was based, not on the innate conservatism displayed by his fellow canons, but on the deep theological conviction that an ancient liturgy, like an ancient church, was something to be treasured because of the love of God which it had for so long expressed and evoked. He saw his chief task at Chester, therefore, as that of preserving the building and the worship. The mystery plays, scheduled to extend over a fortnight, would disturb the rhythm of the cathedral's normal use.

It was fortunate that Cleasby, a wise and conciliatory dean, would not permit sharp personal disagreement to affect his personal relationships, and he and Vanstone became firm friends. And outside the cathedral itself, where the dean and chapter's substantial property holding was also in urgent need of reform, Vanstone – unlike the other canons – gave the dean strong support. Cleasby also greatly valued all that Vanstone offered in personal ministry. Since Vanstone was unmarried, he was allocated a fairly small seventeenth-century cottage, rather than one of the tall, three-storey houses normally occupied by canons. This suited him and he soon became a familiar figure in the close, sitting outside his cottage, tending his little garden, smoking a cigarette, moving to and from the cathedral, with time for anyone who stopped him to pass the time of day or ask some searching question about the cathedral. Or he would stand in the nave or the cloister garden, where he became, in Cleasby's words, 'a resident guru, a holy man available to all'. Visitors from America and other parts of the world attending Evensong were invited to his cottage after the service for a glass of sherry and a biscuit, which led invariably to a long and serious discussion on some aspect of religious faith. Similar discussions went on long into the night – he seemed to need little sleep – after supper parties at which his cookery skills made him both a generous and delightful host.

Yet, like many other highly gifted people, he had an elusive personality that was difficult to pin down. That he was a priest of deep faith and devotion, and of loving pastoral sensitivity, was not open to doubt. He was an engaging conversationalist and a brilliant mimic and teller of jokes – usually with a glass of wine in one hand and a cigarette in the other. He rarely read a newspaper – relying on the radio for news – and he usually travelled by bus or train. But he could sometimes appear arrogant, intolerant and touchy, and had problems with those whom he regarded as superficial in their assessment of issues and situations. He once likened the Church of his day to a swimming pool, where all the noise comes from the shallow end. As he grew older the constant pain caused by an arthritic hip and the frustration of severe deafness also tested his patience. So those who knew him tended to be either very much for him, regarding him as close to sanctity, or very much against him, finding him almost unbearable. He never failed to make an impact.

Besides his personal ministry at Chester, he took under his wing, as part of his responsibility for visitors, the cathedral refectory and shop, and the training and supervision of the welcoming stewards. His sermons, particularly at the Eucharist, continued to be of the highest quality and he was in great demand for sermons and lectures elsewhere, and for the conducting of retreats. He was also a member of the Church of England's Doctrine Commission. Following his retirement in 1990 he moved to Gloucestershire, where he undertook responsibility for the small village church at Beverston, near Tetbury. There he conducted the services in strict accordance with the Book of Common Prayer, took the same great care over his sermons, and became much loved in the village. Though bent and crippled, he was grateful for the opportunity to have returned to his true vocation – that of a parish priest. He died in 1999.

When in the course of his research into Vanstone's life and writing, the Reverend Robert L. Glover, a minister of the Church of Scotland, visited the vicarage at Kirkholt, he was astonished to discover just how much of Vanstone's occasional writing remained. Virtually all of the sermons had been destroyed immediately after their delivery, but a huge number of parish magazine articles, book reviews, lectures and other papers indicated that his books represented the refinement of developing thought extending over many years. The first chapter of *Love's Endeavour, Love's Expense*, which occupies about half of the book, is autobiographical – and necessarily so, since Vanstone's theology is inseparable from his life's experience. He had, he says, attempted over a period of 25 years to unfold or unravel a conviction that 'the outward expression of religion, what Christians call "the life of the Church", is a matter of supreme and unconditional importance'. Rejecting the commonly held belief that the Church exists for the glory of God, since so much of its life is concerned with trivialities, he goes on to affirm that all true creativity, and all material reality, is a work of love – ultimately the love of God – and the Church is, therefore, to be seen as part of the wider expression of the divine love. It follows from this that even if it could be shown that the Church was of no importance for man's temporal well-being, it might still be important to his eternal well-being.

This leads to an examination of the nature of God's love, which can, he says, be discerned only through an examination of the character of human love. There is no other source of reliable information. 'If we can discover what love ought to be, we need enquire no further what the love of God is.' Careful analysis leads him to conclude that authentic human love is unlimited, makes no attempt to control others, and is never detached but always completely involved. God's love must therefore be limitless, precarious and vulnerable – imprecise, ambiguous concepts when applied to the eternal, but attributes clearly displayed in the life of Jesus, the Christ.

God's creative activity, he goes on, is – because it is a work of love – vulnerable and always poised between the possibilities of triumph and tragedy. Which of these it turns out to be depends on the response of creation, and there is always the tragic possibility that 'when all is given in love, all may be given in vain'. That is the cost of love – divine and human. What therefore is the appropriate 'Response of Being to the Love of God' (the book's subtitle)? Three areas of response are delineated. First is that of nature – of which human beings are a part. This must fulfil its true purpose, that is to say 'come right', rather than 'come wrong', and in this human beings have a part to play. Herein lies the second possible response – that of freedom, freedom in the midst of the crises of human life and the disorders of nature to choose those actions that will aid the triumph, rather than the tragedy, of the love of God. The third possible response is that of recognition, and here Vanstone points out that if a gift of love is to be realized in its fullness, it must be received and recognized for what it is. Thus the limitless self-giving which expresses the divine love requires recognition by its recipients, and it may be necessary for God to await this recognition before his work is completed.

This leads to the final chapter, on the specific offering of the Church in the context of the total response of creation. The Church is called to be 'the enclave of recognition' – a role that is far wider than its own ecclesiastical domain, but nonetheless requires form. 'The Church is what a man is and does when he recognizes what is happening in the being of the universe.' It seeks to further love's triumphs and to redeem its tragedies as an expression of its own responsive love. The reform of the Church is therefore a matter of extreme delicacy and difficulty:

The task is not simply to bring the spontaneity of the present age within the Church: it is to form that spontaneity into the costly offering of love. Reform of the Church requires more than sociological insight into contemporary trends and attitudes: it requires also the artist's understanding and the lover's experience of the costly discipline of love.

There follows a discussion of the importance of church buildings, prayer and preaching – all to be seen as 'the articulation and offering to God of whatever gratitude and responsive love a district may contain, and thus an important and even irreplaceable service to the well-being of man'.

Love's Endeavour, Love's Expense will not yield its treasures to a superficial reading, though the inclusion of illuminating illustrations drawn from its author's own experience assist the process of understanding and assimilation. The same is no less true of *The Stature of Waiting*. Vanstone again brings into dialectic human experience and divine revelation and applies this to the enforced passivity experienced by, for example, a hospital patient or an elderly person in the closing stages of life. After a detailed and illuminating exposition of the Passion narratives in the Gospels of Mark and John, and deep theological reflection, he challenges the current view that men and women are only ever fully human, truly alive, when they are active. He rejects the long-standing belief that because human beings are 'created in the image and likeness of God' they must of necessity be sharers in his ceaseless creative activity. And this is because in the being of God there is passivity as well as activity.

Vanstone's starting point is the role of Judas during the final hours of Jesus' life and he notes that although he is said, in the English text of St Mark's Gospel, to have 'betrayed' Jesus, the original Greek word for 'betrayal' appears only once in this Gospel. On all the other occasions Mark uses a similar Greek word which means 'handed over'. Thus Judas handed over, rather than betrayed, Jesus to the chief priests, there being no need for betrayal since he was exercising an open ministry and could have been arrested at any time. In any case, if the death of Jesus was necessary for human salvation it would presumably have taken place whether or not Judas was involved.

This might seem at first sight a somewhat slender thread on which to hang an unorthodox doctrine of the being of God, but Vanstone goes on to observe that the 'handing over' of Jesus marked a distinct and highly significant turning point in his life and work. Whereas he had previously exercised an active ministry of preaching, teaching, healing and caring, from this moment onwards he became passive – 'Jesus is no longer the man who does, he becomes the one who is done to'. In

St John's Gospel the point of transition is marked by a different way of handling the activities of Jesus. Between the third and seventeenth chapters there is great emphasis on the 'works' of Jesus. He is portrayed as being intensely active in obedience to the Father's will and entirely free to respond to God in this way. But after his being handed over to the chief priests he is bound and loses his freedom. He can now do no more than wait.

Vanstone goes on to discuss the true meaning of the word 'passion' – used by the Church to signify the period of intense suffering endured by Jesus immediately before and during his crucifixion. The Greek word from which 'passion' is derived actually means 'to have something happen to me'. It appears therefore that the earliest Christian believers understood the handing over of Jesus as his transition from the free activity of a subject to the passion of receptivity of an object.

The second half of *The Stature of Waiting* considers a number of human predicaments in which individuals find themselves in a position of helplessness and are required to be passive recipients of the ministry of others. These situations, the number of which is bound to increase, are normally resented or denied and public opinion accords the highest worth to individuals who manage to move from passive acceptance to independence, and to institutions that facilitate or 'enable' individuals to become self-reliant or self-sufficient. But this attitude is based on questionable assumptions that will not stand up to scrutiny. Nor will the long-standing Christian belief that human beings, because of their relationship with God, are called to be constantly industrious. Jesus revealed a different sort of God – one who hands himself over, the one who may in some circumstances be passive, one who waits, one who suffers. Thus man may live an authentic human life in either an active or a passive mode, and this raises passivity, waiting, to a new stature with positive implications for everyone who, at some time or other in their lives, finds themselves in a situation of helplessness. The implication for the expectations and ordering of society are no less radical.

Superbly written and with a devotional as well as an intellectual component, *The Stature of Waiting* gives theology a good name. So it is perhaps not surprising that some of Vanstone's readers, hungry for further exciting illumination, were a little disappointed with his third and final book, *Fare Well in Christ*. Written over a period of five years when he was in retirement, and published in 1997, this is a very different kind of book. The exploratory element in his thinking had given way to mature reflection on the central truths of the gospel, focused on the meaning of grace. Many more analogies from his own pastoral experience are included and it seems in some ways surprisingly conservative. It is also much less intellectually demanding than his previous books and would serve as a valuable introduction to the Christian faith for almost any thoughtful enquirer. In the context of the twin mysteries of existence and identity, the final chapter is on life after death. It ends:

> By comparison with these mysteries the death of my body is a rather unimportant event, and I am inclined to echo John Donne's words, 'Death be not proud, though some have called thee mighty and terrible; for thou art not so.' There is a reality which transcends and enfolds the dying of my body and its return to dust and ashes . . . And the name of that reality is God; and the grace of God has been disclosed to mankind in Jesus Christ.

22

Canons Functional or Canons
Theologian? Looking Ahead

At various times in their long history the English cathedrals have
undergone reform, most recently as a consequence of the Cathedrals
Measure 1999, yet the substance and structure of their life is not
fundamentallydifferent from that of the Middle Ages. A com munityof
priests, recently reinforced by a few non-resident laypeople, is responsible for maintaining a daily round of worship at a high standard in a
majestic building. By means of preaching and other methods of com-
munication the faith of Christian believers is to be strengthened and
the unbelief of others challenged. The cathedral remains the bishop's
church, even though his freedom of action within it is still limited, and
it has therefore a particular relationship with its diocese, though the
parochial character of the Church of England means that this relationship is not close.

The status of the canon residentiary is also unchanged. He is
appointed to an office in which he has a marked degree of independence and, inasmuch as he has almost certainly been previously in a
position of leadership in some other sphere, this is what he might
reasonablyexpect and is the best way his gifts will be exercised. On the
other hand, he is appointed to a corporate body in which a measure of
collaboration is required, and if the activities of that body increase and
become more complex so the need for closer collaboration increases.
The dean is still the focal point of the community's life and the central
figure in its administration. But he is not a managing director to whom
the canons relate, as if they were departmental heads or line- managers.
Neither do they relate to him, and now to her, as curates relate to a
rector or, for that matter, as archdeacons relate to a bishop. The dean
is first among equals and, while accorded certain rights, privileges and
responsibilities by the cathedral's statutes, his freedom of independent
action is severely constrained. The chapter must act together or not
at all and majority voting is generally regarded as a final, regrettable
resort in special circumstances.

The most significant consequence of the recent reforms is to be seen already in the method of appointing canons residentiary and the kind of priests now being recruited. This is greater than it might at first sight appear and more substantial than envisaged by the reformers. Whereas in the past, cathedral stalls have been given for the most part to priests with a strong record of pastoral or academic achievement, and with the prospect of a longish period of occupation unless preferred to a deanery or a bishopric, a new pattern is emerging. Seven-year tenures of canonries, which may or may not be renewed for a further three years, is leading, as anticipated, to the appointment of relatively young priests to a particular function within the life of the cathedral or the diocese. These posts are invariably advertised and, in accordance with the bureaucratic tendencies of the age, those wishing to be considered are invited to e-mail or write to the cathedral administrator's personal assistant for an information pack and an application form. The shortlisted candidates are usually interviewed by the dean and the other canons if the stall is confined to cathedral ministry – the bishop being involved in the final choice. If the stall is required primarily for diocesan ministry the bishop will choose, having first consulted the dean.

This open method of appointment has several advantages over the former procedure, which relied on the bishop's knowledge of likely candidates or by recommendation from sources behind the scenes. With the field now wide open there seems every likelihood that the English cathedrals of the near future will be staffed, no longer by grave, ageing dignitaries but by lively young priests who will bring their vigour to particular aspects of a cathedral's ministry before moving on to another form of service. These priests may perhaps be accurately, though not legally, described as canons functional – a role clearly intended by the reformers and one that should bring clear benefits to a vitally important area of the Church's witness. But there is a price to be paid for most things and in this instance it is safe to assume that none of the distinguished churchmen whose lives have been outlined in the preceding pages would have stood the remotest chance of appointment as a twenty-first-century canon residentiary, except in the small number of cathedrals where a professorial chair is attached to a stall.

It also seems fair to assume that few, if any, of them would have wished to be appointed to a new-style, functional canonry. The learned scholar, the social reformer, the political agitator, the original thinker – none of these would have been attracted to a small world of incessant meetings and regular financial crises. Some might also have wondered about their own financial position, since the Archbishop's Council has decided to erode the stipend difference between the cathedral canon and the parish priest to an insignificant figure, with stipends now at £24,000 and £20,000 per annum respectively. In a perfect Christian society all would doubtless receive the same, though there is nothing in Christian ethics to prohibit greater rewards for greater responsibility. Moreover, in the present, imperfect society a priest moving from a university or a school to a cathedral close is required to sacrifice at least £10,000 per annum – a level of sacrifice not required in any other sphere of the Church's ministry.

Those in the know might also have wondered whether in the not-so-long term there might be money available to pay them at all. Notwithstanding the fact that the Church Commissioners' initial substantial capital was derived from surrendered cathedral estates, and that by way of compensation the commissioners agreed to be responsible in perpetuity for the stipends of the deans and the canons, there is now constant pressure from the General Synod for the commissioners to make block grants to dioceses towards the stipends of all their clergy, apart from the bishop and the dean, leaving the distribution of the grants to be determined locally. Such a decentralization has much to commend it, but a number of key elements in the Church's ministry would be left vulnerable to lack of vision or naked prejudice. Among these the cathedrals, because they are not greatly loved by the parishes and are often regarded, perhaps with envy, as all-consuming monsters, would almost certainly be among the first to suffer. It is only too easy, therefore, to envisage the number of cathedral canons being reduced to one or two in order that the parochial ministry may be maintained in its traditional form, or some other kinds of local ministry developed. Such a policy would be disastrously short-sighted and only hasten further the marginalization of the Church's witness and influence.

Nothing has disturbed my conviction, outlined in *The Deans* (SCM Press, 2004), that the future of the cathedrals can be properly determined only in the light of a radical reappraisal of the Church's mission as a whole in a world far removed from that of a thousand years ago, in which the parochial and cathedral systems were first devised. There is argument about the degree of secularization now affecting Britain, but there can be none concerning the dramatic decline in church attendance and in the number of clergy, and concerning the acute financial crises, which demand substantial retrenchment as well as appeals for greater generosity. Similar challenges face virtually all of the major Churches of western Europe. My belief is that in England most of the parish churches should be served by locally recruited non-stipendiary clergy and readers, and that a reduced, but more able and better-trained, corps of stipendiary clergy, perhaps 100 per diocese, should be employed to support the parish ministries and also to engage in forms of non-parochial ministry. These clergy would be attached to the cathedral and to, say, five other large churches in key geographical locations in the diocese, and would become the dynamic, driving force in a mission-orientated church life.

Such a reform of the Church of England's structure would bring many more clergy into a direct relationship with their cathedrals and, while their chief responsibility would lie well beyond the confines of the close, some of it would at times be closely linked to activities within the cathedral or its ancillary buildings. In many though not all places lay canons are already undertaking responsibility for substantial administrative work. What, then, will be the best use of the canon residentiary?

It is unlikely that the dean alone would be able to manage a cathedral on the lines envisaged, and provision might be needed for at least one canon with a functional role. But, however many may be required, there should be no abandoning of the role of the canon residentiary who has sufficient leisure to study and to think. For several reasons, not simply financial, it is unlikely that a sufficient number of these can any more be recruited from the academic sphere, and in any case much academic theology has become too technical to be useful to the Church. But in spite of the serious decline in clergy numbers there is still among the parish clergy a significant number who have undertaken post-graduate research. Among these are bound to be some who, with further opportunities for appropriate study, might be encouraged to embrace the vocation of a missionary theologian.

In *The Bishops* (SCM Press, 2002) I pleaded for the liberation of diocesan bishops from their current role of pastoral managers, in order that they might become strategic thinkers, exercising pioneering leadership in the new missionary situation in which the Church now finds itself. If the bishop had available within the life of his cathedral a small group of canons theologian whom he could regularly consult and who would stimulate his own thinking, this could only be to the advantage of the diocese, as well as the cathedral itself and sometimes the wider Church. And in case this might appear to be an unrealistic, revolutionary concept it may be recalled that it is not very far removed from the original relationship between a bishop and his *familia* and the circumstances in which the title of Canon came first to be used.

Bibliography

The serious student of cathedral life cannot neglect Philip Barrett's *Barchester: English Cathedral Life in the Nineteenth Century* (SPCK, 1993), a mine of scholarly information about deans and chapters in the nineteenth century. His early death prevented the writing of a much-needed companion volume on the twentieth-century cathedral. Professor Stanford Lehmberg's recent *English Cathedrals: A History* (Hambledon and London, 2005) provides a useful general introduction to its subject, but the chapter on the twentieth century is somewhat sketchy.

The following list of biographies and autobiographies is provided for readers who may wish to know more about some of the canons whose lives are briefly treated in the present volume. Second-hand booksellers should be able to help and most can be located through the Internet – visit www.abebooks.com.uk.

Henrietta Barnett, *Canon Barnett: His Life, Work and Friends* (2 vols), John Murray, 1919

Alan Bell, *Sydney Smith: A Biography*, Clarendon Press, 1982

Perry Butler (ed.), *Pusey Rediscovered*, SPCK, 1983

Susan Chitty, *The Beast and the Monk: A Life of Charles Kingsley*, Hodder and Stoughton, 1974

Diana Collins, *Partners in Protest: Life with Canon Collins*, Victor Gollancz, 1992

Brenda Colloms, *Charles Kingsley*, Constable, 1975

Nan Dearmer, *Life of Percy Dearmer*, Jonathan Cape, 1940

Emmanuel Amand de Mendieta, *Rome and Canterbury: A Biblical and Free Catholicism*, Herbert Jenkins, 1962

F. W. Dillistone, *Charles Raven: A Biography*, Hodder and Stoughton, 1975

F .W. Dillistone, *Into All the World: A Biography of Max Warren*, Hodder and Stoughton, 1980

David L. Edwards, *F. J. Shirley: An Extraordinary Headmaster*, SPCK, 1969

W. H. Elliott, *Undiscovered Ends: An Autobiography*, Peter Davies, 1951

Donald Gray, *Percy Dearmer: A Parson's Pilgrimage*, Canterbury Press, 2000

Peter Green, *The Town Parson*, Longmans Green, 1924

G. H. Hains, *Vernon Faithfull Storr*, SPCK, 1943

F. E. Kingsley (ed.), *Charles Kingsley: His Letters and Memories of His Life* (2 vols), Kegan Paul, 1877

C. F. D. Moule (ed.), *G. W. H. Lampe: A Memoir by Friends*, Mowbray, 1982

Hesketh Pearson, *The Smith of Smiths*, Hamish Hamilton, 1934

Robin Pittman (ed.), *Fred Remembered: Recollections of John Shirley*, John Catt, 1997

Michael Sadleir, *Archdeacon Francis Wrangham. 1769–1842*, Bibliographical Society, 1937

H. E. Sheen, *Canon Peter Green*, Hodder and Stoughton, 1965

Edith Sichel, *Life and Letters of Alfred Ainger*, Nelson, 1906

Alec Vidler, *Scenes from Clerical Life: An Autobiography*, Collins, 1977

Max Warren, *Crowded Canvas: An Autobiography*, Hodder and Stoughton, 1974

James M. Wilson, *James M. Wilson: An Autobiography 1836–1931*, Sidgwick and Jackson, 1932

Index of People

Index of Places